Essex
BOYS

Essex
BOYS

KAREN BOWMAN

AMBERLEY

For my own Essex Boys, my father William, husband Bob,

Amberley Publishing
The Hill, Stroud
Gloucestershire, GL5 4EP

www.amberley-books.com

British Library Cataloguing in Publication Data.
A catalogue record for this book is available from the British Library.

ISBN 978 1 4456 0853 2

Typeset in 10pt on 12pt Sabon.
Typesetting and Origination by Amberley Publishing.
Printed in the UK.

CONTENTS

ACKNOWLEDGEMENTS

Illustrations in this book are reproduced by kind permission of the following: Bob Bowman; George & Julien Courtauld; Discovery Point, Dundee Heritage Trust; Essex Record Office; Hylands House; the Museum of Witchcraft, Boscastle; Robert Hallmann; York Castle Museum. Other illustrations are from the author's own collection.

Thanks also to the staff of Rayleigh Library who managed to locate some rather obscure books for me, Ben Turner of York Castle Museum, Julie Merick of the Dundee Heritage Trust, Graham King of the Witchcraft Museum, Boscastle, Mike Howard of *The Cauldron Magazine*, the staff of the Essex Records Office, Ciara Canning, curator of Community History at Colchester, and Ipswich Museum Service.

Thanks also to Julien Courtauld who gave me permission to use the photographs of his father, August, and pointed me in the right direction as to where to find them.

Also a very big thank you to my family and friends, who continued to encourage me during this venture.

INTRODUCTION

Men have always challenged the world in which they lived. Far-reaching and adventurous in both word and deed, they did not fear the unknown but wished to explore it, did not hide from adventure but embraced it, did not avoid the insurmountable but set out to tame it. A man was not so much by a woman's side as striding ahead of her. Essex Men were no different.

The Essex Man's passions, be they good or bad, lay in his quests for justice, love for his country and his woman, and the longing for success and to improve the world with his practical and intellectual ideas. Yet there were obstacles. While women struggled for recognition and equality, a man might feel the sting of the Navy lash, experience brutal schooling and cut-throat business practices.

Yet throughout, the Essex Boy was undaunted. Able to make something from nothing, go places from nowhere, find courage where there was none, be he a barrister or a barrow-boy, he has always been the eternal entrepreneur... the discoverer of wonders – and the companion of kings.

The gentlemen and rogues contained within the pages of this book are Essex Boys of varying degrees. Not all can claim to have been Essex born but all can claim to have given to the county's history, enjoyed its bounty or suffered by its hand. You only have to read this book in the spirit it was written to understand why each and every one of them deserves to be mentioned...

1

LANDOWNERS, PRINCES & KINGS

EUDO DAPIFER, NORMAN OVERLORD (*d.* 1120)

He eased the oppressed, restrained the insolent, and pleased all.

Philip Morant, *The History and Antiquities of Colchester*

At the end of battle on 14 October 1066 the blood of the slain soaked deep into the mire of Senlac Hill as did the hopes of every English shire. Seven thousand, five hundred Norman soldiers had done what neither Roman, Saxon nor Viking had been able to, and had taken over a country of 1.5 million souls. As the first of a new breed of Norman landlords, William I set about putting his stamp upon Britain by word and deed; in stone and in law. He initiated major changes both legally and socially. Latin became the official language of government; native Englishmen were systematically dispossessed and castles stood sentinel over a vanquished Saxon populace. By 1086 the Domesday Book reveals that only about 5 per cent of land in England was left in English hands, the loss of most native landholdings having taken place in the south of the country. By the time he died, William had left his mark on almost every part of English life. What he could not do himself he charged others to do on his behalf. Two of those men with connections to Essex were his half-brother Bishop Odo of Bayeux, and Eudo Dapifer.

Eudo was the youngest son of Hubert de Rie of Normandy, the liege lord of the small town of Rie, his father having been a great favourite with William in Normandy. It was Hubert who had once, in 1047, saved the young duke's life and later, as the king's ambassador, successfully persuaded Edward the Confessor to appoint William his successor for the throne of England. For these efforts, Hubert was promised the office of Steward of the Household as soon as William became the new British king. As it was, the appointment had to wait, as William, concerned by unrest at home in Normandy, asked Hubert – whom he considered 'prompt of hand and good at council', to return with his three eldest sons, Robert (Ralph), Hubert and Adam to maintain peace. Eudo, the youngest, and by far the most able and distinguished of Hubert's four sons, remained in England receiving possessions and lordships in several counties. Widespread in the east of England, these holdings amounted to no less than sixty-four manors; twelve in Bedfordshire, ten in Suffolk, nine in Norfolk, seven in Hertfordshire and one in Berkshire. In Essex, however, Eudo became the overlord of twenty-five.

Eudo's correct family name was actually FitzHerbert, but he became known for the office he held, which was 'Seneschal' or High Steward, and so the name Eudo 'Dapifer' became his moniker. Certainly not born in Essex, he qualifies, for the purpose of this book, as an Essex man by virtue of many entries in early Essex documents, the first being this entry in Domesday, which states, 'Eudo – one house and a court or hall, one hide of land and 15 burgesses in Colchester which had belonged in Edward's time to Thurbernus.' Eudo is also credited with having had '5 houses and 49 acres of land and a fourth part of St Peter's church'. An entry in the Colchester Chronicle written in the thirteenth or fourteenth century records that 'William Conqueror gave Colchester to Eudo the year after it was burnt by the Danes – and should start building his castle straight away'.

That year was 1069. A large Danish fleet, having been sighted off the Kent coast, had slowly journeyed north attacking Dover, Sandwich and Ipswich as it went. Colchester, according to a rector of All Saints Colchester writing in the eighteenth century, recorded that 'being on the way North was burnt by the Danes and having ravished the citysens wifes, the Conquereor gave Colchester to Eudo'. It was after these events that Colchester was granted to Eudo with instructions that he build a defensive castle on the strategic route between East Anglia and London. The castle was completed in 1076. The result was that Colchester's new fortress became the largest building of its type in Europe, completed just before William's White Tower in London.

Colchester Castle then, as it still is today, was impressive. It consisted of a large enclosure and a great keep at the centre, measuring 151 by 110 feet. As it is estimated that a medieval keep could be built at the rate of 10 feet per year, something the size of Colchester would have taken about ten years to build. It was built over the ruined Roman Temple of Claudius, incorporating the ancient structure's solid base so as to give the castle's foundations formidable strength. The remains of Roman Colchester were plundered for quality stone that to this day is not available in the county, resulting in tons of Roman tile still being evident in the walls of the castle. The castle was also crenellated at some time during the original construction, the massive keep hurriedly fortified, perhaps against an impending attack. These battlements too are still visible today. They were never dismantled but, as building continued, were simply incorporated into the upper floors of the castle. When finally completed around 1101, Eudo's castle stood an impressive three stories high.

Eudo was not only Colchester's castle-builder, he was also its benefactor. During his years as overlord he dominated the town, having outright control over various properties and authorities in Essex, but equally was well respected by all of Colchester's citizens, whether Norman or Saxon. In 1096 he founded St John's Abbey just south of the walled town, on the site of an original wooden church that had been dedicated to St John the Evangelist. Eudo himself laid the first stone. Not only did the townsfolk benefit from a substantial new place of worship, but also from a four-day fair granted by Henry I in a charter of 1104, to be held in the grounds annually in June. He was also responsible for founding the Leper Hospital of St Mary Magdalene in Colchester, and he restored St Helen's Chapel.

When Eudo Dapifer died in 1120 it was not in England but in France, at his castle at Preaux in Normandy. He had, however, made it known that he wished to be returned to Colchester and interred within St John's Abbey, the church he had founded. He was seventy-three. His Will contained several gifts left to Colchester Abbey, one being the manor of Brightlingsea. His Essex landholdings were many, including The Rodings, Theydon Garnon, Quendon, Weeley and Pitsea, Arkesden Takeley, Hazeleigh, Manuden and Purleigh, yet with no son to inherit, his lands largely reverted to the crown. His daughter Marguerite by his wife, the daughter

St John's Abbey church, Colchester, was founded by Eudo Dapifer in 1095/6 and completed in 1133. After the Dissolution of the Monasteries, the lands passed to the Lucas family of Colchester.

of Richard Fitz Gilbert, eventually married William de Mandeville and became the mother of a dynasty. Her son was an Essex boy through and through, being none other than Geoffrey de Mandeville, created 1st Earl of Essex in 1141.

HENRY VII (1457–1509)

Slender but well built and strong; his height above the average, his face cheerful, especially when speaking; his eyes were small and blue.

Description of Henry VII in his mid-forties

Hunting does not automatically spring to mind when thinking of Henry VII. His public image was one of a careful man, a man too preoccupied with his own safety to ride with the hunt; too practical to enjoy music, dancing and festival. But Henry VII was an avid hunter. It was something he pursued in the Essex forests of Epping, Hainault, and Havering-atte-Bower while they still sprawled untamed across the county; the Abbeys of Waltham and Barking, still standing magnificent on their woodland boundaries, enjoyed the privilege of seasonal hare hunting supplemented each year with a generous grant of venison.

It was Henry who instilled in his son, the future Henry VIII, a love of hunting. He strongly believed that a prince's body, as well as his mind, should be prepared for monarchy, and skill at arms was a necessary accomplishment. Hunting was 'a proper physical exercise', a way to keep a man fit and psychologically prepared for war, and so deer hunting, as well as archery and sword play, was practised by most youths from around fourteen years of age.

Henry VII was the first Tudor monarch to make night hunting in private forests a punishable offence. An Act of Henry VII's first Parliament in 1485 brought in the death penalty for poachers caught after dark with their faces obscured or disguised. If poachers were caught in daylight with their faces plainly visible they continued to invoke only a fine or imprisonment, the standing penalty for trespass.

Like anything else in life, when an obstruction is encountered a way is sought to go round it. The ban on night poaching did not deter the determined lawbreaker; instead it inadvertently popularised the use of greyhounds for illegal hunting, as their swiftness and agility coupled with their colourings (black, red, fawn, and brindle) made the dogs hard to spot against the woodland backdrop. By contrast those that hunted legally made a point of employing white or spotted dogs that could be easily followed by both hunters and spectators alike. Over the coming centuries, English aristocracy would be known for believing that 'you could tell a gentleman by his horses and his greyhounds'.

Wanstead Hall, a relatively small building until 1499, when Henry VII acquired it as a hunting lodge, was to become a favourite residence of the king. It was at this time, ten years before his death, that Henry looked more and more to Wanstead as a retreat. The hunter and sportsman he once had been was gradually succumbing to advancing age, physical disability and failing eyesight as indicated in the Treasurer of the Chamber's account books, which record not a single entry after 1499 of the king playing the 'real tennis' he so loved and had been so physically suited to.

Henry spent vast sums of money on Wanstead Hall, his *maison de retraite*. Interestingly he also received large amounts of money while on the premises. This was where Henry VII or his closest attendants collected fines and non-Parliamentary taxes, away from the gaze of the nobles in other royal palaces; his 'slush-fund', as leading Tudor historian David Starkey has been known to call it.

Such privacy was paramount to Henry. He relished the solace that the now much-refurbished hunting lodge afforded him over that of nearby Greenwich Palace. Wanstead also offered him seclusion as his health failed. In February 1507 he was reported to be very seriously ill of 'a quinsy' – a severe throat infection which made it almost impossible for him to eat or drink – and his life was despaired of but he rallied later that year and once more hunted, if at his own pace, in Wanstead's magnificent parklands. However February 1508 saw him once again gravely unwell and by July the same year he was found to be in the last stages of consumption (tuberculosis).

To this author's mind Henry VII, the first Tudor, died much misunderstood. He had gained a reputation as a money-grabbing, cold-hearted king, yet when news reached him in 1502 that his eldest son and heir to the throne Arthur had died his first reaction was to comfort his wife Elizabeth. When she in turn died a year later in 1503, just days after eminent astrologer William Parron had predicted she would live until she was eighty, the distraught king 'privily departed to a solitary place'. It may well have been Wanstead.

HENRY VIII (1491–1547)

*By God's Body I would rather that my son should hang than study
literature. It behoves the sons of gentlemen to blow horn calls correctly, to
hunt skillfully, to train a hawk well and carry it elegantly. But the study of
literature should be left to clodhoppers.*

Anonymous gentleman, 1517

It is rumoured that in his youth Henry VIII wore out eight horses a day while hunting. An exaggeration perhaps, but it shows the passion Henry had for the great outdoors and the fact that nothing fired the king's blood quite like the thrill of the chase. A regular visitor to the Great Forest of Essex, 'his majestie' (the new title that Henry had styled for himself), would often leave his palace at Greenwich, take the royal barge, cross the Thames and head for one of at least four royal Essex residences, namely Langfords at Buckhurst Hill, the Palace of Havering, Pimp Hall below Friday Hill in Chingford, and the 'Kings greate standing', later the hunting lodge of his daughter, Queen Elizabeth.

It is easy to understand that a man like Henry who had control over so many other things in his life would also have had some measure of personal control over the laws and customs of the forests he patronised. In fact he insisted on it.

From its beginnings at the time of the Norman kings, the Great Forest of Essex had been managed by men in specially created posts, the highest being the steward or lord warden. From him, others ranged down through lieutenant of the forest, deputy warden and master keepers (often the lords of the manor) until it levelled out at under keepers, regarders, woodwards and reeves. Henry himself appointed the lord warden of the forest, setting the precedent for it to become a position by royal appointment only.

The king himself added new legislation to the existing rules of the forest. He also adhered to them and expected his subjects to do likewise. During midwinter, when stag could not be hunted, royals and their nobles took to hawking. A noble was only allowed to hunt and kill one stag at a time for the requirements of a feast or a banquet. Dogs, except those belonging to clergy, were 'lawed' (claws removed) so they were unable to chase deer. No fences within the forest were to be at a height that would restrict the movements of a doe with her fawn and farmers were not allowed to drive the deer from their crops. All trees and scrub such as holly, blackthorn, hawthorn and crab apple, which were food for the deer, were also protected. In 1543 the king issued an Act of Parliament, declaring that all 'coppiced' trees should be enclosed and left untouched for at least four years to prevent the over-stripping of timber. After Henry had dissolved the monastic buildings of Essex he ordered a survey to be carried out of all 3,000 acres of the woodland of Hainault Forest. The details were collected and presented back to the king by his Essex 'Woodwards' George Maxey and William Mildmay.

For those that flouted forest law Henry VIII imposed the heaviest penalties, but interestingly in 1533 he introduced legislation that actually contradicted existing laws designed to protect game and birds' eggs. Alarmed at the damage rooks and crows caused to both crops and the thatch on the roofs of cottages and barns, the Act declared that every parish must keep nets for catching the offending birds and allowed anyone who had previously been refused by a landowner to 'trespass' upon his property to catch and destroy the birds without fear of reprisal.

Henry VIII hunted until his last years and records exist of the payments he made to people in the forest for providing him with services and entertainment.

In 1543 a document describes how George Maxey was paid £30 for work at the 'Great Stonedeings' [sic] and for laying out and enclosing the king's 'new deer park at Feyremeade' (Fairmead) all in Chingford.

Though Writtle Manor, approximately 2 miles outside Chelmsford, was considered suitable for a hunting lodge, it is not certain if the king ever used it as such. He did, however, make many visits to the area; one occasion in 1527 was mentioned in a dispatch dated 31 July which informed Cardinal Wolsey (the king's advisor) that Henry would be in Essex in August for the hunting in Waltham Forest and that he would be visiting Castle Hedingham and the royal estate at New Hall Boreham.

Prior to the Norman Conquest in 1062, New Hall had first belonged to the canons of Waltham Abbey. The Crown acquired it in 1491; it was granted to the king by the Earl of Ormond, Sir Thomas Boleyn, father of Henry's second and most enigmatic wife, Anne. The estate was sold back to the king in 1516 for the princely sum of £1,000; Henry spent £17,000 immediately on re-facing the old house in majestic brick. It was after this that Henry renamed the house Beaulieu, meaning beautiful place. Was it just Henry's desire for splendour and beauty that prompted him to invest in what was, by royal standards, a fairly moderate Essex estate? There was, of course, the possibility that Henry was building a palace 'fit for a prince', the live heir he much needed, a royal babe that would be his and wife Katherine of Aragon's fifth child.

Henry had given the order to build Beaulieu eight months into Katherine's pregnancy, hoping beyond hope that she would be delivered of a son. Having married in 1509 their first child, a girl, had been stillborn on 31 January 1510, followed exactly a year later by a son, Henry, Duke of Cornwall, who lived for only fifty-two days. The years 1513 and 1514 saw the births of two more sons, the first surviving no more than a few hours, the second delivered dead. Four children promised then snatched away was nothing less than a tragedy for the king and queen and must have seen both Henry and Katherine despair.

But adversity appeared to have turned to hope and then gratitude when, almost at the end of Katherine's fifth pregnancy, Henry ordered plans for the transformation of Newhall, the subsequent delivery of a live and healthy baby prompting a genuine joy in the king. Henry certainly set out to make a statement, incorporating eight courtyards and two massive gatehouse towers. Years later in 1547, a housekeeping record listed twenty-nine great beds, four bathing rooms with wooden floors and a library. The enlargement and enhancement was undertaken without a hint of disappointment that it was Princess Mary who was the royal couple's only heir. Always believing he would sire more sons in the years to come, Henry, in those early years, cherished Mary as the 'greatest pearl in his entire kingdom'.

Henry was at Beaulieu again in July 1527 but this time not with his wife Katherine. With a much-reduced court and now in the company of his 'mistress' he was spending a month away from London, with its sweltering high-summer heat and foul-smelling Thames, to enjoy the charms (those she would allow) of Anne Boleyn. Rumour has it that it was here, in the early stages of trying to obtain a divorce from Katherine, that Henry entertained the idea of asking the Pope to permit him to commit bigamy! The idea was dropped once discovered by Cardinal Wolsey.

May 1528 saw Waltham Abbey play host to the king when, accompanied by both queen Katherine of Aragon and Anne Boleyn, he fled Greenwich after an outbreak of the sweating sickness. He returned the following July while on 'progress', this time just with Anne. It was three years later that he and Anne revisited the monks of Waltham Abbey. Henry was still in pursuit of a divorce and Anne was still keeping him at arm's length, and for five days the king 'hunted' the frustrations out of his system in Epping Forest and in the hunting park of Copped Hall.

Henry and Anne were familiar figures in the forest while Anne was the king's favourite. The forest was also the place Henry came to on the day of Anne's execution, wanting to be out of London but near enough to hear when the Tower of London's guns announced that Anne was dead. Upon hearing it Henry exclaimed ungallantly, 'The day's work is done, uncouple the hounds and let us further the sport' – he was at High Beech. Later he rode to Theobald's in Waltham Cross, into the arms of Jane Seymour, whom he married very soon after.

Henry, after finally daring to believe he was a king that could at last have both a compatible wife and much-longed-for son, had one snatched away by fate, which then waited impatiently for the other. At Royden, in 1531, an estate high in the north-west of the county close to Harlow and within touching distance of neighbouring Hertfordshire, the king was to share both his sorrow and joy with its inhabitants. For here, in the hall Henry had previously bought for Anne Boleyn in exchange for Bromhill Priory in Norfolk, Henry poignantly presented to the villagers the newborn infant prince, Edward, the son neither Katherine nor Anne had been able to give him; the son Jane had produced to her cost.

Of all the nobles who entertained the king at their Essex residences – Ingatestone's Sir William Petre and Sir Thomas Darcy of St Osyth, to name a couple – it was Lord Henry Marney who, in knowing Henry as both prince and king, was a respected friend. Marney had fought in the Battle of Bosworth and had subsequently been knighted. He had also been present that All Hallows' Day (1 November) in 1494 when the young Prince Henry, who was never born to be king, was created Duke of York. The Christmases of 1508 and 1509 saw Marney receive handsome gifts from the newly crowned King Henry VIII, then just eighteen.

Henry VIII on the morning of Anne Boleyn's execution, hunting in Epping Forest. Henry was to proceed to the home of Jane Seymour once he had heard the Tower of London's guns announcing Anne was dead.

Marney had become Lord Privy Seal, Vice Chamberlain of the Household and Captain of the Yeoman of the Guard, a body of men created by Henry VII for his own personal safety. Add to that Chancellor of the Duchy of Lancaster, Steward of the Duchy of Cornwall and the award of the Honour of Clare in Suffolk and you have a man who, almost overnight, became one of the richest office holders in the kingdom. In the words of the king himself, Marney was one of those 'scant but well born gentlemen; and yet of no great lands till they were promoted by us and so made a knight and lord'.

Henry Marney certainly lasted in the king's employ and was one of the few men to have 'great authority and credit with the king'. His home, Layer Marney Tower, was always an open house. It must have been in various states of construction when the king visited in August 1522, as Layer Marney Tower was built between 1515 and 1525. Designed to rival Cardinal Wolsey's imposing Hampton Court on the river at Richmond, Henry VIII certainly found his friend's house impressive, if unfinished. Alas Henry Marney died in 1523, leaving the estate for his son to complete, but he too died soon after. Between them, however, they had finished the church, stable block and magnificently decorated front side of the courtyarded palace. Today we can still marvel at what was then and is now the tallest Tudor gatehouse in the country.

As well as occasionally sharing the homes of his subjects, Henry also owned hereditary palaces such as the one at Havering-atte-Bower, traditionally the property of the queens of England. Here, Henry repaired the ruinous palace of Pirgo (spelt Portegore by Henry VIII's officials), just north-east of Havering village, and in 1536 imparked the land for hunting, allowing a steward to remain there to oversee the estate. It was here (it is said) that in 1542 that Henry called together his estranged daughters, Mary and Elizabeth, to his new house at Pirgo and, 'being pleased with them', was said to have made the decision to reinstate them in the succession to the crown.

Further east towards the marshes and islands of the Essex coast, Rayleigh and Rochford were also haunts of the king, with Rochford Hall being an estate of the Boleyns and Rayleigh part of the royal deer park, which regularly replenished the stocks of does and bucks at Greenwich Park.

With England's security high on Henry's housekeeping list, he made many inroads into Essex to see for himself the state of his sea defences along the Thames estuary. Henry's divorce from Catherine of Aragon had left England politically isolated, and he had concerns as to what would happen if Harwich, one of the South's valuable deep-water harbours, should fall into the hands of an invader. Should that happen he knew that London could find itself under attack after less than a day's march. Thus Henry visited Harwich in 1543 and under a new coastal defence programme of Device Forts, three blockhouses were built to protect the strategic port from seaborne attack. Perhaps to check the progress of his plans, Henry at times oversaw the work on site; a document of 1544 ordered the bailiffs of Colchester to prepare provisions for '1,600–2,000 horse accompanying his Majestie to Harwich'.

Tilbury was also a concern and in 1539 Henry had five coastal blockhouses built to defend the sea route into London should the French or Spanish attempt an attack. One of these blockhouses was built on the Essex bank at West Tilbury, the site his daughter would visit in her own right as queen, to rally her troops against the threat of the Spanish Armada in 1588.

PRINCE ALBERT EDWARD (1841–1910)

The Prince along with the Princess of Wales, Prince George, Princesses Victoria and Maud will travel to Easton Lodge on Monday afternoon arriving at Takely station by special train between 3 and 4 o'clock.

Essex Standard, December 1889

At the other end of the princely scale we have unlikely Essex boy Albert Arthur George Saxe-Coburg Gotha, later King Edward VIII, who frequently visited the county while conducting his affair with Francis Maynard, Lady Warwick. Just one of a famous bevy of mistresses of 'Bertie' she, however, was known to have been the most passionate love of his life and entertained the man who would be king for just under a decade.

Known to be a lover of fast horses and even faster women, Edward's sober upbringing was almost certainly a factor in his 'live for today' playboy lifestyle. His mother, Queen Victoria, was so besotted with her husband, Albert, that she had little time for her children, and given that this was a time when infants were soon given to wet nurses a deep bond with her son did not take place. Named after his father but unfortunately not resembling him in any other way, Albert, who was also not as clever as his intelligent elder sister 'Vicky', was thought by Victoria to be 'backward'.

Intense study was thought the answer to improve the young prince, so much so that in later life the Prince of Wales said, 'I had no boyhood.' He was even made to forfeit family holidays at Balmoral in favour of study alone with a tutor. Though his father's namesake, young Albert was always referred to as Bertie, reputedly for a time only being referred to as 'the boy' by his mother who explained, 'I do not think him worthy of being called Albert yet.' Unfortunately in her eyes he never was.

The Prince of Wales's relationship with his parents remained strained well into young adulthood, the royal couple believing him to be a liability. Albert once described his son as 'neither fish nor flesh', while Victoria wrote in letters to his sister Vicky, the Crown Princess of Prussia, that her brother Bertie was never going to be handsome 'with that painfully small and narrow head, those immense features and total want of chin'. Victoria, not a monarch who could hide her disappointment, continued to lament, 'You cannot imagine the awful anxiety for the future which he causes us!'

Such disapproval did not go unnoticed and Victoria on one occasion was reproached for her lack of feeling toward her son by her half-sister. 'Do show him love, dearest Victoria. I know that he thinks you are not fond of him.' It had the opposite effect and when news reached Victoria of Bertie's first sexual encounter, it stretched her relationship with her son to breaking point.

How such an encounter came about was a piece of brilliant engineering on the part of his fellow Army cadets given that in 1861 the prince was spending ten weeks at Curragh Army training camp in Ireland. 'Minded' day and night by two Grenadier officers and a colonel, Bertie even slept in the general's quarters, yet knowing that Albert was a sexual novice, his companions smuggled local actress Nellie Clifton into the prince's bedroom via a secluded window. Evidence in his engagement diary during September 1861 shows Albert enjoyed a second and third encounter with 'NC', obviously taking to this new-found activity with enthusiasm.

When newspapers reported his liaison with the young actress the news caused his father 'the greatest pain I have ever yet felt in this life'. Albert, in relating the affair to the queen, informed her she was not to hear 'the disgusting details'.

As a consequence, Prince Albert first wrote to his son, by now studying at university, then chastised him in person by visiting him and walking for hours with him out in cold, damp weather, impacting his own weakened health. Thus when Prince Albert died not long after on 14 December 1861, Victoria hysterically blamed the Prince of Wales and the episode at the Curragh for his father's death. 'That boy,' she wrote to her daughter Vicky in Germany, 'I never can, or ever shall look at him without a shudder.' They never made amends.

In 1863 Edward married Princess Alexandra, the eldest daughter of King Christian IX of Denmark, and fathered five legitimate children in quick succession between 1864 and 1869. He was in love when he married and cared for his wife, but with Alexandra heavily involved with her children and her charity work, Bertie's passions were ultimately catered for by a plethora of mistresses. Between Lillie Langtry, whose affair with the prince lasted from 1877 to 1880, and his last companion, Alice Keppel, whom he installed as his mistress from 1898 till his death in 1910, Edward's eye fell upon the wife of Lord Brooke. Francis Evelyn Greville (née Maynard), the Countess of Warwick, who liked to be known by her childhood nickname 'Daisy', was the woman with whom he fell deeply in love.

Daisy had married Lord Brooke in 1881 and, like Alexandra, had provided her husband with three children very quickly. Having produced a son and heir, Daisy had been open to the infidelity accepted in the aristocratic circles in which she moved and was already the lover of Lord Beresford, an engaging and ambitious young naval officer. With adultery a social convention, there was no need for divorce, and affairs in high society were almost to be expected. With the scandal of divorce far outweighing the reasons for it, liaisons were conducted with discretion, even Daisy herself declaring that 'a scandal was a romance until it was found out'.

Fortunately for the prince it was Daisy's own rashness that saw her seek his assistance in order to retrieve a furious letter she had written to her lover deploring the fact he had dared make his wife pregnant while declaring his love for her. The letter had since fallen into his wife's hands and was threatening to ruin her. By securing a favourable outcome, Bertie found himself on the receiving end of Daisy's gratitude. Their affair was to last almost a decade, the backdrop to their meetings being both her Essex estate of Easton Lodge, and Warwick Castle, inherited by her husband Lord Brooke in 1893.

In truth the prince had known Daisy since her childhood and he confessed to being fascinated by her on many levels. She rode dangerous racehorses from her stepfather's stable, had been to the theatre with Disraeli and, most shockingly, she had thwarted the plans of his mother Queen Victoria to marry her to his youngest brother, Prince Leopold. In short she was headstrong and impulsive. She was also part of the prince's Marlborough House Set, a section of aristocracy who were named after the prince's London residence. It was a place that proved to be a thorn in the side of Queen Victoria and her straight-laced retainers who remembered the vulgar 'Carlton House Set' of the debauched George IV. Considering his relationship with his mother, Bertie made no apologies for his or their conduct.

With no paparazzi, Edward appeared free to indulge himself without the fear of being exposed in the newspapers. Yet with discretion being the by-word of the era a mechanism was still needed by which the prince could pursue his 'interests' with the minimum of reportage. Thus the concept of the 'country-house weekend' was born. An outward sign of gentlemanly pursuits, it provided hunting and shooting by day and sport of a different nature by night. In his book *Royal Mistresses*, Charles Carlton discloses that the country-house weekend was essentially an elaborately choreographed game of musical beds; 'some helpful hostesses even posted name plaques on the doors to help the wanderers locate their quarry'.

Scandalously, 'tea time' was the optimum time for assignations. Late in the afternoon the men would come in from sport and the ladies would be waiting dressed in specially made loose diaphanous garments known as tea-gowns, devoid of corsetry and petticoats, designed for ease of movement and to appear a tempting sight for the gentlemen. Daisy's gowns were usually bought from Paris, designed by the great French designers, Charles Worth and Doucet. A surviving description of one of Daisy's gowns from a contemporary magazine reads, 'Lady Brooke [Daisy] defied all competition in a soft green gauze gown held to her waist by a band fastened with an emerald and diamond buckle and finished at the neck by a deep falling collar of chinchilla.'

Daisy was the most passionate love of Bertie's life. He showered her with jewels, as he did all his mistresses, but to his stunningly beautiful Daisy he gave the ring his parents had given him on his confirmation. Big and gold, it bore the initials 'V&A' and was the most personal and intimate item he had ever given anyone. He wrote her letters in a Latin code, usually ending affectionately, 'My own adored little Daisy wife'.

A less flattering label, namely that of 'Babbling Brooke', was also assigned to Daisy, the moniker stemming from the fact she was unable to keep gossip to herself. But both Daisy's husband, whom she called 'Brookie', and the prince were devoted to her. Her husband stated he would rather be married to Daisy, with all her faults, than to any other woman in the world. Thus Lord and Lady Brooke entertained the prince at Easton Lodge frequently during the 1890s.

The newspapers kept pace with the prince's many visits into Essex, one of the earliest being in June 1886 when both the Prince and Princess of Wales visited Easton Lodge. The *Essex Newsman* informed the reader that their Royal Highnesses were to spend a weekend visiting Lord and Lady Brooke at Easton Lodge and that they were travelling by train and expected at Takely or Elsenham stations and would return via Dunmow. Afterwards 100 men from the 2nd Volunteer Battalion Essex Regiment would form a guard of honour at the Dunmow railway station on Monday to see them off.

However, three years later visits by the prince were becoming a singular affair, with the *Essex Standard* reporting in September 1889 what was fast becoming a familiar headline, namely 'The Prince of Wales at Easton Lodge'. This time the paper stated that 'The Prince of Wales paid a hastily arranged private visit to Lord and Lady Brook, at Easton Lodge, near Dunmow', the visit having been kept very quiet, with officials unaware of who was on the 12:47 train from Takely until it arrived. Even the stationmaster had been kept in the dark. It was said the visit was unannounced so as to avoid 'anything like a demonstration'. After shooting and attending church on Sunday the prince left on Monday morning catching the train to Stortford and continuing on to St Pancras where, 'accompanied by Lady Brook', he continued on to Scotland.

In December 1889 the prince visited Easton Lodge and of course Daisy, with the papers reporting he was 'adding hunting to his Christmas festivities'. The following year in November the Chelmsford Chronicle covered the

Albert Edward as king. For almost ten years he was a frequent visitor to Easton Lodge, the home of Lady Warwick.

arrival of distinguished guests at Easton, the Prince of Wales among them. On his departure it reported that the prince 'had enjoyed his brief stay at Easton Lodge very much' and expressed himself as 'remarkably well pleased with the arrangements made for his comfort'.

Weekend visits seemed a favourite, as in 1892 the prince was again with 'Lord & Lady Brooke'. The newspaper delighted in professing that the visit was of 'a purely private nature', pointing out with its literary eyebrow raised that 'when the prince left on Monday morning it was Daisy who drove him to the station'.

The manner by which the prince was transported was to become a feature of all royal reports. Such small snippets of information spoke volumes about his relationship with Daisy. Theirs was an equal partnership. He did not see Daisy solely as a sex object, he enjoyed her companionship and she in return enjoyed a measure of control over her royal suitor. Daisy was no Victorian shrinking violet, as can be ascertained by her insistence on always collecting her prince from the station.

By 1895 Edward's ability to visit his mistress became easier and thus more frequent, as Daisy and her accommodating husband had paid for a small station or halt to be built at Easton Lodge out of their own pocket. Convenient though this strategically placed station would become for Bertie and Daisy, it could not and did not stop the inevitable.

Their affair ended in 1898 when she was supplanted by Alice Keppel, the mistress at his side until he died. But though their passion cooled their friendship did not. In fact it was one of Edward's virtues that he was able to leave a relationship with as much chivalry as he had started it with. Not a possessive lover, Edward was a kind man and seldom made an enemy of a mistress or indeed their husbands. He never disparaged the women he had known, and though Alexandra, his wife, suffered his infidelities in private she was never humiliated in public, causing her to say of her husband, 'if he were a cowboy I would love him just the same'. Daisy too said of her prince, in a letter long after their trysts at Easton Lodge had become romantic memories, that 'he was a very perfect, gentle lover' adding that 'anybody would have been won by him'.

When Daisy died in 1938 her obituary in *The Times* made light of her nine-year affair with Bertie, the whole episode diluted down to no more than a grudging reference: 'Above all she enjoyed the friendship of King Edward VII both as Prince and sovereign ... King Edward liked her for her wit and vivacity, and beside there was a bond of union in their interest in the common people.' A report in *Hello* magazine it was not...

2

WARRIORS

He himself was tall of stature standing above the rest.

Byrhtferth's Life of St Oswald, tenth century

The Bayeux Tapestry is unarguably the most famous work of embroidery surviving today; an epic battle picked out in thread, woven forever into the very fabric of our history. But it is not the only tapestry to record such events. The Battle of Maldon in 991 was also depicted in such a fashion. The poignant commemoration of this earlier Essex battle could well have been the inspiration behind the embroidery that recorded in such detail the history-changing events of 1066. But it was first and foremost a labour of love; it was commissioned by Aethelflaed, the widow of Maldon's fallen hero, who presented it to the Abbey of Ely, her husband's final resting place.

In the Liber Eliensis, a tenth-century account about life at Ely, it was described as 'a curtain woven and depicted with the deeds of her husband as a memorial of his virtue'. That fallen hero was Byrhtnoth, Earl of Essex. The location for this epic battle between Saxon host and Viking hoard was 'on Pantas stream', known to us now as the River Blackwater.

To all intents and purposes 'Byrhtnoth' was a prophetic name. Composed of Old English, *beorht*, meaning 'bright' and *noth*, 'courage', history records this giant of a man as *Byrhtnoþ* or *Byrhtnoð*, *Byrihtnoð*, *Brihtnoþ*, *Beorhtnoþ*, *Beorhtnoð*, and *Baeorhtnoð*. History also records – when his bones were discovered and examined at Ely in 1769 – that he, at an estimated 6 feet 9 inches – would have stood head and shoulders over his men, a leader of imposing physical appearance. He was also a man of immense wealth.

Saxon marriage customs of this period required a husband give his bride a 'Morgengifu' or 'morning gift' (that was hers alone) at the time of the wedding and Byrhtnoth gave his prospective bride, among others items, the village of Rettendon (or Retendune) in Essex, a parish that she in turn gave to the monks of Ely on the occasion of her husband's death. After her own death her Will mentions her sister (the second wife of King Edmund) and her husband, with whom she shared interest in many other Essex locations, namely Peldon, Mersea and Greenstead, Fingringhoe, Woodham, Barking and Wickford. Byrhtnoth himself gave the manor of Lawling to the monks of Canterbury in the very year of that famous battle in AD 991.

It was not, however, his wealth or appearance that saw this man renowned. Byrhtnoth must be one of the few military commanders who earned his place in the annals of history for a defeat rather than a victory. Yet events leading up to that defeat were lauded in literature, written into an epic work to rival that of Beowulf; the poem 'The Battle of Maldon', applauding not so much winner over loser, but courage and determination in the face of oppression and conquest. Though the battle's outcome effectively changed the course of English history, Byrhtnoth's heroic stand has become the stuff of legend and is now a defining characteristic of the British as an island race.

We know most about this man from sources written after the battle, embellished perhaps, but 'The Battle of Maldon' was probably written by someone who knew the area and had good knowledge of the event. Remarkably the text is in Old English at a time when most learned men still used Latin. Hence we know of 'Pantan' stream (Blackwater), where the waters 'locked', as they still do today, whenever the tide returns and the waves meet across the causeway. Then the waters were narrow enough for an arrow to easily find its mark on the opposite shore, and it was possible for no more than three archers to keep the Danes confined on the small island of Northey, where they were encamped. Northey was larger then. As with all military engagement it is preferable to engage one's enemy hand to hand and on open ground. It's what the Danes wanted and ultimately what Byrhtnoth gave them.

The road to Northey for the Danes begun in AD 991, when Olaf Tryggvason, later King of Norway, arrived off the Kent coast with ninety-three ships and harassed the towns and villages from Sandwich to Ipswich, which they sacked. Then they turned to Maldon. Encamped on Northey until the tides allowed them access to the mainland, it is possible they did not initially seek battle as a messenger shouted across the sea-washed causeway that bloody battle could be avoided if sufficient 'tribute' was paid. Byrhtnoth, who had instructed his men in their positions, shouted back his unmistakable answer: 'Spear-point and sword-edge first shall appease us, grim play of battle, ere we grant tribute.' Byrhtnoth, bent on revenge for those already slain, was not going to give in without a fight.

With the eventual ebbing of the tide and the realisation that they were easy targets for Byrhtnoth's Saxons, the Danes requested to be allowed to cross

Following the expulsion of Erik Bloodaxe from York in 954, England had enjoyed a quarter-century of respite from Viking attacks. One of the two men responsible for their resumption was Olaf Tryggvason. Earl Byrhtnoth and his Saxon thegns led the English against Olaf and his Viking invasion. When Olaf addressed the Saxons, promising to sail away if he was paid with gold, Byrhtnoth replied, 'We will pay you with spear tips and sword blades.' The battle ended in an Anglo Saxon defeat. (Bob Bowman)

to the mainland. Incredibly this was granted and the Vikings then rushed forward, first hitting the Saxon warhedge or shield wall before slicing through into the main body of men, who rushed at them with equal ferocity. 'Bitter was the battle-rush,' the poem tells us. 'Fighters fell on either hand; young men lay low.' Byrhtnoth's nephew Wulfmaer was among the butchered. 'The slain fell to earth. Steadfast they stood. Byrhtnoth incited them…'

As bloodied as his men, Byrhtnoth himself was wounded, but killed his assailant. He was then wounded again, and seeing his leader falter, a young squire pulled the spear from his body and in turn killed the attacker. Losing strength, Byrhtnoth eventually fell at the hands of a Dane, but not before thanking God 'for all of those joys I have known in the world' with his dying prayer.

As with many battles, once a leader falls men lose heart and leave the field, but although some of Byrhtnoth's men ran to the woods, his *húskarlar*, or housecarls, stood firm. It would appear Byrhtnoth commanded such respect from his men that they were willing to die for him as a matter of honour. The poem shows us this devotion, when Byrhtwold, an ageing retainer, finds these words:

Temper must braver be, keener the heart,
courage the greater, as our strength lessens.
Here lies our leader all hewn down,
the good man in the dirt. May he ever mourn
who thinks to turn now from this battle-play.

I am grown old; I will not hence,
but beside my lord do I
mean to lie, nigh so dearly loved a man.

Byrhtnoth's 'precious gems, raiment and rings, and well-wrought sword' were taken as war trophies but it brought the Vikings themselves no joy as we know from sources that, despite the victory, they were so badly depleted in both body and spirit that they 'could hardly man their ships'.

The Anglo-Saxon chronicles tell us that 'afterwards that same year it was decided to pay tribute to the Danes for the first time to the tune of ten thousand pounds'.

With the benefit of hindsight it is easy to question Byrhtnoth's decision to let the Danes bring the fight to him rather than the other way around, after all he did initially have the upper hand. But research has thrown up the argument that Byrhtnoth, knowing he could have easily beaten the invaders, chose not to in accordance with Saxon war etiquette. Such pride and arrogance were qualities frowned upon in a leader. Thus we can blame an ancient code of conduct, not misjudgment, for Byrhtnoth's defeat, and applaud a man who sacrificed his life but not his honour.

Byrhtnoth. (Bob Bowman)

SIR JOHN HAWKWOOD (c. 1320–1394)

*Syr Iohan Hawkwoode … and many others whoes names shyne gloriously
by their virtue noblesse and actes that they did in the onour of the odre of
chylvalry.*

Nineteenth-century author

Legend has it that his mother gave birth to him in a wood, having been frightened by hawks, but it is more likely that John Hawkwood's family name derived, like so many other medieval names, from a location. 'Halke' is Middle English for 'nook' or 'corner'. Scant few records remain regarding the Hawkwoods, and what there are deal mostly with land dealings and tax records of John's father Gilbert de Hawkwood. What is known is that by the time John was born his family had risen to the level of minor gentry. These records, featured in Christopher Starr's book *Medieval Mercenary*, show the slow increase in fortune that had seen Gilbert de Hawkwood become the owner of property in Gosport, Finchingfield, and Sible Headingham.

It is most likely John's birth occurred at Headingham, with documents stating he was 'the son of a tanner'. As John's father was a man of substance, it is more than likely he owned a tannery instead of being employed by one. Plus Gilbert de Hawkwood's Will, dated 1340, indicates that the Hawkwoods were far from poor. Gilbert's eldest son was left approximately £100 in bequests; £6 of that was in coin of the realm, the rest made up of 'my yoke of 6 stots and 2 oxen in the messuage of Sible Headingham', the messuage being Hawkwood Manor situated in Potter Street, later known as Swan Street.

As a second son, John was to receive from his elder brother 'a quantity of grain, a bed and a sum of twenty pound' which was by no means ungenerous. But with his elder sibling in receipt of the lion's share of their father's estate and already a man of some substance in his own right in the employ of the powerful De Vere family at Castle Headingham, there was little John could do but look further afield to better himself.

The rumour that he was apprenticed to a tailor in London is questionable. It far more reasonable to assume he automatically joined the ranks of men he saw volunteering for the private armies of his local lords, such as the De Veres, the Bourchiers of Halstead and the FitzWalters of Henham and Woodham Walter. These lords, already on John's doorstep, were actively looking for men to join their private armies fighting on the Continent in support of Edward III's claim to the French throne. It was a conflict that would later become known as the Hundred Years' War.

It is also reasonable to believe John Hawkwood offered his services to the Army as an archer. The bow was a weapon every man in every English village was required by law to master from boyhood, honing his skill 'atte the buttes' every Sabbath, usually before church. Some churches still bear the scars of arrows sharpened on the bases of stone pillars throughout particularly boring sermons. As late as 1541, Henry VIII, in order to stem the 'decay of Archery' stated all men under the age of sixty and 'men-children between Seven Years and Seventeen shall have a Bow and 2 Shafts'. Once seventeen, men were obliged to 'keep a Bow and 4 Arrows'.

In Hawkwood's England the longbow, or warbow, reigned supreme. It was greater in length than the 4-foot bow used on the Continent, and so gave English archers an unsurpassed advantage. It is maintained by Geoffrey Trease, in his book *The Condottieri,* that the bows used by the fourteenth-century mercenary troops of Sir John Hawkwood were as 'tall as themselves or a fraction taller'. As rule of thumb an archer's bow was always a hand's breadth taller than he himself. Given that the average height of a medieval soldier was between 5 feet and 5 feet 2 inches, this makes a longbow a considerable length. Accurate and deadly, a longbow's range was anything from 180 to 248 yards, plus it had a rapid rate of fire, at ten to twelve arrows a minute. Relatively cheap and simple to make, in an army of practiced hands it could literally rain death down on an enemy. Resulting injuries were nothing short of horrific with wounds measuring 3 inches long by 2 inches wide and 6 inches deep. It was no wonder the longbow was the national weapon of the English army.

Hawkwood spent twenty years in France as a soldier; his basic pay as a mounted archer was *6d* per day. Wages were not generous but they were supplemented by a *regardum,* a 'reward' or bonus, which most captains of retinues agreed to pay. Yet even when supplemented by the 'reward', wages were not enough and irregularly paid. The real source of profit was exploitation of the enemy, in the form of ransoms of prisoners, loot from captured towns, booty seized on the battlefield, and land captured and settled by Englishmen in France. It is assumed that Hawkwood fought in the landmark Battle of Crecy in 1346, the commander of a troop of 250 archers, and again ten years later in the Battle of Poitiers where it is thought he was knighted by the king, or if not that he assumed the title himself with the support of his fellow soldiers, but evidence of this has still to be found.

The Treaty of Bretigny in 1360, under which Edward renounced his claim to the French throne, was the truce that saw an end to the fighting between France and England and effectively halted Hawkwood's military career in its tracks. That he had earned distinction in the army of the English is without doubt, though it had not been as lucrative as perhaps he had hoped. According to the famous Flemish chronicler Froissart, Hawkwood was 'a poor Knight with nothing but his spurs'.

Unlike Edward the Black Prince and thousands of other troops (including Geoffrey Chaucer who had been captured by the French and ransomed for

£16), Hawkwood decided not to sail back to England. Of the mind that back
in Essex his estate was 'too small to support his title and dignity', he joined the
hundreds of out-of-work soldiers who headed south towards Avignon to sell
their military prowess to the highest bidder. By the autumn of 1360, groups
of these soldiers had formed themselves into small mercenary 'free' or 'great'
companies led by captains elected by the soldiers, and sub-divided into smaller
companies called 'routes' led by marshalls then constables. In 1361, records
point to Hawkwood being a marshall of one such company. The same year
he served under Albrecht Sterz, the commander of an Anglo-German body of
men, who was in the paid service of the Marquis of Montferat, who led his
mercenary army over the Alps to fight against Milan.

Deciding his future fortunes lay in Italy, the only time Hawkwood returned
to France was in 1362 at the start of his mercenary career. It was to fight in
the Battle of Brigaise, probably for booty. It was the Froissart Chronicle that
records the battle as being a godsend, as by now many men badly needed funds.
It appeared they 'all grew rich on the good prisoners'. During Hawkwood's
service to Edward III, rules had been established governing the sharing out
of ransoms and booty, called the 'rule of thirds', which dictated that a soldier
making the gain could only keep one-third of its value, the other two-thirds
payable to the captain of his company and the king. An official known as a
butiner was even employed to ensure this division of loot. Now, as captain
of a free company, Hawkwood was no longer bound by such regulations.
Brignaise was undoubtedly a lucrative move for Hawkwood but not enough
to keep him in France. Recognising money could be made wherever there
was conflict and that Italian cities preferred to hire mercenaries instead of
forming standing armies themselves, he stayed in Italy, where conflict was on
his doorstep.

After Brignaise, Hawkwood's career as a mercenary became legend. In 1363
he rejoined Sterz's company, before commanding his own 'White Company'
in 1364, the name deriving from the scrupulously polished 'shining' armour
Hawkwood demanded from his soldiers. Exploiting the shifting allegiances
and power politics of Italian factions for his own benefit he earned the name
'Condottori' from the numerous contracts (*condotta*) he undertook from
anyone and everyone throughout his career. He was even paid not to fight,
as in 1375, when Hawkwood took up arms on behalf of the Pope against
Florence in the War of the Eight Saints. Florence made an agreement with him
and he accepted a significant sum for not attacking those who hadn't paid
him, for three months.

The results of these contracts and counter-contracts enriched him enough
to be able to acquire estates in the Romagna, in Tuscany, and a castle at
Montecchio Vesponi. His greatest earnings in the years 1377 and 1381
amounted to 82,000 florins and 67,000 florins respectively, the income of a

small town. The least he earned one year in Pisa was 600 florins but that was still ten times the annual income of an average English baron. Despite his rudimentary education and contemporary accounts of his lack of oratorical skills, he was far more 'able with hand and industry than with tongue', revered for his integrity, loyalty to one master at a time and his refusal to knowingly fight against the English Crown or her interests abroad. His tactics too were innovative. Unlike his Continental enemies he favoured the art of surprise and night attacks, plus he fought long into the year, choosing mercenaries as tolerant to cold and rain as himself to fight by his side. Fair to his men, he would always pay them before he took his share of the spoils, thus ensuring their loyalty, plus it kept many fellow countrymen – William Gold, William Boson, John Brice and Richard Romsey, who had come to Italy with him – at his side. He led his men by example, his 'Englishness', a trait he retained throughout his life, instilling in his men steadiness and discipline in battle.

Hawkwood, in all his years as a mercenary, was not deemed unduly cruel. That honour was taken by the Hungarian and Breton companies who seemed predisposed to kill for pleasure with incredible savagery. But Hawkwood's massacre at Cesena in February 1377 cursed him with the unflattering title 'un diaudo incarnato' or 'devil incarnate', on account of the 5,000 men, women and children that were slaughtered. Rumour has it he even ordered that a captive nun be cut in half to stop two soldiers fighting over which one had the right to her. Such was his reputation after the atrocities of the 'Cesena bloodbath' that Italian mothers frightened their children with the threat that 'Giovanni Acuto' (the sharp one) would come for them if they disobeyed their parents.

In the last decade of his life Hawkwood became the commander of the army in Florence, effectively safeguarding her independence against Milanese expansion. In return Florence had given him citizenship and a pension. He died at his villa, San Donato, in Polvarosa close to Florence, of a suspected stroke in March 1394 and in a show of outward gratitude for his years of loyalty, the state of Florence buried him in the Basilica di Santa Maria del Fiore, the main church of Florence, also known as Duomo. After lying in state for several days he was interred in the north wall of the choir, a document of May 1394 recording that provision was made for bread and wine to be available for the mason who carried out the work, plus his assistant.

When news of Hawkwood's death filtered back to England, Richard II, who had previously appointed Sir John his ambassador to the Roman Court in 1381, requested his body be returned to his native country. King Richard saw it as his duty to repatriate English lords who had died abroad, having only months earlier asked for the return of Robert de Vere who had not died on English soil. Moreover, it was a request that reflected the high regard in which Richard held Hawkwood. In a letter of 3 June 1395 it was accepted by the Florentines...

Our devotion can deny nothing to the eminence of your highness. We will leave nothing undone that is possible to do, so that we may fulfil your good pleasure. So, therefore, although we consider it reflected glory on us and on our people to keep the ashes and bones of the late brave and most magnificent captain John Hawkwood, who as commander of our army, fought most gloriously for us and who at public expense was interred in the principal church of Santa Reparata ... Nevertheless, according to the tenor of your request, we freely concede permission that his remains shall return to his native land.

In answer, preparations were made to receive Hawkwood's body and reinter him in his native Essex in a tomb in St Peter's church, Sible Hedinghan. However, there is, and always has been, historical and scholarly confusion as to whether his body ever left Italy.

Archival evidence, of which there is far more in Italy than anywhere else, shows Sir John Hawkwood fathered at least five sons and two daughters by several different women, though he did have two legitimate wives, the second, Donnina Visconti, being the daughter of the Duke of Milan. It also points to Hawkwood in the year before he died liquidating his estates and collecting money owed him to finance a proposed retirement back in England. Letters exist that show Hawkwood dispatched his 'wellbeloved Squyer' (squire), John Sampson, to England several times in order to arrange things with the trustees of his English landholdings, one of them being Thomas Coggeshalle. In a letter dated 20 February 1393 Hawkwood asked Sampson to obtain 'safe conduct for his return'; Sampson's answer was that he would ensure five men and horses would accompany him home via Calais.

Further evidence supports Hawkwood's intention to return to Essex. He arranges the marriages of his two eldest daughters, Janet, aged fifteen, and Catherine, aged fourteen, to an Italian noble and prominent German mercenary respectively, while Anna, at only six, was to accompany him and his wife, Donnina, home to England.

His death in 1394, however, meant his trustees in England, instead of receiving him home, had to implement the conditions of his Will. This was rife with mismanagement and resulted in Hawkwood's wife Donnina and his young son John unable to take possession of the 'great sums of gold' Hawkwood had sent back to England throughout his career. It also meant land he had provided for them in Sible Headingham could not be claimed.

Hawkwood's son, John Hawkwood, never did fully inherit his father's estates. He died young and childless before the age of twenty-one when he would have come of age. Plus there were no more heirs as Hawkwood's male line had died out within fifteen years of his own death, his bloodline in England continuing only through Antiocha, the daughter from his first marriage, who had married William de Coggeshalle. Her daughters, Alice and Blanche, married into the Essex gentry, Alice becoming the wife of John Terrell (Tyrell), a family which has held prominent office throughout English history.

There is one possibility, however, that John Hawkwood's mercenary legacy lived on. There are tantalising references to a Thomas Hawkwood, reputedly a bastard son, but a man after his father's own heart. Taking up arms as a young man, he too rose through the ranks, but this time in the service of John Tiptoft, a governor of Aquitaine. Records show a Thomas Hawkwood taken in battle in 1376 outside Bologna and subsequently ransomed in Venice.

BATTLE KNIGHTS:
SIR JOHN GIFFORD & SIR THOMAS STAPEL

And the knights come down on them, faceless men clad in all steel, and the iron thunder of their charge seems to fill the world.

George R. R. Martin

Men like Hawkwood were mercenaries and adventurers; men out for blood, money and glory, but for some, the ancient medieval law of 'fealty' was the reason men, of all ranks, followed their lords or masters into the thick of battle. Feudalism, introduced by William the Conqueror, was based on the exchange of land for military service, a reward he gave his knights for their part in his conquest of England. As the king's vassals (not to be confused with villains or slaves) these lords would in turn bestow land and favours to those in their 'manors' or 'domains' on the swearing of an Oath of Fealty and an act of homage in a commendation ceremony. Designed to create a lasting bond between vassal and lord, fealty was the key element of medieval social system. It also proved to be a pyramid of power that any ambitious man could climb.

Essex men featured in nearly all medieval foreign wars. Sir John Gifford, whose family gave its name to Bowers Gifford, a village deep in the south-east of the county, was with Edward III's army at the victorious Battle of Crecy in 1346. The Giffard family (an earlier spelling of Gifford), beginning with Sir William, is recorded in the parish as early as 1243 in a Feat of Fines or record of a property transaction. Sir John himself resided at the largest of seven farmhouses in the area called Earls Fee, which was situated towards the Benfleet creek on the marshland just below St Margaret's church. Today, Bowers Gifford is a united benefice with North Benfleet but then there was a sizable population concerned mainly with the keeping of sheep both for their wool and for the production of a good, strong-flavoured cheese, an apparent favourite with sailors. As well as holding the farm,

Sir John Gifford in addition rented 500 acres from Sir John de Vere, 7th Earl of Oxford, for which he had to pay sixpence per year and also to provide 'Silver Spurs for a Knight's Horse'. He is commemorated in brass, in his coat of armour, preserved in the church of St Margaret.

Another Essex man commemorated in brass from the locality was Sir Thomas Stapel; sergeant-at-arms to Edward III, his likeness in full armour is featured on a medieval coffin lid (1371) in the Norman church of All Saints, Sutton, having been relocated from the demolished ancient church at Shopland.

Sergeant-at-arms was a respected rank, both on the battlefield and surprisingly also in the shires. Essentially the king's bodyguard, the Household Ordinance of 1318 ordained there should be thirty sergeants, each one armed, equipped with three horses and resident at court. Four were to sleep outside the king's chamber at night and the remainder within earshot in the hall. When the king travelled all were to precede him on horseback. There were times when the sergeant-at-arms became unpopular, namely during the Peasants' Revolt where a few used the grievance to further their own ends, but generally in times of peace their numbers were low and their duties generally consisted of dealing with matters of local administration and justice.

As Edward's rudimentary police force, the more power he gave to his sergeants the more power he effectively had in his shires, and some men stayed at this post for upward of twenty years.

One of Thomas's recorded duties was to stop a comparatively new crime which had taken a hold, especially in wool-rich counties of Essex, Suffolk, and Kent, which was that of smuggling. It had first emerged about 1300 during the reign of Edward I and was a reaction to the first customs tax charged on the export of English wool, which was in great demand in Europe. This was the first permanent customs system established in England, and until it was set up all trade in and out of England was free. The initial duties started quite small, but as the Hundred Years' War progressed, so the tax went up, to help pay for the troops and fighting.

At first the Customs Service was only there to collect the duties at the ports, and not to prevent smuggling. However merchants soon found it easier to land the goods in the local Cinque Ports where there were few Customs officials. In the Kent Lay Subsidy Roll of 1334/35, the names of Thomas de Stapel and John Staple (possibly his son) with six others occur as 'Men of Liberty of the Cinque Ports'. If this is indeed the Thomas de Stapel in question it is proof of his involvement in the fight against wool smuggling.

In 1364 Thomas and two local men were commissioned on the Thames and Essex coast to deal 'with a matter close to the king's heart', though is not mentioned in the history books what that matter was.

Thomas de Stapel's career as a sergeant-at-arms rewarded him accordingly. As well as grants of land he was commemorated at his death in 1371 with a fine brass in his parish church, St Mary's, Shopland, which read 'Thomas Stapel in armour with pointed bascinet, camail and cinquefoiled crocketed canopy and shields.' The brass made the short journey a mile north-west to Sutton church when Shopland's church was demolished in 1957.

PEASANTS' REVOLT IN ESSEX

Tax has tenet us alle, probat hoc mors tot validorum.
(Tax has ruined us all, death of so many worthy folk proves it.)

Contemporary poem of the Peasants' Revolt, Richard I's reign

As early as 1377, Essex, disenchanted with England's long war with France, was a simmering hotbed of discontent. Along with all other English counties, Essex was about to be asked, yet again, to dip into its empty pockets and help fund the king's ongoing French war, but this time tempers were fraying, and the introduction of the new poll tax was about to tip villains, burgesses and townsfolk alike over the edge. At first the poll tax was greeted with resignation. Taxes were a part of medieval life, and most people paid their dues with varying amounts of hardship but this tax, initially a charge of 1 groat levied on every man and woman over the age of fourteen, was to increase three times in three years. Pockets of resistance were to turn into open rebellion, yet this would not be a fight led by captains and generals. As this was to be a grievance felt by every man, woman and child in England, then every man, woman and child would fight it.

In 1379 the tax, known by those in power to be a growing issue, was graduated, with the intention of gleaning more revenue from the rich than the poor. The age at which it was to be paid rose from fourteen to sixteen, a duke was to pay 10 marks (approx. £7), a Justice of the Peace £5, a 'great merchant' £1, lesser merchants between 6d and 13s, and for all others 'above a beggar' 4d. The tax was to be collected by official assessors who in turn made use of local 'best and most discreet men' who would supply information on every inhabitant and so collect all charges due.

The tax brought in far less than expected. It appeared rich and poor alike reacted the same way and did their utmost to disguise who they were, what they did and how many of them were doing it. Just as this tax was intrusive, so the people were twice as elusive. Family members 'disappeared' as heads of households lied about the sizes of their families, how many dependents they had and the numbers of eligible children over the age of fifteen who were at home. In fact records show that during the poll tax years 1377–80, the whole Essex population miraculously dropped from 47,962 to 37,740, from what can only be described as fraud. Locally the population of Colchester alone almost halved, going from 2,955 to 1,609.

With such a shortfall in revenue a third tax was imposed at 3 groats per person eligible with the motto that 'the strong might aid the week' in the raising of the money. Discontent grew stronger and the frauds greater. Even those who had been entrusted to collect the tax found themselves letting people off or turning a blind eye to the lies being told in order to evade full taxation. But by March 1381 the government had become aware of this and as a consequence all poll tax returns were to be checked and shortfalls rectified. Commissioners were dispatched, and instructed to go 'from town to town and place to place and search out and examine those who ought to pay'. Sir John Gildesborough, an Essex JP, was to head a concession of six Essex commissioners authorised to pry as deeply as necessary into the lives of those charged with the tax in order to obtain the true measure of their circumstances. He could also demand any monies due. On 30 May 1381 he and several other Essex JPs – including one John Bampton – arrived in the quiet town of Brentwood.

Unfortunately things did not remain quiet. Among those in Brentwood ordered to appear before Gildesborough were several men from Fobbing in the Barstable Hundred. They had encountered JP John Bampton before when he had collected their village's poll tax. The experience had not been a good one and rumour had it that he had pocketed the money himself and here he was now demanding they pay all over again. The men refused outright to pay. The crowd was threatened with arrest but instead they attacked the commissioner and his fellow JPs 'with bows', encouraged by the support of other Essex men such as John Stalworth, a prosperous Chelmsford barber, and others from as far away as Bocking.

Thomas Baker of Fobbing had led the attack, a man nominated by the inhabitants of the tiny Essex village to be their leader. Under fire, Bampton fled back to London and a replacement, Robert Belknap, was dispatched back to Brentwood to restore law and order. Thomas Baker stood up to him too, making Belknap swear an oath to leave and never return, beheading six of his accompanying clerks in the process and burning all the official documents.

The simmering passions of men, who since the Black Death (1348–9) and the emergence of new civil liberties, were still being 'kept in great servage', finally bubbled over. It was a period known as 'the time of the great rumour' and was referred to later in charges against the Brentwood rioters as 'when men rode about armed in a land of peace and did many evil deeds'. In evidence, court records for Bradwell-on-Sea show that Richard Proudfoot threatened to kill John Gerveyn at a town meeting in Burnham if he didn't join in the revolt. Violence was beginning to spread.

In North Essex, men from Bocking, Braintree, Coggeshall, Stisted and Dunmow had sworn an oath to kill the king's subjects and follow no other laws than their own. To underline this threat they attacked the Sherriff of Essex, John Sewale, at his home in Coggeshall and terrorised the clerk with him so that 'their lives were despaired of'. The rebels then moved on to the home of King's Treasurer, Sir Robert Hales, who was also prior of the Order of St John of Jerusalem at Cressing Temple. Several hundred converged on his home including the Fobbing baker, Thomas, who had started the uprising, plus men from Onger, Benfleet, Hadleigh and Leigh. Men from the three Hanningfields had joined up, led by their own bailiff, John Geffrey, plus men from Barking, Felsted, Goldhanger and Maldon. Unfortunately for the mob, Robert Hales was not at home when they arrived and in frustration they sacked the manor and drank his wine before setting fire to the buildings, leaving only the tithe barns standing.

Returning to Coggeshall the rebels once again looked for the Sheriff, but were unsuccessful, and so carried away all official documents instead. When the rebels did finally catch the Sheriff in Chelmsford some days later, he was assaulted and all remaining treasury accounts containing the written evidence of their feudal servitude and monetary obligations were destroyed.

The burning of documents as a way to release themselves from taxation was seized upon by peasants throughout the county. In Asheldham the Court Rolls were destroyed as were those of the Manor of Woodham Fitzwalter (Woodham Walter). The rolls from the Bishop of London's Manor at Southminster were taken plus those of the Bishop of Stansgate. In Mayland the house of John Bourchier was ransacked. Today, for Cold Norton there is no Court Rolls record for 1381 although they exist up to 1380, and after from 1382. Men who burned the Moulsham Court Rolls were both rich and poor Chelmsford citizens alike: William Chypenham, a wealthy brewer; Geoffrey Andrew, a tailor and John Baldwin, a cobbler. Fishmonger Stephen Pays, and John Fletcher, plus two men from Boreham and one from Hatfield Peveral were also involved.

Record burning was also accompanied by trespassing and no doubt the confused situation was used to settle personal grudges. Wood was taken from Tollshunt Major. Rebels in Childerditch took control over manor land by seizing an enclosed croft and making all the servants there leave their work. In Abbess Roding, rebels stole their lord's timber, firewood, hay and cattle and at Bacons in the Dengie Hundred twenty cows and 200 sheep were driven by serfs and tenants onto manorial land. Some landowners were unwilling to acknowledge their property was being attacked by their own serfs, preferring to believe the atrocities were carried out by 'unknown malefactors', but with Great Bromley in Essex 'all the tenants of this manor in bondage' were accused of involvement.

Men known to have carried out lesser acts of violence were Simon Skynner and Henry Taylor from North Weald, Simon's father, William, being a 'pelter' by trade and wealthy enough to own some of the most valuable property on Chelmsford High Street. John Brid, a chandler and alehouse keeper, joined in the destruction of the charters at Bromfield in the possession of lawyer, Richard Stacey. As if more proof were needed that rich and poor alike both had grievances with the judicial system, the ringleader of the Moulsham troubles was actually the town 'Franklin' Richard Baud, the wealthiest man in the hamlet.

However, serious personal violence towards lords was unusual. The Lady of Great Bromley was only 'insulted' by those who broke into her manor house to burn tax documents and that was probably only because she confronted them. Those that were seriously hurt or killed were those in an official position and deliberately singled out for punishment.

Yet this wholesale burning of documents later proved a double-edged sword. Documents burned may have destroyed records of what the peasants owed the crown but it also destroyed records of what the peasants themselves owned. In 1393 John Heyward and his wife could not prove to the authorities that they were the owners of a house and lands acquired thirty years before because 'in the time of the rumour the rolls of the court of former years were burned'. As late as 1408, Joan, widow of Roger-atte-Noke, had to pay to have her own copy of her original house and land documents re-enrolled on the manor records.

The revolt by the men of Essex, led by Jack Straw, was now heading for London, and the men of Kent joined them under the leadership of Waultre le Tieuliere, more commonly known as Wat Tyler. By mid-June 1381, the men of Kent were assembled on Blackheath, while the Essex Army, with Robert Baker, William Prentys Thomas Osteler, William Saresson, William Chypenham, Stephen Pays and John Spicer – all from Chelmsford – camped outside the City walls at Mile End. Their intention was only to speak to their king, but the teenage monarch, hearing of an invading peasant army, had fled with his ministers from Westminster to the Tower of London. Unaware the king was now in hiding, the peasants made for the heart of the capital.

Perhaps it was the bravado of youth that saw the boy king leave his safe haven to find out exactly what his angry subjects wanted, and, agreeing to an arms-length meeting with the rebels, headed a small flotilla of barges which met them at Rotherhithe. For safety's sake he stayed aboard his boat but listened to the rebels' demands, which were not directed at him but those who had implemented the poll tax. Unable to satisfy the mob, the king returned to the tower leaving the rioters on the river bank.

Aggrieved, the rebels then marched on to Southwark, venting their anger on the way. When the mob reached the residence of John of Gaunt, the young king's uncle, they proceeded to sack his palace, the Savoy, as they believed it had been built with money from the poll tax. It was plundered to destruction. With London in chaos, the king agreed to meet the rebels face-to-face, and on 14 June 1381, rode out to meet them at Mile End and hear demands for an end to bonded labour, freedom to trade, the reduction of land rent and a pardon for all those that had rebelled. The king, it appeared, conceded; even when the rebels demanded the heads of two of the most hated of the king's ministers still in power, Sudbury and Hale. For the first time in two weeks the situation seemed defused. Believing their cause to be just, the peasants trusted their king, let down their guard and began to drift back home. All, that was, except Wat Tyler and a body of hardcore peasants who wanted further change to the social order. The king once more agreed to meet the rebels, this time outside the City walls at a place called Smithfield.

Assembled under the flag of St George and with few arms, the peasants met the king's men who were dressed in steel and had swords by their sides. Richard listened to Tyler's new demands and, at length, during a disturbance that took place Wat Tyler was wounded and taken to nearby St Bartholomew's Abbey where he was tended by the monks. It wasn't long, however, before the king's men dragged him out again and, making an example of him, cut off his head. The Revolt was over there and then. Seeing Tyler's head paraded on a spike, the rebels gave up their weapons and begged forgiveness.

Richard's backlash to the revolt was ferocious. William Walworth, the Lord Mayor of London, was appointed to secure the city and its suburbs and on 22 June the king, his council, plus 40,000 men left the capital, rode into Essex and set up government at Waltham Holy Cross. On 23 June the king received rebels who had regrouped at Billericay and who'd come to see the king fulfill his promises to them. They were bluntly told that 'Villains ye are and Villains ye shall remain'. Though the king allowed them to leave unharmed he immediately outlawed all unlawful assembly and set up a commission to deal with treasons, felonies, and trespass committed in Essex during the uprising. Richard and his council then moved into Havering where he proclaimed that all his subjects, 'without murmuring or resistance', would return to work for their masters as they had done before the uprising. The last serious stand in Essex was at Norsey Woods in Billericay, where men who had been living as outlaws were massacred on 28 June.

For almost a week Chelmsford was the seat of English government, with the king taking lodgings near Writtle. Hoping to see the king, approximately 500 Essex men converged on Chelmsford to beg the king's mercy. As the rebellion had originated in Essex they did not get much quarter and justice was meted out immediately and harshly. Names of 145 ringleaders were offered up, unsurprisingly the man at the top of the list being Thomas Baker of Fobbing.

The guilty men died a traitor's death on the gallows situated half a mile outside Chelmsford by the Writtle road, today Primrose Hill. Some of the men's names are known. As well as the Fobbing baker there were twenty-seven others from that village; Richard Baud of Moulsham, two men from East Hanningfield – John Geffrey and John Field the Miller – plus Chelmsford barber John Stalworth, who was accused but escaped. Possessions and lands of the dead and fugitive traitors reverted to the Crown; John Stalworth's belongings did not amount to much, being simply a basin, towel, bed and tablecloths, a platter, a brass pot, three shovels and two irons: in total no more than 40 shillings. John Baud's were more valuable and his lands and tenements in Moulsham were granted to one of the king's servants. Besides traitors, who were hanged, drawn, and quartered, nineteen other rebels were hanged for lesser crimes that same week before the king left for St Albans to punish the rebels there.

For those who had evaded capture, an amnesty was declared on 14 December so men, including escapee John Stalworth, could return home, in John's case to his wife Agnes and his business. It is recorded that he went on to become a respectable householder in the town and occupied a small high-street corner house on the north side of Springfield Lane. Eleven years after the revolt in 1392 he is also noted as giving an annual offering of 2 shillings towards the upkeep of a light at the Holy Cross. Other rebels managed to return to Chelmsford and continue their trades, William Prentys, Thomas Osteller, and Robert Baker among them. John Spicer survived too, returning to what was probably the most valuable site on Chelmsford High Street, namely 'Spicerestenemnt', known centuries later as the Saracens Head.

By 1382 all village administration resumed with the winter court, but the feudal system was crumbling. As men became old and forgetful the scarcity of written evidence confused exactly who owned what or who served whom, and possession of property and rights became hard to prove. One example was the year 1399, when it took a jury of twelve most senior men to swear whether a man named William Pauln was a bondsman or not, when it had been written down and was common knowledge in 1381 that he was. When men appealed against the work they carried out for their masters, the means by which they could have proved otherwise no longer existed.

Though personal servitude on the medieval scale has long died out there is still a relic of those times in our property references. The term 'copyhold' derives from the term 'copy of the kings roll', the very documents that were burned in anger all those years ago.

SIR CHARLES LUCAS (1612/13–1648)

*Rough, proud, uncultivated, 'morose', and, off the battlefield, intolerable ...
but very brave in his person, and a gallant man to look upon and follow.*

The Earl of Clarendon

Just as many warriors before him, Sir Charles Lucas was renowned more for the manner of his death than for the brave and capable way in which he lived his life. Executed after the surrender of Colchester in 1648, he has probably become the foremost Royalist martyr of the Civil War. Whether he should have been executed at all raised serious doubts at the time. The contentious decision still raises hot debate in Essex today, even after almost four centuries.

Sir Charles Lucas, born 1612/13, was the youngest son of Sir Thomas Lucas, gentleman of Colchester, and his wife Elizabeth; the Lucases had long been a prominent Essex family. Sir Charles's grandfather, John Lucas, born in St James, Colchester, in 1535 and an ambitious young man, had been eager to build up the dynasty and at a relatively young age was elected to his late father's seat as Member of Parliament for Colchester. Favoured by Queen Elizabeth I during the following decades, he held many government posts. As a Justice of the Peace he sat in judgment over local malefactors and as Recorder of Colchester he oversaw the town's legal affairs. He was three times High Sheriff of Essex, an annual appointment made by the queen herself.

By now Colchester was one of the largest towns in Britain, a full mile across, with a population of around 10,000. Timbered houses with tiled roofs lined the streets, and fresh water came into the town from springs in the surrounding countryside. Thomas as a leading citizen managed his estates to maximise his income, investing his profits in substantial land purchases, and by the time he died in 1611 at the age of eighty, the Lucas family were one of the richest in Essex with an income of £3,000 – £4,000 per year. Yet it was Thomas's captaincy in the Essex militia that was most important to him and it was as a cavalry commander that his grandson Charles would credit his family.

Young Charles Lucas was privately tutored in Colchester, as were his older brothers, Thomas and John, and sister Margaret, later to become the Duchess of Newcastle, known also as 'mad Madge' due to her free thinking and outspokenness. He entered Christ's College, Cambridge in June 1628, aged fifteen; later, in 1637, he served in his elder brother's troop of horse in the Netherlands. Although he gained valuable fighting experience, he did not stay there long. With unrest brewing north of England's border, the Lucas brothers, known for their experience at fighting abroad, were sought out and 'elected' to serve the king, Charles; they were knighted by the monarch at Berwick on 27 July 1639. A year later he was commanding a troop of horse in his brother's regiment in Yorkshire, and by September he was garrison commander at Richmond. Needless to say, by 1641 he had established himself as a most able and responsible officer. By 1642, with discontent and discord slowly simmering into the heat of the English Civil War, Charles was more than ready to defend the realm.

Gaining a reputation for fighting 'resolutely and bravely', Lucas fought in all the major battles between Royalty and Roundheads in the years 1642–4. At Marston Moor (1644) his horse was shot from under him and as Thomas Fairfax's prisoner, he was taken around the field to identify the Royalist dead, so that they might be given an honourable burial. A deeply disturbing event for anyone, Lucas is said to have wept at their numbers. He was later released by exchange before being captured again in 1646 in what was the last major engagement of the First Civil War, but highly regarded as 'a soldier of reputation and valor', he was not discredited. Released on parole he was made to swear that he would never take up arms against his country again.

It was while on this parole that Lucas took a commission in Essex at the request of the Prince of Wales, who wished to capitalise on Lucas's local connections. Closely pursued by Lord Fairfax and his Parliamentarians, Lucas marched to Colchester, arriving on 10 June 1648 and immediately dispatched his drummers to walk the town 'beating for volunteers', recruiting a good number of poor weavers and other tradesmen who wanted employment. Nearly 800 men joined his regiment. Word had it that Fairfax was regrouping at Billericay after leaving Horndon-on-the-Hill and was now approaching Maldon. Lucas was soon joined by fellow Royalist Lord Goring who, promising Colchester's townsfolk His Majesty's protection, settled his troops, placed more cannon in St Mary's churchyard and ordered fresh fortifications to the town's walls and gates.

When Fairfax arrived, he made Lexden, barely 2 miles away, his headquarters and after four days of attempting to take Colchester by storm, opted to besiege the town. Neither side knew the stalemate that had started on 12 June would continue for seventy-six days until 28 August. As with most military situations, negotiations took place over terms of surrender, but in this case matters were made worse by Fairfax refusing to deal with Lucas directly. For Fairfax, Lucas 'was not capable of command or trust in Martial affairs' as he had broken the terms of his parole and was still in his eyes his prisoner, therefore forfeiting his 'honour and faith'. Though Lucas responded with an excuse for his breach of parole, it was disregarded. The siege was a bitter and brutal affair with atrocities committed on both sides; Fairfax's troops torturing a messenger boy and desecrating graves in the Lucas family vault while the Royalists allegedly used 'poisoned bullets', otherwise shot that was roughened and rolled in sand to cause gangrene in wounds. Plus it was a conflict as much about pride as it was about hunger and sickness. In the early days when morale was still high and before Fairfax had instigated a blockade of Colchester as well as a siege, it was possible for daring raids to take place outside Colchester's walls under cover fire, some led by Lucas.

At one point Lucas and a small party of men were able to bring in a quantity of provisions, sheep and black cattle. Another time some corn-filled hoys, which had come up to the Hythe, were relieved of their contents and taken back within the walls. About a week into the siege Lord Goring was even able to add to the town's defence 'some great guns brought in from some ships at Wivenhoe'. Attacks upon the besiegers were also carried out and prisoners taken, but once Fairfax received a further 'forty pieces of heavy cannon' from the Tower of London and all roads to the town were blocked, a number of cattle from the country and five wagons laden with corn were the last bulk provisions Colchester received.

By 18 July the town 'began to be greatly distressed'. Some soldiers deserted; others would gladly have died with their swords in their hands had a fight with the enemy been forthcoming. Provisions were low and despite the thatch being systematically stripped from the roofs of people's homes to feed the army horses, the animals were now unfit for service and were being killed for food, though in 'Diary of a plan of the Siege of Colchester, by the Parliament Forces, written in 1648' it was recorded that on Thursday 20 July, 'One butcher ran away rather than he would do it.'

By 2 August the soldiers, having lived for several weeks on horseflesh 'as lean as carrion', rifled the houses of the townsfolk for food. Those of the army that remained were now sickly and dying of the flux, yet Colchester would not surrender. As the relationship between the Royalist forces and the townsfolk became 'uneasy', Colchester's mayor and aldermen asked Goring and Lucas to petition Fairfax and ask him to let the townsfolk leave so they should not perish. Goring agreed but Fairfax refused. Days later the townsfolk rioted, clamouring for surrender and 'bringing women and children, who lay howling and crying on the ground for bread'. The men were beaten back, but the women and children would not go, hoping that the soldiers might kill them, declaring they would rather be shot than be starved.

Moved by the plight of the townsfolk, Goring again petitioned Fairfax, but all Fairfax returned were his terms of surrender and what he called his last offer of mercy. To Lucas and Goring these terms, which declared all men under the rank of captain were to have quarter and those above none, were unacceptable. When another riot took place, Colchester opened its gate and told the people to go to Fairfax, thinking that this time when faced with the poor and hungry he would not refuse them. Not only did Fairfax refuse Colchester's townsfolk, but his guards shot at them, driving them all back again.

Despite brave talk and courage in the face of unimaginable deprivation, on 28 August Colchester did surrender. It was the prospect of mutiny that sealed the town's fate, with those soldiers below the rank of captain who knew they would be spared declining to join in with a last rush at the enemy devised by Lucas and Goring. The surrender terms dictated the following: that all prisoners who were lords and gentlemen were prisoners at mercy; common soldiers had passes to go home to their dwellings, but without arms, an oath not to serve against the Parliament and the town to be preserved from pillage. On top of that was to be a payment of £14,000 in coin of the realm.

The death toll during the seventy-six days of the siege was staggering, yet there were still 3,526 army personnel alive at the surrender. A separate war council was called to discuss the fates of those in command and it was decided that Lords Goring, Lucas, Sir Marmaduke Gascoigne and Sir George Lisle would be shot to death while others awaited further orders under guard.

According to a letter contained in the Clarke papers (Secretary to the Council of the Army, 1647-9) there is a poignant description of the last moments of Sir Charles Lucas and his companions that fateful morning of 28 August. It is a long letter, but tells how when Lucas was first brought into the yard of Colchester Castle as a prisoner he proudly quantified his actions to those in attendance by saying that he had come to Colchester to do his duty 'in the Prince's service' and that since then he was not guilty of any wrongdoing. Due to his religion he thanked those that had allowed him to receive the sacrament, then embraced Sir Bernard Gascoigne, also a prisoner, at which point Gasgoigne declared that it was an honour to die at his friend's side. Lucas then asked the minister to advise his parents of his demise and that they should not think badly of him.

Only then did he inquire of the officers how he was to die and 'by what means'. A Captain Packer then replied, 'That which is most proper to soldiers, to be shot.' Sir George Lisle, also by Lucas's side, then expressed a wish for more time to repent his sins and contested the necessity of such severe punishment for their actions 'especially so suddenly'. The letter also speaks of Lucas's conversation with Sir Henry Ireton, one of Cromwell's generals and his son-in-law, where Ireton pressed home the charges against Lucas, charging him with treason. 'Prove mee one, before you condemne mee to be a traitor' was Lucas's impassioned reply. After a moment of prayer with his companions, he announced, 'Gentlemen, I now die like a soldier.' These were almost his last words before he requested to be laid out decently when he had fallen and that he would have a decent burial in the family vault where his ancestors lay. After hearing the words 'Oh Father, Son, and Holy Ghost, receive my soule', six dragoons armed with fire locks discharged first their shot into him then into Sir George Lisle. Sir Bernard Gascoigne, who had removed his doublet expecting to be shot next, was told to stand down, unexpectedly reprieved.

Both Lucas and Lisle were privately buried in St Giles's church, but in 1661, after the restoration of Charles II and on the anniversary of their entry into

Monument in the grounds of Colchester Castle. The inscription reads, 'THIS STONE MARKS THE SPOT WHERE ON AUGUST 28. 1648 AFTER THE SURRENDER OF THE TOWN THE TWO ROYALIST CAPTAINS SIR CHARLES LUCAS AND SIR GEORGE LISLE WERE SHOT BY ORDER OF SIR THOMAS FAIRFAX THE PARLIAMENTARIAN GENERAL.' (Robert Hallmann)

the king's service, they were commemorated with a magnificent funeral in Colchester Cathedral, attended by gentlemen, soldiers and dignitaries. The victims had become the victors.

DANIEL MENDOZA (1764–1836)

Intelligent, charismatic but chaotic...

In Brentwood cemetery lay the last mortal remains of Daniel Mendoza, bare-knuckle Heavyweight Boxing Champion of Britain from 1792 to 1795, the only Jew to hold the title. An Essex man by virtue of this resting place and the matches he fought in this county, he was regarded as the father of scientific boxing. This was at a time when boxing still had no rules or regulations; matches were vicious affairs where the final bout was over only when one fighter, bloodied and bowed, could no longer stand.

The origins of boxing can be found in the Roman gymnasia when, along with wrestling, it was called Pancratium. Together they were thought to 'recreate and strengthen the body and mind'. Once the Empire had fallen, the sport descended into a fairground attraction; a sideshow of brute strength where the contestants were woefully mismatched and all was a foregone conclusion. In the nineteenth century, bare-knuckle boxing was outlawed altogether. Matches were consigned to secrecy, taking place only in dim and dingy places, a favourite location being the Essex marshes and islands. But previously, in the eighteenth century it was, for a time, elevated to the 'noble art' it had once been.

'Noble' in connection with boxing was used for the first time by the original boxing champion of England, James Figg, who retired unbeaten in 1730 after 300 matches. In order to promote his London Boxing Academy, at the Adam and Eve Inn north of Oxford Street, he issued business cards. These, designed by the artist William Hogarth, became the first known form of advertising associated with the sport and the caption on the cards referred to Figg as 'master of the noble science of defence'.

But Daniel Mendoza was the first to truly put the 'science' into boxing. A relatively small man at only 5 feet 7 inches and weighing a mere 160 pounds, he relied on defensive movements, such as side-stepping, ducking, blocking, and most of all, by using his agility he was able to avoid punches from his larger, slower opponents. Employing these 'new' methods Mendoza became a very popular fighter and from 1792 to 1795 became England's sixteenth Heavyweight Champion, the only middleweight to ever win the Heavyweight Championship of the World. Of Spanish origin and proud of his faith, Mendoza always billed himself as Mendoza the Jew.

Mendoza was born in Aldgate in July 1764 to Abraham Mendoza and Esther Lopez, the third son of seven children. He grew up in poor surroundings and worked as a glass cutter, labourer, greengrocer's assistant and an actor before making a career of fighting. At the start of his boxing career, he was employed in the service of a Jewish family and, in his memoirs, he comments on how the anti-Semitic feeling of the time often gave him an excuse to train on the streets of East London; 'I was here frequently drawn into contests with butchers and others in the neighbourhood who, on account of my mistress being of the Jewish religion, were frequently disposed to insult her.'

His first recorded prize-fight was a victory over Harry the Coal-heaver, whom he dispatched in forty rounds. In 1787 he defeated Sam Martin, also known as 'The Bath Butcher', a feat which established Mendoza as one of the highest-ranking fighters in the country. Soon he had the patronage of the Prince of Wales (later George IV); he was the first ever boxer to attain this honour. His acceptance by the British royal family elevated the position of the Jew in English society and he is recorded as being the first of his faith to speak to King George III.

Mendoza married in May 1787 and he and his wife Esther would go on to have nine children. In the early years of his marriage and boxing career he also embarked on a series of three fights with his former mentor, Richard

Daniel Mendoza.

Humphries. These were reported fully in the newspapers of the time with all the hype one would expect in the sport today. One paper, the *Hereford Journal*, dated 6 May 1789, began by recounting, 'Yesterday the much talked about match between Humphries and Mendoza was decided before a vast concourse of people who were assembled on the occasion' and went on to elaborate,

> Several hundred people paid Half a Guinea a piece to gain admission within the paddock where the stage was raised. The paddock was well defended against the multitude by Tring, Ryan, Dunn and a great number more of the strongest men in England, who with clubs looked like so many giant; but who can resist the shock of the English mob? The paddock was broken down and the Torrent rushed in. The combatants mounted the stage exactly at 'One' and after the usual salutations, Mendoza began the onset with all the heat and impetuosity of a man determined on Victory.

Mendoza lost that first match, though 'several blows of Mendoza had their effect', one cutting Humphries under the left eye. But after 'they had fought eighteen or nineteen minutes Humphries began to manifest his superior skill and the bets changed in his favour'. The match lasted twenty-nine minutes, after which Mendoza 'was carried off the stage totally exhausted and seemingly lifeless'.

In the rematch the following year, Mendoza thoroughly dominated Humphries, winning in fifty-two minutes. Mendoza also won the third encounter in fifteen minutes. Mendoza was now so popular that the London

Draws by C.R.Ryley

Engraved by J.Grozer

DANIEL MENDOZA & RICHARD HUMPHREYS

This Boxing Match took place at Doncaster Sep.29.th 1790 on a Twenty four feet Stage and was the third Public Contest between these two pugilists. It lasted for about an Hour & five Minutes & was decisive in favour of Mendoza

Published as the Act directs by W. Richardson York House N° 11 Strand

Daniel Mendoza fighting Richard Humphries at Doncaster in 1790.

press reported news of one of his bouts on 4 July 1789 ahead of the Storming of the Bastille, which marked the start of the French Revolution. In 1791 Mendoza laid claim to the English boxing title when the prevailing champion, Benjamin Brain, retired. This was contested by another top boxer, Bill Warr, and in May 1792, the two met to settle the matter. Mendoza was victorious in twenty-three rounds. Warr and Mendoza met again in November 1794, and this time it took Mendoza a mere fifteen minutes to dispose of the challenger.

As champion, Mendoza toured England, Scotland and Ireland, demonstrating his skills as part of the Aston Circus. While in Ireland, Mendoza thrashed Squire Fitzgerald, who had made derogatory remarks about Mendoza's skills and ethnicity.

Mendoza held the title until 1795 when he fought 'Gentleman' John Jackson for the Championship at Hornchurch in Essex. It was a comparatively short fight, ending after a mere quarter of an hour, but it was still enthusiastically reported in the papers. The *Ipswich Journal* of 17 April reported,

The battle between Jackson and Mendoza took place on Wednesday upon a stage at Hornchurch in Essex. Johnson was second to Jackson and Ward to

Mendoza. The contest continued 10 minutes and a half and consisted for the whole time of hard blows without shifting. Mendoza nearly lost the sight of both eyes and was beaten. Jackson was wounded over the left eye but was not otherwise much hurt being from the beginning too powerful.

Another paper, the *Derby Mercury*, carried the Essex-based story word for word except for an addition at the end, which read,

Mendoza, however writes to his friends that he gained as much credit as if he had won the battle. He says 'I should have won if he had not been drove to the unmanly act of fastening on to my hair, which he declared he would to his friends who backed him, and who have since declared it to me in the presence of several of my friends. I could not have my hair cut off on account of my present employment, although it was the advice of my friends. I have received no injury except a few blows in my face, and my friends are willing to back me for 1,000 pounds if I will have my hair cut off.'

In truth Jackson was five years younger, 4 inches taller, and 42 pounds heavier. The bigger man won in nine rounds, and as Mendoza had said, Jackson had seized him by his long hair and, holding him with one hand, had indeed pounded his head with the other. As a consequence it has always been the case that from that day to this, boxers have always worn their hair short.

Despite his failure to hold on to his title, Mendoza remained popular. Songs were written about him, and his name appeared in scripts of numerous plays. His personal appearances filled theatres, portraits of him and his fights were popular subjects for artists and commemorative medals were struck in his honour. Mendoza retired from the ring but not from boxing. He ran a boxing academy and wrote on the subject his book, *The Art of Boxing*, referenced by all subsequent followers of the sport. He did make the occasional appearance for financial reasons, as in 1806, when aged forty-one he fought and won a match with Henry Lee.

Mendoza made and spent a fortune. He was known to be 'intelligent, charismatic but chaotic' and he tried a number of ventures to support himself in his latter years, even appearing one more time in the ring as a boxer in 1820. Though he lasted twelve rounds, his age, now fifty-six, worked against him and he lost. He died at the age of seventy-two, sadly leaving his family in poverty, but leaving the sport of boxing a legacy still widely used by fighters to this day.

3

MEDICINE MEN

PETER CHAMBERLEN (1601–1683)

Great talent and wide celebrity, energetic and eccentric, but at the same time highly practical.

J. H. Aveling, 1882

Today we take medicine very much for granted. The past was not always as reassuring, but Essex has always had its share of capable physicians. Peter Chamberlen, doctor of physic and owner of Woodham Mortimer Hall, was one of them, and a man ahead of his time. When he died in 1683 at the advanced age of eighty-two, he was laid to rest in St Margaret's churchyard, Woodham Mortimer, in the shadow of his former four-gabled home. Unfortunately the secret to his unique means of easing childbirth for women was buried with him. In his lifetime he had been physician to three kings and queens, husband to two wives, Jane Myddelton and Ann Harrison, and father to fourteen sons and four daughters, with sixty-five grandchildren and fourteen great-grandchildren.

Chamberlen himself was the eldest of eight children and of Huguenot descent, baptised at the French church in Threadneedle Street. Chamberlen's grandfather had been a religious refugee in Elizabethan times, and had established himself as a 'man-midwife' when such medical practitioners were a novelty. Educated at the Merchant Taylors' School in London, Peter, then aged only fourteen, went on to Emmanuel College, Cambridge where he admittedly did not stay long, commenting afterwards, 'I merely piddled there in surgery.'

His serious medical education was taken at Padua University where he gained his MD on 16 September 1619 and became a doctor of medicine aged only eighteen. Before the age of twenty he was also Doctor of Medicine at Oxford and Cambridge. His first application to become a member of the

College of Physicians was turned down on account of his extreme youth. His second attempt, five years later, was accepted but by now he had become a fashionable gentleman of town and appeared at the college wearing velvet, frills and a feathered hat. This time he did gain his scholarship but also a lecture on what a doctor was and was not expected to wear. He was subsequently made a Fellow of the college in 1628.

Deputising for his uncle, in 1630 he attended and assisted in the birth of Charles II and was later, in 1642, made 'physician-in-ordinary' to Queen Henrietta Maria. But his obvious success was not without criticism from his colleagues, who questioned his motives as well as his methods. In 1634 his fellow medics petitioned the College of Physicians against what they saw as an attempt by Chamberlen to gain control of the London midwives by suggesting that they broke away from Church control and became better educated, as he thought them ignorant and incompetent. He had also proposed that he became the governor of a college for this purpose. He was attacked for his lack of knowledge on the subject, being only a physician and not a surgeon, under whose responsibility childbirth fell.

In his defence he published a pamphlet called 'A Voice in Rhama', or, 'The Crie of Women and Children', attacking the way the Church licensed midwives purely on random testimonies and the substantial payment a potential midwife needed to pay before practising. He expounded the virtues of a college for the purpose of the advancement of midwifery, for 'instruction and order', so that the average figure of 3,000 women a year dying in childbirth in London alone would be significantly reduced. Noble as his suggestions were, it was thought unworkable. In reality many women practised as midwives without obtaining a license, paying a fee or having any medical knowledge at all.

Having fallen foul of the Royal College for many reasons, including supporting Cromwell in the Civil War, Chamberlen was expelled from the College of Physicians in 1649 and retired back to Woodham Mortimer Hall, the Essex home he had purchased in 1638, where he could practise unrestricted, and without interference. Chamberlen claimed that he alone could successfully deliver a difficult birth when everyone else had failed. He had devised an early set of forceps modelled after midwives' spoons. He kept his new invention so secret that the machine was taken to a confinement in an ornately carved gilded box, so heavy it took two to carry it. He went to great lengths in his pursuit of profit and secrecy. It was not enough for him to rely on the prudery of the times, which dictated medical administration be conducted under the bedclothes to preserve a lady's modesty – Chamberlen insisted the poor woman be blindfolded as well.

At the Restoration in 1660 he was reinstated to his royal appointment by Charles II who recalled 'he had attended our happy birth' and was therefore 'one of our first servants'. Although reappointed, Chamberlen was never again called to court.

When he died in 1683, his futuristic invention died with him, lost and forgotten, hidden in a box at his Essex home. Not until 1813 was his device rediscovered. At his death, Chamberlen's widow had hidden several sets of medical instruments, among them obstetric forceps in various stages of development, plus a few small, curious trinkets, including 'my husband's last tooth' in a box carefully hidden beneath a trapdoor in the floor of the attic. The heads of the screws had been carefully plugged with wood to disguise them and it wasn't until one of these 'plugs' eventually worked loose that the hiding place became known.

Today, correctly applied, the use of forceps is safe. The halo of metal around a baby's head protects as well as assists in the extraction of the child during a difficult labour. Straight not curved, and probably made of wood or steel padded with leather, Chamberlen's invention was at least effective. Yet jealousy, pride and greed all conspired in keeping the instrument out of the reaches of the lower classes. Not until Queen Victoria was introduced to the pain-numbing effects of chloroform during her own pregnancies was there to be another breakthrough in midwifery on the same scale.

Of his fourteen sons, three continued in medicine, Hugh being the one to continue in royal service. He also envisaged that 'every family might be served much better and cheaper than at present, with Visits, Advice, Medicine, and Surgery' – an advocate of the National Health Service 250 years before its time.

Hugh's son, also named Hugh, was a friend of the Duke of Buckingham. He is the one who finally freed the obstetrical forceps for general use at the beginning of the eighteenth century, ending the countless preventable infant deaths that the keeping of his family's secret had caused.

Hugh later sold his secret in Holland, where the Medical-Pharmaceutical College of Amsterdam was granted permission to license physicians to use the technique of the Chamberlens, but for a fee. Eventually they became freely available to the public.

About the same time, a Dr De la Motte addressed the Paris Academy of Medicine, and declared his contempt of anyone who might invent a successful instrument: 'he deserves to be tied to a barren rock and have his vitals plucked out by vultures' if he kept it a secret for his own profit.

From Chamberlen's second marriage only one child survived, his son Hope, and it was he who erected this monument in the small churchyard next to Woodham Mortimer Hall. The epitaph reads,

The said Peter Chamberlen took ye degree of Doctor in Physick, in fever all Universities born at home and abroad and lived such above three

The magnificent tomb of Peter Chamberlen, 'Doctor of Physick' in the churchyard beside his home at Woodham Walter. (Bob Bowman)

score years being physician in ordinary to three Kings and Queens of England. viz. King James & Queen Anne; King Charles ye first & Queen Mary; King Charles ye second & Queen Katherine; & also to some forraine Princes; having travelled most of partes of Europe and speaking most of the languages.

As for his religion he was a Christian keeping ye Commandments of God & faith of Jesus. being baptized about ye year 1648, & keeping ye 7th day for ye saboth above 32 years.

To tell his Learning and his Life to Men: Enough is said by here lyes Chamberlen.

JONAS ASPLIN (1771–1842)

A respected man, eminent in his profession

Chelmsford Chronicle, 6 May 1842

Jonas Asplin was Doctor of Prittlewell and later Rayleigh, where he died, his obituary in the *Chelmsford Chronicle* dated 6 May 1842 paying tribute to a 'respected' man, 'eminent in his profession'. Born seventy years earlier, his childhood home had been Wakering; his father Francis Asplin had inherited Little Wakering Hall from his father, also Jonas Asplin. He began his medical career on 2 December 1786 by becoming an apprentice to William Miller of Avely, himself a surgeon, going on to become doctor to the English residents in Paris. On his return he kept diaries of meticulous detail between the years 1826 and 1828, when he was in his early fifties. These works, however, do not give us much evidence of his earlier life. This has had to be pieced together by random facts and events.

Much of Jonas's early years were taken up by his studies, but in 1799 he married a lady named Elizabeth Launceley Burchell, daughter of the wonderfully named Golden Burchell and his wife, Eleanor Lodwick. With the early years of the nineteenth century filled with apprehension that the French would land an invasion force on the north bank of the Thames on the orders of Napoleon, Asplin became involved not only with his medicine, but in the various defensive schemes being installed around the county.

No fighting ever took place, but war fever waxed and waned and in 1803, with fighting spirit running very high, volunteers were enrolled by the thousand. Signal stations were established at Foulness Island, Wakering, Shoebury and Southend and a new force called the Sea Fencibles, men of the seafaring population not eligible for impressment, were to supply coastal defence at the princely wage of 1 shilling a day. In Rayleigh and Rochford, infantry detachments were raised, and in 1803 Jonas Asplin of Wakering and John Lodwick of Southend recruited a troop of volunteer cavalry to resist any attempted invasion.

Seven years later in 1810 Jonas was described as 'Esquire' when he appeared on the electoral register for North Shoebury, but it was a troublesome year for Jonas when he found himself embroiled in a libel battle with Peter and Thomas Lodwick. It was a serious case, tried at the highest court for common pleas in the country, the King's Bench. On Tuesday 5 June that year the *Kentish Gazette* reported that Peter Lodwick, for libeling Jonas Asplin Esq., 'was sentenced to six months imprisonment in the King's Bench and to find security, himself £100 and two securities of £50 each to keep the peace for three years'. The following day the paper reported that Thomas Lodwick 'was brought up to receive judgment for libeling Dr Jonas Asplin, a physician at North Shoebury, in Essex by fixing placards in Chelmsford, and the neighbouring towns'. He too was sentenced to six months.

Asplin, as the eldest son, had inherited Little Wakering Hall after the death of his father, but it passed to his brother Charles, possibly when Asplin left for Paris. Returning to England, Jonas and his wife took a house opposite Prittlewell church and settled down once more to medical practice in Southend. In 1826 Asplin's elevated position saw him entitled to vote, as part of the Borough of Maldon, in the general election, and he showed himself to be a moderate Tory. Socially minded, he applauded the apprehension and transportation of felons, but deplored the abysmal on-board conditions. He also voiced a concern against his own class, a case in point being the Earl Winchelsea, whose death in 1826 he deemed 'no loss'. Owning 'fine farms in Foulness', it appeared Asplin's neighbour demanded such high rents 'as to oblige the old tenants to leave them and ruin those that have taken them'. For Asplin, had 'Winchelsea's death taken place earlier it would have been better for all concerned'.

Though the majority of his visits were to middle-class patients, Asplin treated poorer people whenever they needed him and sometimes operated on them in the parish workhouses, to all intents and purposes the only hospitals for people unable to pay for treatment. By now Asplin was keeping his famous diary, and among other things for 19 May 1828 was the entry 'Miss Lester came from Wallace (Wallasea) Island and a Mrs Thorby from Southend, whose breast I condemned for amputation.' The very next day Asplin drove to Southend at 10 a.m. to visit Mrs Thorby and make 'arrangements for an operation which has not been performed in this country for 40 years; and then not by any surgeon in the country. Appointed 4 o'clock tomorrow afternoon for the operation.' Dr Asplin invited several colleagues to attend, but not all of them shared his enthusiasm for such progressive practice.

On 21 May his diary records that he indeed operated on Mrs Thorby and removed the whole breast, which was diseased from cancer, and 'succeeded extremely well'. On 25 May his diary noted, 'Mrs Thorby is doing delightfully' and by June it recorded, 'Visited Mrs Thorby, which case cannot go on better.'

In 1841 the doctor appears in the first national census and we find him, with his wife Elizabeth, now moved to Rayleigh, aged sixty-six, described as 'physician' and wealthy enough to employ a female servant, Ann Parmenter, and a young lad called Thomas Farmer to help with the chores.

Asplin died a year later in early May, the *Chelmsford Chronicle* dated 3 June 1842 announcing a 'genteel furniture sale' of Asplin's effects including 400 books on medical and other subjects and a variety of excellent surgical instruments in cases. Perhaps his widow found Rayleigh Place, their home, too large to keep on without her husband? Whatever the reason, it served as a rare glimpse into the life of an extraordinary Essex doctor.

4

SEA DOGS

HADDOCKS & SALMONS

Leigh mariner Richard Haddock was one of seven captains and two admirals given to the Navy by his family in the seventeenth and eighteenth centuries. Born only yards from the quayside in what is now known as the Crooked Billet public house, he would have witnessed Leigh trade her butter, grain, and coal under a forest of masts and sail. Thirty-two masters and 230 mariners lived in Leigh in 1565, and in the 1580s it was the major port between London and Harwich, benefiting from an allowance of five shillings on the tonne for any ships built at 100 tonnes or over. The Spanish ambassador, taking stock of England's naval capacity prior to the Armada, reported home that he'd sighted two ships of 100 tonnes at anchor, two of 60 tonnes and twenty ships of less than 80 tonnes only recently built. An embarkation point for soldiers, 300 men could be mobilised from Leigh in four days, and with it being a vital deep-water anchorage, a complete war fleet could put into harbour for a refit.

John Haddock was a Leigh landowner in 1327. A Richard Haddock is commemorated in a brass plaque in Leigh church in 1454, along with two wives, a son and assorted nephews and nieces, but it was in the seventeenth century that a Richard Haddock began a naval career that brought him great maritime distinction. Becoming a captain, he supported the Parliamentary cause and on his death in 1666 he had received £40 from Parliament for public service.

Likewise, Richard's son William distinguished himself at sea. For commanding the *America* in 1653 against the Dutch, Cromwell's Parliament awarded him a gold medal, a copy of which is in Southend Museum.

His son, another Richard, joined the Navy quite young, and at twenty-eight was in command of the frigate *Abragon*, which patrolled the Channel waiting to intercept Spanish marauders. He was knighted for his heroism while captaining the *Royal James*, a 100-gun first-rate ship of the line in the opening conflict of the Third Dutch War, one of the few times England has fought alongside France to defeat a common enemy. Though he was involved in many campaigns, Richard's letters to the Admiralty show that life in the Navy was not all blood and thunder. A correspondence of 1673 has him requesting 'Suffolk and Ipswich canvas, 50 bolts of each', while later that year he thanks the Admiralty Board for 'the horse boats which will be of great service'. Cavalry often had to be carried abroad, and these boats fitted with tight stalls on two decks were towed behind the fleet. Most importantly, he asks the board 'to remind Secretary Samuel Pepys of the Admiralty about his pay owing'.

Unfortunately, in 1674 Captain Haddock became a casualty of Pepys's Navy-reforming zeal. The practice of allowing naval vessels to carry bullion for British merchants, in order to thwart piracy, was being abused. So lucrative had service in the Mediterranean become, that ships refused to engage the enemy for fear of losing precious cargos. Pepys made an example of Richard Haddock, sentencing him to six months in prison, and ordered him to pay all profits to 'the Chatham chest'. If he served his sentence it did him no harm. He went on to become 'Comptroller of the Navy'.

Richard's eldest son and namesake held the same office as his father for fifteen years, while Nicholas, his youngest son, became a captain at the age of twenty. Nicholas saw action with the Spanish off Sicily, borne out by a request by him in 1738 for a 'pilot for the Alborough fireship'. Manned by a skeleton crew, or towed, these old vessels were filled with turpentine, cordage, or old sail. Once set alight, the men would 'lash the rudder', escape in a small

Sir Richard Haddock was born in Leigh-on-Sea in 1629 and died 26 January 1714 in London. He rose to the rank of admiral in the Navy, having held the command of HMS *Dragon, Portland, Royal James, Lion, Royal Charles* and HMS *Duke* during his career. He is attributed as having fought in the battles of Holme's Bonfire, Solebay, Schooneveld and Texel.

boat and watch 'the yardarms burn' entangled in the enemy's rigging. He was eventually promoted to admiral. He died in 1746 and is buried with sixteen others of the family in the churchyard of St Clements. It has been said that such an amazing tradition of naval eminence in one family has never been known before, and is unlikely to occur again in England's history.

Robert Salmon, 'borne in this towne' in 1566 and buried in 1641, is also laid to rest in St Clements church, Leigh-on-Sea, a bust of him on display beneath a gloriously beamed ceiling resembling the upturned hull of a great ship. A wealthy merchant, his family had connections with Leigh since 1472. One of his forebears, 'Thomas Saman', and his grandson both died on the same day in 1576, the general view being they both drowned. Robert himself held the coveted office of Master of Trinity House. This institution was the result of the fusing of two guilds of pilots, one at Leigh, the other at Deptford. The Fraternity of the Most Glorious and Invisible Trinity and St Clement, to give it its full name, was formed to ensure the welfare of those who made a living from the sea, the relief of mariners, and their dependants in distress. Occasionally it also had a military function, for example when Elizabeth I, fearing a Spanish invasion in 1588, ordered Trinity House to prepare for war. In response, Captain Robert Salmon (Master of Trinity House 1588–9) informed Lord Burghley, the queen's advisor, that he could fit out thirty merchant ships in four days and have them at the disposal of the Lord High Admiral, Lord Henry Seymour. Consequently Lord Seymour commanded Captain Salmon to 'go with his galley and make ready to guard the mouth of the Thames'. Fortunately Salmon's Trinity ships did not encounter an armada, but it was proof that if needed, Trinity House and its power was a valuable asset.

Salmon's son, also Robert Salmon (1599–1636), held the same distinction as his father, as well as being a prominent member and director of the East India Company. In his capacity of Master of Trinity House he was often called to deal with that scourge of early seventeenth-century shipping, namely Turkish pirates. Such men operated from the ports of North Africa, often finding winter refuge in Holland and at Flushing, both within easy reach of the Essex coast. The hardship of sailors taken as prisoners kept in chains and tortured until they 'turned Turk' are all too evident in poignant petitions made to Trinity House by wives and mothers. As master of the corporation Salmon would have been closely involved in helping to raise money by levies on shipping to finance expeditions to Algiers against the Turkish pirates. Closer to home he would also been involved in the authorisation of certificates designed to address the misfortunes of seamen and sometimes ship owners themselves. Such certificates enabled those who had lost everything in an unfortunate voyage or through capture by pirates to obtain a license to beg, and not fall foul of the vagrancy statutes.

PRESSED MEN

Better one volunteer than three pressed men...

Local historic records are littered with the evidence of men having been taken into the Army as well as the Navy in times of war, against their will. As early as 1591/2, Robert Haselwood of Hadstock, in his Last Will and Testament, described himself as 'pressed for a soldier in her majesties service beyond the seas'. Later, in 1599, John Lytherland of Coggeshall, a clothier, and Mark Ashtyn of Great Braxted, a carpenter, were both pressed into Her Majesty's Service to fight in the Netherlands.

Impressments were used as a deterrent. They were a legalised form of kidnap used as a way of swelling the ranks of the country's services. In 1585, recorded in the Michaelmas Sessions Rolls of Halstead, a letter written by a constable of Bumpstead, Thomas Gent, to the Justices of the Peace, told how he had bound over a man named Thomas Keape 'to be of good behaviour' after six weeks of living in a disorderly fashion. Keape was warned that if his behavior did not improve he would be presented to the magistrates as a 'master-less man'. At this, Keape 'very rudelye and disorderlye did rayle of the constable with opprobrious wordes' and then threatened to beat him, and 'did not onlye contynewe his stubborne behaviour towardes the constable, but also did very proudly and disorderlye many wayes behave himselfe before us'. It seems that the constables warning did no good as Thomas Keape later found himself up before the JP and was 'viewed and 'pressed for her majesties service'.

According to Session Rolls dated Easter 1599, John Hawkins was bound and charged by the constables of Stanford Rivers to appear at Epping sessions to be pressed for Her Majesty's Service into Ireland, as a soldier – but he refused to make his appearance.

To be pressed meant hardship for the families left behind or for those maimed in the service of their country. In 1593 Baltazar Coole from the 'hamlett of Coxell' (alias Coggeshall) petitioned Her Majesty's lieutenants Sir Thomas Myldmay and Sir John Petre, knights for parish relief, having been pressed from his home to be 'a Servitor under the chardge and bonde of Captayne Cristmas and so imployed in her Service in the lowe Countries wheere he receyved many a mayme and hurte'. In response it was decreed that he would receive the relief needed to alleviate the 'poore distressed estate wherein I my poore wiefe and childe stande in', preventing him from begging as a means of support and so avoiding the laws and punishments usually metered out to 'rogues and vagabonds'. In 1656 there was a petition from Barking fishermen for protection from the press gang.

In 1617 William Stonard of Stock applied for alms from the parish, giving the reason that he had at one time been pressed in to the Navy to fight in the Low Countries in which he was hurt and maimed. He was fortunate as he was allowed during his life a yearly pension of 40 shillings to be paid quarterly by the treasurer for maimed soldiers for the Hundred of Chelmsford, with 10 shillings payable immediately. The documents were signed by the Justices of the Peace at that time who were Lord Petre, Barrington, and Lord Maynard.

At the much later date of 1672, Quarter Session Rolls of the Liberty of Havering contain a complaint against pressing men who were not seamen from Hornchurch. This included the waggoner's man. Apparently he was apprehended by the pressmen while on a journey to London, the horses and wagon subsequently left unattended and abandoned.

The question of parish relief for pressed and maimed soldiers was an ongoing one. In 1647 the court in session at Easter granted double relief for John Dawe, a maimed soldier who had been born in High Easter but pressed for the service of the Parliament against Charles I, by the constables of Aythorp Roothing. By virtue of his connection to both parishes it was decreed that 'as long as his impotence continued', his relief of 2 shillings a week was to be shared by the two parties. In 1656 William Hutson claimed he was pressed as a soldier into Parliament's service and was wounded at the Siege of York, thus rendering him unable to maintain his wife and children. The court ordered he be paid 30 shillings forthwith on condition he be 'of no further trouble therein' to the parish.

Thomas Hewes of 'Burneham' in Essex made a humble request for relief of the Essex quarter sessions at Michaelmas, 1655, on account of him having been pressed to serve as a drummer in Scotland in the service of the state and 'was there long since maimed'. This was also endorsed by the complete inhabitants of Burnham who also verified that he had been in receipt of a small pension allowed him toward his relief but this had stopped once he had been able to resume some paid work. Now he was 'past his labour' and too old to be gainfully employed he was reapplying for help from the parish. He was successful. The Treasurer for the East Division ordered that 'for charitable uses,' he was to be paid 'out of the Countyes Stocke Fourety Shillings a yeare towards his releife' at 10 shillings per quarter, 'the first payments to begin this present Sessions and to continue during his life'.

As one of many county nobles heavily involved with recruiting parish men for the services in time of conflict, Sir John Bramston was almost daily in receipt of letters from Naval officers. On 11 January 1664/5 he received from James, Duke of York, Lord High Admiral, a letter of instruction 'to send any men impressed to his Majesty's ship, rideing in the Hope'.

On 27 December 1664 James, Duke of York, Lord High Admiral, again wrote to Sir John Bramston requesting that he impress 200 able mariners or seamen. He was to pay them 1 shilling for press money and 1 penny per mile conduct money, and those Bramston chose to undertake the task were to be un-corruptible men whom would not bargain for freedom with any pressed in their charge.

Impressment was to be avoided at all costs. On 28 February 1672 Bramston received a letter from the Duke of York expressing his concern that 'sev[er]all of ye Seamen in ye said County have deserted their habitations and are gone upp into ye County thereby to avoid ye presse'. He therefore authorised the sending of tickets and press money to parish constables to entice the runaways back.

The need for men was relentless. February 1671/2 saw Sir John Bramston receive a letter from the Admiralty explaining that 'These Easterly Winds w[hi]ch have kept our frigotts blockt upp in ye River, hath alsoe kaused mee to keepe till now ye Orders enclosed from his R.H. for pressing Men in yo[u]r Jurisdiction'. He went on to express hope that 'in a few dayes some of ye Kings shipps wil be at Harwich to receive ye Men'.

Acting on instruction from the Duke of York, Bramston drew up many warrants and letters in order to implement the requests of the Admiralty. In 1672 he issued a warrant cataloguing an account of which ships the men were put on board and from where they were impressed, together with charges and disbursements. The men were listed by port, including Brightlingsea, East Donyland, Manningtree, West Mersea, Tollesbury, and Wivenhoe, with press and conduct money paid and to which ships the men were assigned. Separate accounts left to the historian include payments to constables of Leigh and Dunmow, giving names of men impressed. Those for Leigh include men from Loughton, Bobbingworth, Chigwell, Kelvedon, Lambourne and Theydon Garnon, as well as parishes in the Rochford Hundred area. The payment also includes £1 3s 4d for the feeding of 'a file of Musquetiers sent from the fort at Shearness to tend the prest men – 5 days at 8 pence p[er] diem'.

There was more to impressment than merely the capture of drunken men.

In 1696 Aubrey de Vere, 20th Earl of Oxford and Lord Lieutenant of Essex, received a letter from the Privy Council requiring 'a speedy supply of able Seaman for completing the number of eight thousand men which are wanting to man his Majesties Fleet'. All parish constables were to make lists complete with the ages of eligible men both ordinary working men as well as boatmen, bargemen, watermen, and fishermen. Once compiled this list was to be sent to the commander of the Admiralty and the vice admiral of the county. The vice admiral was then to raise 300 men and appoint 'Prestmasters' to do so.

As the Lord Lieutenant of Essex, Aubrey de Vere was then required to ensure that those men designated to do the 'pressing' did not abuse their office. Once 'pressed' these men were to be conveyed to Harwich, and the Nore, where the conductor would be paid 6d per man per day. The letter also stated all seamen that had retired 'into the Country to Husbandry Worke' especially be sought and pressed into service, as they would already 'know the ropes'. In this task the vice admiral was to be assisted by the deputy lieutenants and Justices of the Peace. Contrary to the widespread belief that impressment was a small-scale operation involving the capture of drunken men at sword-point from inns and taverns, records show it was a concerted effort by those in authority, both high and low, to ensure the king's ships were adequately filled in both peace and war.

RICHARD PARKER (1767–97)

30 years old – of a robust form – dark complexion and black eyes; his figure was five foot eight inches in its height, and both in his feature and mould of person he was entitled to the term of manly comeliness.

The Gentleman's Magazine, c. 1796

If the fact can be appreciated that the Nore, the famous anchorage lying in the Thames estuary, has featured many times in Essex history then perhaps the imagination can be stretched a little further to accept that Richard Parker, hanged from the yard arm of his own ship as a stark warning to anyone daring to challenge the brutality and indifference of the eighteenth-century Navy, can at a pinch be counted as an Essex boy.

Well educated, Parker entered the Royal Navy as midshipman and, in 1783, aged sixteen, became an acting lieutenant on the *Mediator*. His career looked set to take off, but, a quarrelsome man, Parker was his own worst enemy and after a heated disagreement with his captain he left the Navy under a cloud, married Miss Ann Machardy, and settled in Scotland. But the sea was in his blood, and restless, he rejoined the Navy in 1793 as an officer, before a court martial saw him reduced once more to the rank of common seaman for refusing to obey an order. A year later he fell ill and returned home to try his hand at school teaching, though it appeared a strange living for a man with a quick temper. This only led him into debt and imprisonment and so on his release, knowing himself to be a competent sailor if nothing else, he once more turned to the sea, took the king's bounty money, which at £20, more than covered his debt, and rejoined the Navy.

Parker was drafted to the crew of the *Sandwich* and found his fellow seamen at the Nore in a miserable condition, the long three-year war with France responsible for unbelievable deprivations, mostly due to conditions and pay that had not risen since the days of Charles II. Even if pay had been regular, their meager nineteen shillings a month would not have fed their families, and prevented wives claiming parish relief. To add to this, sailors were usually confined to the ship when at port, to prevent those press-ganged from leaving, even if their families were starving and they could have worked on land for a time to help out at home. It appeared the victorious naval battles won on the backs of the Navy were forgotten by the government, though officers' pay was regularly raised and volunteers like Parker were highly rewarded. Expendable and exposed to the arbitrary will and tyranny of their commanders – one captain killed a seaman with his bare hands – it was evident that even the lowest-born soldier had more worth than his seaborne brother.

To say Parker found the crew of the *Sandwich* 'agitated' when he joined her at anchor was an understatement. The air reeked of rebellion, with rumours from the Channel fleet at Spithead that they themselves were about to mutiny. One man, Henry Long, aboard the ship *Champion* had even written to the Admiralty, 'Damn my eyes if I understand your lingo or long proclamation, but in short, give us our due at once and no more of it.' Independent and energetic, Parker took the men's side, immediately winning their trust.

In early May 1797 Parker and his men secretly received men from *Spithead* who had taken things into their own hands and indeed mutinied on 16 April. Tired of their treatment they had removed their officers, flown the red flag of insubordination and were now waiting for their demands to be met. With an air of uncertainty as to their ultimate fate, they had come to their fellow seamen at the Nore to see if they would rise up and stand with them. Parker and his men unanimously agreed.

The mutiny was set for 12 May when all captains would be attending a court martial aboard the sixty-four-gun *Inflexible* and thus when the rebel crews were to take over the ships the highest ranking officers they would encounter would be lieutenants. Parker was elected leader and, just as planned, when the captains returned to their duties they found all Naval authority in the hands of mutineers. All, that was, except Admiral Buckner who, not returning to his command on the *Sandwich*, left the way clear for Parker to effectively become 'Admiral of the Fleet'.

When Richard Parker joined the crew of the *Sandwich* at the Nore he found the men ready for rebellion, seen here complaining of their rations, just one of the issues that would see them mutiny.

Unexpectedly, the Admiralty took the uprising calmly, knowing the *Spithead* mutiny was well on the way to being resolved and assumed the Nore mutiny would follow suit. Thus for eight days the Nore mutineers were a law unto themselves, ruled by none but Parker, and free, possibly for the first time in their lives. It was, however, a well-ordered affair. Riots were not allowed, drunks dealt with and the officers that remained on board were well treated. The prostitutes on board were retained on condition of no fighting over favours. Eventually Admiral Bruckner returned to the *Sandwich* with reports that the *Spithead* mutineers had dispersed and it was time for the Nore men to do the same.

Parker refused, instead issuing further demands both to the Admiralty and to the government. After six days of deliberation, delegates returned to the Nore with the stark answer that they would consider nothing but 'surrender and a prayer for pardon!' The government had run out of patience.

Anticipation of civil unrest, should the mutineers enlist the help of sympathisers ashore, prompted military units to be mobilised. The *Hereford Journal* dated 1797 reported that 'the mutiny at Sheerness and the Nore had got to such a height as demands more vigorous measures than have yet been used. There has been enough of concession and the refractory seamen must be brought back to their duty by other than lenient and palliative measures.' Strong words indeed, but they were backed up by the actions of the 23rd Regiment of Foot who marched from Chelmsford barracks for Southend in order to intercept the mutinous crews should they attempt to land.

With the government's firm stand and negotiations at a stalemate, the mutineers took the only further action left to them. The vessels at Sheerness joined those at the Nore and a combined force of at least twenty-four ships proceeded to block up the entrance to the estuary, preventing all but a few craft, which had to acquire a 'passport' from Parker himself, passage up or down the river. After a few days the mutineers had detained a vast number of vessels kept in order by ranging all the captive ships of the line at a considerable distance from one another with their broadsides pointed at the merchant vessels, which were positioned in-between. According to eye-witnesses on shore, the whole appearance of the assembled ships was described as both grand and appalling. To add to it all, the red flag flew from each one of the mutineers' ships, adding alarm to the uncertainty that was gripping London.

The stalemate gradually had the effect of making the mutineers uneasy, especially as the government had taken the measure of removing all the buoys from the mouth of the Thames and the Essex and Kent coasts, so that any vessel now wishing to escape would have no way of knowing when or where they would run aground. It did not however stop the ship *St Fiorenzo* or the frigate *Clyde* from deserting with a combination of officers and seamen at the helm. These vessels were fired upon but ultimately escaped only to be replaced by a sloop and four men-of-war, which, having left from their posts at Texel in Holland, joined the stand-off.

Yet by 10 June the mutiny was dissolving. Other vessels began to defect and place themselves under the protection of the fort at Sheerness. Merchant vessels once more were allowed entry into London and it was said that never had so many vessels entered London on one tide. By 12 June only seven ships were flying the red flag and by 16 June all ships had been returned to their commanders; the mutiny was over.

As the proven leader of the rebellion, Parker was taken from the *Sandwich*, his trial occurring aboard the *Neptune*. He accepted his sentence with the words, 'I shall submit to your sentence with all due respect, being confident of the innocence of my intentions and that God will receive me into his favour; and I sincerely hope that my death will be the means of restoring tranquility to the Navy.' On the morning of 30 June the yellow flag (of death) was hoisted on board the *Sandwich*, where Richard Parker spent his last night and where he was to meet his fate. With the whole fleet ranged within sight of the *Sandwich* each crew of every ship was piped on deck to see Parker, washed, shaved and in a 'suit of deep mourning', step with great composure from below, take prayers between two chaplains and drink a glass of wine as 'salvation for his soul and to forgiveness of his enemies'. He was strung up to the yard-arm at half past nine, and a dead silence reigned as he met his death.

One would have thought Parker's actions and those of the other mutineers to have been a purely Naval affair, when in fact it had almost split the nation. This was evident in the account of his wife's desperate race to save his life, discovering his involvement with the mutiny at the last moment while at home in Scotland.

In her desperate attempt to get to London before it was too late, she travelled to Edinburgh to catch the mail coach, but was arrested on suspicion of carrying mutinous letters. This found to be incorrect, she made her way to London where she paid a man a guinea to write a letter of petition to the king, delivering it herself to St James's Palace. A lord-in-waiting informed her that petitions were being heard for the mutineers but not for Richard Parker, whose fate had already been decided, adding that he was not at liberty to inform her of the outcome. Immediately she took another coach to Rochester, and there was told her husband was to be executed the next day.

Sitting up all night waiting for the tide, she then, at 4 a.m., went to hire a boat to take her alongside the *Sandwich* but was met with boatmen who were less than enthusiastic to comply with her request. 'No, I cannot take one passenger,' came the reply from one man she asked, 'the brave Admiral Parker is to die today and I will get any sum I chooses to ask for a party.' Finally she got passage on a market boat, though as they got close to the *Sandwich* a waterborne guard threatened to fire at them. Parker's wife did see her husband briefly on deck appearing between two clergymen and heard him call out, 'There is my dear wife from Scotland.' Unfortunately the shock overwhelmed her and, collapsing back in the boat, she was taken ashore, missing, perhaps to her benefit, her husband's execution.

Unable to accept his death, Ann once more hired a boat out to his ship only to call out for him and be told his body was back on shore and was already buried. When she arrived at the churchyard she found her husband's corpse was indeed buried, but not deep, as it was expected the surgeon would return to the churchyard that night to disinter the body for anatomical research. Alarmed, she managed to enlist the help of two women and five men sympathetic to her husband's cause and her plight, and between them they dug up Parker's body and put it on a wagon to Rochester where Mrs Parker, after paying a further six guineas for a fresh team of horses, took it to her lodgings in London on Tower Hill, arriving just before midnight.

The news that Parker's body now rested at the Hoop & Horseshoe Inn sent waves of discontent through the capital and brought London's Lord Mayor to see Mrs Parker to ask her what she intended to do with the body. She replied she would take it to Exeter and finally Scotland but the Lord Mayor, aware that vast crowds had gathered threatening unrest, advised he should be buried without delay, 'least Admiral Parker's remains should create a civil war'. She reluctantly agreed to allow his body to be taken first to Aldgate workhouse, for its safekeeping, and let the crowds settle before a ceremony was conducted with dignity in Whitechapel churchyard.

Parker had for a time both united and divided the country and would, as proved by the writing of his story, be remembered for his actions. His devoted wife on the other hand has been forgotten. For a few years she enjoyed the property left to her in her husband's Will but then she was denied legal claim to it by those in authority who condemned his actions. She was also deprived of the pittance which had formed her maintenance. In 1836 when she was only sixty-nine years old, due to harsh conditions and neglect, she was almost completely blind and living in a hovel in Blackheath. The late King William at one time gave her £10 and then £20, but then, destitute, she was compelled to ask for charity. Eventually her plight was made known to London magistrates and a refuge was found for her.

VETERANS OF SEA & SHORE

When Nelson uttered those immortal words, 'England confides that every man will do his duty', it is what he expected and what England gave him. Of those that manned the guns, spliced the mainbrace and fought hand to hand with a Navy cutlass a good many of them were Essex men. Similarly when Joan Soole made known her remarkable findings in 2005 of how many Colchester men had fought in the Battle of Waterloo she was hoping for one or two. She was surprised to find nineteen – proof, if proof is needed, that when Albion is in trouble Essex men will answer the call and step up to the mark.

Years later, when newspapers featured such men's obituaries, proudly lauding them as 'Veterans of Trafalgar, Waterloo and the Crimea' they also inadvertently disclosed how many of them, returning to ordinary lives, later suffered hardship and betrayal. Poignant and human, the stories of some of these men bring those distant land and sea battles very much to the fore. When Daniel Turner died in Chelmsford in 1871, he was upwards of eighty years old and still working in Tyndal Square, Chelmsford, where he had lived and supported himself since 1847. What surprised the readers of the *Chronicle* was that he was also a veteran of the Battle of Trafalgar.

Essex men such as Eliab Harvey, a distinguished kinsman of William Harvey, who discovered the circulation of the blood (described also as 'a swarthy and testy man who habitually wore a dagger'), received the thanks of Parliament, a medal and a sword of honour for his role as captain of the *Temaraire* in 1805. He was also promoted rear admiral and served as one of the pallbearers at Nelson's funeral. But the ordinary soldier or sailor who had fought well for his country and in later years needed help himself was not always in receipt of the recognition he deserved. Newspapers such as the *Essex Chronicle* or the now obsolete *Essex Newsman* carried many tributes and obituaries of the men who fought in both the Peninsular Wars and the Crimea. On Friday 9 December 1881 Joseph Pudney, aged ninety-one, was recorded as 'of Stanway', Chelmsford, who as a veteran of Waterloo was buried with some military honours. His plain oak coffin, surmounted by a brass plate, was draped with the Union Jack and carried on a gun carriage pulled by horses and met at the gates of Stanway churchyard by Revd Canon Hill, who read the service in 'an impressive manner'. At the conclusion of the service, three volleys were fired over the coffin. Despite this send-off, his widow was from then on was deprived of his pension and faced the workhouse, though it was suggested she would be saved from this fate as a small fund was being raised by the parishioners.

This was by no means an isolated case, as all wives of veterans were automatically exempt from their husband's pension and so faced straitened circumstances. And it was not only the wives who suffered in this way. Many service men found themselves with a pitiable pension and had to work to supplement it. This was acceptable when he was young and strong enough to do so, but when he became infirm the meager pension often meant periods in the workhouse when things were particularly tough.

In 1880 William Thorpe, who at eighty-four was a veteran of Waterloo, died in the Romford Union Workhouse. He had been through most of the Waterloo campaigns and had taken his pension when it was time for retirement and settled in Romford for the last twenty years of his life. He managed to eke out a living collecting unwanted items door to door in the summer months, but in the winter he voluntarily took refuge in the workhouse. It was here he died. No military honours for him.

The same happened to Waterloo hero Edward Wiseman, who died in 1873 aged seventy-nine in the Maldon Union. He had received a bayonet wound in the foot during the great battle, but had recovered and afterwards served in America. He received a pension but when his injury and infirmity held him back he entered the workhouse. His lot however was rendered 'as comfortable as possible' as he received the 'greatest consideration from the guardians and the master Mr Timpaly'.

By virtue of it taking place a good forty years after Waterloo, those veterans whose theatre of war had been the Crimea often received a small pension as standard. This was the case with William Nunn, who died at Dumow in 1923 at the age of eighty-seven. A native of Ingatestone, he had been 'brought up to the forge' and at only sixteen had gone to Crimea to work as a shoeing smith. He later received a pension for volunteering for active service and spending time in the trenches at Sebastopol and Balaclava.

Aged ninety, Joseph Peer was living on a small pension in 1925 from his time on the railway after his time in Sebastopol. Volunteering to take out a pair of horses for the removal and burial of the dead at the outbreak of the war, he duly stayed two years. He died in Hornchurch, in the house he had returned to, raised a family in and inhabited for almost seventy years.

The Crimea was also where Thomas York of Woodham Ferrers spent his fourteenth year serving as a boy first class aboard HMS *Aeolus* in the

Gunboats of the Baltic Fleet during the Crimean War. (*London Illustrated News*, 1855)

war's Baltic campaign. At his funeral in 1930, the Last Post was heard at his graveside, sounded by a bugler from Warley barracks. Likewise, James Stevens enlisted as a drummer boy in 97th Foot where he had sounded the bugle calls at the signing of the peace at Balaclava and was present at the siege and capture of Lucknow. He was laid to rest in Barking in 1924.

But perhaps the most startling series of events was brought to the attention of the guardians of the Romford Union Workhouse when it was discovered that those in charge had deemed it fit to send the destitute poor who had died on the premises to the school of dissection, something apparently allowed by an ancient anatomy law. This had gone unnoticed until it was deduced from records that a man recently dispatched this way was in fact an Indian Mutiny veteran. Dismay and outrage brought the full weight of disapproval down on the heads of those responsible, who were accused of carrying out a 'cowardly and selfish act'.

As a result the school of anatomy was asked for the body back, the War Office informed and asked by the Union if the man could be given a military funeral. From then on it was to be the case that any future inmates who had served their country and died on the premises were to be made known to the War Office and given the burial they deserved.

5

MARTYRS

ARDLEY, CAUSTON, DRAKES & TYMS

Near this spot suffered for the truth Thomas Causton, 26 Mar: 1555, John Ardley 10 June 1555, who in reply to Bishop Bonner said 'If every hair of my head were a man, I would suffer death in the opinion and faith I now profess'. Also to commemorate Robert Drakes, Minister of Thundersley and William Tyms, curate of Hockley suffered in one fire at Smithfield, 24 April 1556.

Martyrs Memorial, Rayleigh

There is a body of work by a man named Foxe which bears the title *Book of Martyrs* in which he records the names and details of all those who perished by fire in the terrible days of the Marian persecutions. For five catastrophic years Henry VIII's eldest daughter, Mary Tudor, set about returning England to Catholicism, which she considered 'the true faith'. It plunged England into a chaos that saw her behead traitors and murder heretics. In the case of three women burned at the stake in Guernsey, an unborn child also suffered her fanaticism, one of the three being pregnant. It is said it was born at the time of her burning and, falling from the burning pyre, was thrown back into the flames. It begs the question, 'What made Mary so merciless?'

Mary's position at court and within the royal family had always been precarious. As a child, she was, to her father King Henry VIII, 'the most precious pearl in my Kingdom'; she then found herself a bastard in favour of her half-sister Elizabeth. Later, this time alongside Elizabeth, she was declared so again when Henry's son by Jane Seymour, Edward, was born. Through Jane's efforts, both girls were ultimately reunited with their father and reinstated as princesses of the realm, respectively as second and third in the line of succession. But with her father's death and younger brother's reign under the protection of staunch Protestant advisors, Mary could only despair as her Catholic world began to crumble and everything she had ever known begin to disappear.

It had a devastating effect on her health, but she would not give up her religion, even when Edward beseeched her personally to embrace the new faith. The Mass was central to her very being, as it had been for her mother Catherine of Aragon, and though it was taking every ounce of strength she had to resist the constant pressure of Protestant factions; she was not going to let anyone take it away from her.

For Mary, all Protestants were 'heretics', the word deriving from the Greek 'to chose', with Mary believing Protestants were 'choosing' to deny her the religion she cherished. Matters were made worse once her young brother died of consumption and she expected to become queen, as she had not reckoned on Edward's desperate bid to keep Catholicism from returning by declaring the crown would not be going to her but to the young Protestant Lady Jane Grey.

Luckily for Mary, Jane was swiftly deposed after a brief nine days on the throne, but it had not been so much an affair of religion that deposed her as of blood. England wanted a child of Henry VIII to continue to rule the nation and so it was on that point alone that Mary was cheered into London in 1553, both Protestants and Catholics supporting her rightful place as the true Tudor queen. But by now Mary was a pale and bitter woman of thirty-seven, entrenched in her religion and determined to bring England back to Rome and godliness. After years of confusion and personal turmoil she was also determined to punish those that had corrupted her Church and made her life a misery.

Mary's plan to cleanse the English Church of the Protestant curse turned into a bloodbath. In the first three years of her reign she executed almost 300 heretics, which is more than the Spanish Inquisition and the notorious Chambre Ardent (the French court of justice set up solely to try cases of heresy) for the same period. Reinstating the medieval Heresy Act of 1401 gave Mary the power to condemn heretics to flames in her belief that to purify the soul nothing could be left of the body. Determined that the burnings were to produce the maximum effect, Mary is known to have remarked, 'Touching the punishment of heretics, methink of it ought to be done without rashness, that it may be evident to all this realm how I minister true justice.' To underline her intention, the first burnings were of the bishops Latimer and Ridley on 16 October 1555. The persecution of popular country preachers followed, usually at the hands of Mary's zealous Catholic Bishop of London, Edmund Bonner. Their burnings were carried out in town squares all over the country, usually on market days, to cater to the 'maximum effect' that Mary so desired.

The names of four particular Marian Martyrs have a particular significance for The Fitzwimarc School in Rayleigh. They represent the four divisions of the 'house' system into which every child on entering the school on the first day of their very first term is introduced. The school's adoption of these men becomes clear should you read the inscriptions on the Martyrs Memorial in the high street opposite Crown Hill, formally Crown Lane. Erected in 1908, the granite obelisk proudly remembers the strength and ultimate sacrifice the martyrs made.

JOHN ARDLEY

John Ardley was not born in the parish of Rayleigh, but met his death there, as prescribed by Queen Mary, in the marketplace. Ardley was, by trade, a husbandman, a small farmer who worked, rented land and rarely earned more than ten pounds a year. He came from Great Wigborough, approximately 18 miles to the north of Rayleigh, and was condemned by Bishop Bonner after being apprehended with another from his parish, namely John Symson, both receiving their sentences of death on 22 May 1555.

During his examination by Bonner, Ardley had been charged with 'great stubbornness' and possessed of 'vain glory'. He on the other hand had said he was perfectly happy to 'yield to the Queene all his goods and lands so that he might be suffered to live under her', but insisted he wished to keep his 'conscience free from all idolatry and papistical religion'.

Both men were then delivered to the sheriffs in London before being taken to their places of execution on 10 June that same year. Symson and Ardley were not burned together, though they probably travelled from London in the same cart. Rochford town square was to be Symson's place of execution, and with a modern train of thought that had the sixteenth-century main route into Essex passing through Rochford and then on to Rayleigh, Symson may have been taken to his place of execution first, leaving Ardley to make the last leg of his final journey alone.

When Ardley stood on the crude platform built around the stake to which he was bound, and around which faggots had been stacked, he must have prayed the wood was dry enough to afford him a hasty death. Green timbers would only have smouldered and he would have choked to death before he was burned. He may also have hoped that he would perish in a great blaze as occasionally 'small fires' were ordered to be lit, the flames remaining low and burning away the legs, eventually causing the body to slide down into the flames, before asphyxiation due to smoke inhalation had taken place. It is said both John Symson and John Ardley died rejoicing that they were accounted worthy to suffer.

THOMAS CAUSTON

One cannot mention Thomas Causton without including Thomas Higbed, also known as Highbed/Hubbard, of Horndon-on-the-Hill. Foxe, in his *Book of Martyrs*, describes them both as being 'zealous and religious in the true service of God' as well as being two 'worshipful and worthy' gentleman in the county of Essex. He also recounts that 'in a time of blind superstition and wretched idolatry' it was almost impossible for the friends to hide from being spied on, and information about them reaching the wrong ears, as they had no intention of giving up their Protestant faith or their worship of God in what they considered to be the true religion. They were eventually arrested on the orders of Bishop Bonner and were detained in Colchester Castle. With them was Thomas Causton's servant, who was as dedicated to the Protestant religion as his master.

With both Causton and Higbed being men of some standing, or as Foxe put it 'two gentlemen of worshipful estate and great estimation in Essex', Bishop Bonner thought it wiser to visit them to privately ascertain their guilt rather than summoning them to his court in London. An astute tactician, Bonner did not wish to ignite a riot over their arrest at such an early stage as he knew it would only raise local feeling against him higher than it already was.

Bonner arrived in Colchester with several others, including a Master Fecknam to assist him in persuading Causton and Higbed to see the queen's reason and adopt Catholicism. By all accounts Bonner firstly tried to cajole them with 'large promises and flatterings' but later, losing patience, resorted also to 'terrors and threatenings', eventually leaving them both to deliberate on their plight. When it was evident Causton and Higbed were not about to conform to Catholicism, Bonner left Colchester, taking both men plus several other prisoners to London to see if, once in the capital and confronted with the gravity of their situation, they would 'revoke their opinions'.

Not even incarceration in London and further attempts by Bonner and his chaplain's could make Causton and Higbed recant. On 17 February 1555 they were brought forward to be examined by the supreme ecclesiastical court of St Paul's, the Consistory, where the Bishop of Bath questioned them. This was repeated on 1 March but they would not change their minds and so they were commanded to appear two weeks later to be charged as heretics and to hear of their fate. Thomas Causton was first to hear the charge against him followed by his friend Higbed. They were then delivered into the hands of the London sheriffs, possibly William Woodoffe and Thomas Leigh, who in turn delivered them to the prison at Newgate where they languished for a further two weeks, at the end of which they were taken at four o'clock in the morning through the streets to Aldgate where they were given over to the Sheriff of Essex, who in 1555 was William Harris of Cricksea.

Now they were bound to carts to prevent attempts to rescue them and taken to their respective places of execution. Thomas Higbed was delivered to his home village of Horndon-on-the-Hill, Thomas Causton to Rayleigh, it being the nearest parish to his home in Thundersley and important enough to have a marketplace where a sizeable crowd could be summoned to witness an execution by burning.

Thomas Causton and Thomas Higbed died for their unswerving beliefs, unrepentant, on the same day – 26 March 1555. Land that Thomas Causton held in the Essex parish of Tillingham and which was confiscated at his arrest was restored to his family on the accession of Elizabeth I.

ROBERT DRAKES & WILLIAM TYMS

Robert Drakes suffered the terrible fate of burning to death on 25 April 1556 in the same fire as William Tyms. Commemorated on the Rayleigh memorial, he did in fact die at Smithfield alongside four other Essex men, all from Bocking, their names Richard and Thomas Spurge, John Cavell, a weaver, and George Ambrose, a fuller.

Drakes was minister of the parish church of St Peter in Thundersley, the same parish in which Thomas Causton, who had died the previous year, had lived. Drakes had been made a deacon only three years earlier in 1553, by Doctor Taylor of Hadleigh on the recommendation of the Archbishop of Canterbury, Thomas Cranmer. A year later he was ordained by the Bishop of London, Doctor Riley, Bishop Bonner's Protestant predecessor. He was then presented to the benefice of Thundersley by Lord Rich of Rochford and by Thomas Causton himself. Rich, a man whose allegiance changed in favour of every new Tudor monarch, then betrayed Drake and sent him before the Bishop of Winchester to be persuaded to conform to the religion of the realm as was the law, Catholicism. Drakes, as far from the character of the duplicitous Rich as a man could be, admitted only to abide by the laws of God, and was committed to prison where he remained until his death, which was to take place at Smithfield alongside William Tyms of Hockley.

Tyms had come to be in prison with Drakes as a result of two sermons preached in defiance of Queen Mary's true religion in Plumberow and Beeches Woods in the parish of Hockley. The woods belonged to Master Tyrell, who was soon made aware that 'unlawful assembly' was taking place on his land, prompting him to 'come to Hockley to sort out these proceedings'. A servant of Tyrell's wishing to curry favour with his master suggested it was William Tyms who was to blame for bringing heretic preachers into the parish and so Tyrell charged the parish constables to bring Tyms to him. When Tyms was brought to account, Tyrell made sure no crowds were present as he knew his tenant to be an honest man and that there would have been an outcry if he were 'to open his mouth against Tyms'. But eavesdroppers heard Tyrell finish his exchange with Tyms angrily, after he had called him a traitor.

Tyms was sent to London to be questioned by Bonner and also to be examined by the Bishop of Bath just as John Ardley had been. The constables who had taken Tyms to London spoke of the exchange between the accused and his accusers saying that they had 'never heard the like' before; his eloquence was truly inspirational. William Tyms was such a 'truehearted man' that it appeared to those that heard him that God himself was speaking through him on his behalf. It was the weary bishops who finally called a halt to the exchange, for Tyms had argued his case for over six hours. The constables, Edward Hedge and John James, were dismissed and Tyms returned to his place of detention.

Though Foxe's *Book of Martyrs* was written after the Marian atrocities and presented from the author's personal point of view, one is still able to get a feel for the character of William Tyms. It appears he was a personable man, a man comfortable in his beliefs and in his own skin. His exchanges with his accuser, Master Tyrell, show he was not overawed by the social divide between tenant and overlord. In answer to Tyrell's accusation of treason he is calmly able to remind his accuser that 'in King Edward's days you did affirm the truth that I do now'. This counter accusation saw Tyrell firmly deny that 'nay by God's body, I never thought it with my heart'. Confident in his reply Tyms retorts, 'Well, then I pray you master Tyrell bear with me, for I have been a traitor but a while, but you have been a traitor six years.'

Tyms does not appear openly afraid at his cross-examinations by the bishops either, appearing self-assured in what he is prepared to die for. When he is mocked for appearing in the ecclesiastical court not wearing his deacon's clothing but dressed instead in a coat and coloured breeches he sharply observes, 'Ah, my Lord, my vesture doth not vary so much from a Deacon, but methinketh your apparel doth as much vary from an Apostle.'

But eloquence and wit alone were not enough to save Tyms and on 28 March 1555 he, Robert Drakes and the four others detained with them were taken to the consistory court at St Paul's and condemned for heresy. In his address, the Bishop of London accused Tyms of being a ringleader to which Tyms replied, 'My Lord, I marvel that you should begin with a lie', stating that he only knew the men accused with him from their time in prison together. He further defended himself by saying that he held no other religion 'than Christ preached, the Apostles witnessed and the Church received'. He ended with the words, 'Proceed on, I fear not.'

Bishop Bonner condemned Tyms and his fellow heretics, giving them over to the sheriffs. They were taken as was customary to Newgate and on 14 April 1556 they all burned together in one fire at Smithfield.

The unveiling of the Rayleigh Martyrs Memorial on 23 September 1908 was carried out by Mr Rowland Whitehead MP, who said in his address that he, like everyone, was privileged to 'honour the memories of four men who played their parts as men should, with courage, tenacity, and sincerity, in one of the greatest struggles of mankind'. The height of the monument was reported by the *Essex Newsman* to be 'about nineteen feet', with the cost being £100. A similar memorial was erected in memory of twenty-three other Essex martyrs in the Moot Hall, Colchester.

Ardley, Causton, Drakes and Tyms were among the first men of Essex who died 'joyously' for their beliefs. In the five years Mary was on the throne her frenzied persecution of Protestants was to condemn so many more to the flames.

WILLIAM HUNTER

Hunter's story is made all the more poignant by virtue of his young age, the idealism of youth and that he travelled in the same cart from London into Essex for his execution as John Ardley. He was only nineteen when he was apprehended, to all intents and purposes a godly young man, as Foxe says, 'born of the like godly parents'. William was an apprentice in London during Mary Tudor's first year as queen and it was there he attended worship. At first he must have been able to somehow avoid taking Mass or avoid Catholic service altogether but at one Easter service he was commanded to take Communion in the church in Coleman Street where he was living, as was expected of all the queen's subjects. He refused and was threatened with the prospect of a meeting with the infamous Bishop Bonner. Hearing this, Hunter's master at the time Thomas Tailor, a silk-weaver, asked him to leave his employ, afraid that Hunter's obvious Protestant beliefs would see him and his family implicated in the boy's actions.

Hunter returned to his home town of Brentwood where he stayed with his father, attending the chapel there as he had done before his arrival in London. On one occasion he visited the chapel and, thinking he was alone, picked up a Bible and began to read it aloud. Unfortunately he was interrupted by Father Atwell who as a worshipper of the old order was infuriated that a mere man and not a priest was reading the gospels aloud, interpreting the word of God unqualified. He challenged William, accusing him of meddling with the Bible, to which William replied that all he had done was read the Bible for his own comfort. Outraged, Father Atwell stormed out of the building, throwing away the comment that 'it was never merry since the bible came abroad in English', obviously deeply troubled that common people had such unrestricted access to the Holy Book now that it was no longer in Latin.

Atwell returned to confront William but this time had brought with him the vicar of South Weald, Thomas Wood, whom he had found in the inn next to the chapel. Wood accused the lad of preaching from the Holy Book, which he was not authorised to do. William explained to Wood what he had explained to Atwell but Wood was convinced the boy was reading the Bible aloud wishing to preach God's word, yet as a Protestant was not truly accepting what was written.

William ultimately escaped the chapel and the vicar of South Weald and laid low, but at home his father and the parish constable, Robert Salmon, were sent for and asked where the boy could have gone. When William's father denied all knowledge of a possible hiding place, he was not believed and pressed for answers. Eventually he faced down his inquisitors as any father would; 'Sir would you have me seek my own son to be burned?' he challenged. His appeal fell on deaf ears and he was told that he did not 'need to care for the matter', and that if he did indeed fetch him he would see what would be done for him.

An accidental meeting on the highway brought parent and son together and William, knowing his father was under threat, offered to give himself up without fear of the consequences. Within minutes of his return, William was arrested by the constable and placed securely in the parish stocks. The next time William appeared in the stocks they were those of the gatehouse of the Bishop's London residence, after having first been examined in Brentwood, then passed on to the interrogations of Bishop Bonner. His lengthy interrogation was broken only by incarceration in prison where Bonner commanded the keeper to 'lay on him as many irons as he could bare'. Once when Bonner asked how old he was William answered that he was nineteen, to which the

Bishop replied, 'You will be burned ere you be twenty years old if you will not yield yourself better than you have done yet.' William continued in prison for almost a year.

When William was convicted of heresy his brother Robert Hunter was present. Perhaps in recognition of his youth, before he sentenced him Bonner gave William one last chance to return to the Catholic faith, offering to make him a freeman of the city and give him £40 of good money with which to set himself up in business if he so chose. But William, 'strengthened by God', still refused, his brother hearing Bonner condemn William to Newgate for a time before he was to be taken back to his home town of Brentwood, where he declared that William Hunter, heretic, would be burned. He was a month in Newgate before arriving home on a Saturday, his execution cruelly having to wait until Tuesday as it was currently a religious holiday.

William saw his parents in the intervening days, his father praying he would continue in his courage, his mother professing her joy at having been able to have borne such a child. When Tuesday came William walked to the stake, which had been erected in the vicinity of the archery butts at the end of the town. He was accompanied by the sheriff's servant and his brother Robert. He was still only nineteen years old.

It was said that when Elizabeth I, Mary's sister, ascended the throne in 1558 Bishop Bonner, Bishop of London, was presented to her. He was he only one of her subjects that day who she would not allow to kiss her hand.

6

FELONS & FUGITIVES

DICK TURPIN (1705–1739) & THE ESSEX GANG

5ft 9ins high, of a brown complexion, very much marked with the Small Pox, his cheek bones broad, his face slimmer towards the bottom, his visage short, pretty upright, and broad about the shoulders.

Contemporary account of Richard Turpin

According to the Essex Epiphany Sessions Rolls there were no less than forty-five incidents of highway misconduct in 1721 for the Ongar, Harlow and Waltham Hundreds. One records a man from Theydon Bois alleging he was held up and robbed by highwaymen in the forest. An 'idle fellow', he was later proved to be 'a cheat and a fraud', and found to have slightly obscene playbills, song sheets etc., secreted about his person. But that particular gentleman aside, the Essex forests of Waltham and Epping were indeed the haunt of highwaymen, and one in particular, Richard Turpin. Far from being the 'gentleman of the road' and 'seducer of ladies' as his reputation would have us believe, he was no more than a thug and petty criminal. In fact, Turpin only took to the highway robbery he is renowned for in the last year of his life. Up until then he was a core member of a band of organised criminals led by three brothers – Jasper, Jeremy (Jeremiah) and Samuel Gregory. Later, the sixteen or so members of this disreputable and notorious company of miscreants became known as the Essex Gang. All romance aside, these men including Turpin were hardened criminals known for their viciousness and brutality. When raiding farmhouses in and around London they were always fully armed, and destroyed and burned everything not worth taking. Our creation of them as folk heroes and the subjects of romantic ballads is wholly misplaced.

Born in Hempstead in Essex in 1705, Turpin was definitely an Essex lad. His father was a butcher and innkeeper by trade and Richard received a modest education from the village schoolmaster, James Smith, where sometime before the age of eleven he 'learned to make letters'. At the age of sixteen he was apprenticed to a butcher in Whitechapel, then a pleasant village on the outskirts of London, where he spent five years learning his trade before setting up in business for himself at Waltham Abbey. At this point it is the general consensus that young Turpin had no intention of being a law-abiding citizen, preferring instead the company of footpads and thieves. But the trade Richard had followed his father into was a rapidly changing one, and his descent into a life of crime may not have been by choice. To realise the challenges facing young Richard, we must first be familiar with the workings of the eighteenth-century butchery trades and market laws. It was no coincidence that in the heyday of highway robbery there was an unusually high number of butchers among their fraternity.

In 1720 over one hundred London and country butchers petitioned the City, protesting at their loss of livelihood. They argued that they were being 'ruined and disabled' by the centralisation of city markets and unscrupulous traders who avoided selling their meat and venison in the correct public places, preferring to supply shopkeepers and alehouses directly, usually with goods that would not satisfy market standards. Meat and poultry guilds were inadvertently introducing a class differential between traders, which meant markets such as Smithfield no longer welcomed the itinerant meat seller; the 'cutting butchers' and the 'poulterers'. Small dealers, such as herb women, drovers, carters, small-time higglers and kidders were being squeezed out of the markets into alleyways and dark corners, no longer able to obtain prime selling pitches. Small woodland communities who up until now had always been able to provide meat and venison for London saw their market disappearing.

Turpin was beginning to feel the pinch just as much as his neighbour and poaching was becoming the only way a tradesman could feed himself. Against such odds, was it any wonder that highway robbery was such an attractive option, and poachers became more audacious?

On 4 December 1723 a group of men were hanged at Tyburn for murder and deer stealing, these activities having taken place in broad daylight and not at night as usual. Having blackened their faces, these men had gone to the parks of the nobility and gentry and repeatedly stolen deer, a casualty of these actions being the murder of the Bishop of Winchester's keeper on Waltham Chase. These daylight poachers were known locally as the 'Waltham Blacks'. Such disregard for possession and property made it necessary for 'the Black Act' to be brought in, a measure that elevated deer stealing from a misdemeanor in common law to a hanging offence.

Turpin stayed on the right side of the law for a number of years, marrying a Waltham innkeeper's daughter named Hester Palmer, but then began to supplement their income by stealing cattle. Eventually, to avoid capture, he fled into the wilds of rural Essex, where he earned a living from robbing the smugglers on the coast, sometimes posing as a revenue officer which won him no friends on either side. Forced to flee again, this time he found himself in Epping Forest, the haunt of the 'Gregory Gang', and with them he graduated from smuggling venison into London beneath wagonloads of vegetables to burgling houses on the north-eastern outskirts of London.

The Essex or Gregory Gang varied in size depending on how many outlaws had thrown in with them at any one time (usually around twenty), but there were always the key members, of whom Turpin became one. Turpin could count among his companions Joseph Rose, a thirty-eight-year-old blacksmith with a wife and several children who for several years had taken an active role among the Southern deer stealers. John Field, also a blacksmith, was 'tall of stature' having initially joined the Horse Grenadiers but while serving had been accused of deer stealing. In the autumn of 1734 the other members of the Gregory Gang were: Samuel Gregory, blacksmith; Thomas Rowden, pewterer; Jeremy Gregory; John Field; Abraham Downham; Robert Woodward; Joseph Rose; John Fuller; William Rogers; Herbert Haines, barber & periwig maker turned thief; William Johnson; West Drake; John Coster; John Gassey (Gaskey); William Faulkener; Philip Onyon; Edward Brooks; John Bateman; George Hicks; John Coot; John Wheeler, the youngest at only seventeen, and William Saunders (Saundersson).

The only woman was Mary Brazier, a core member of the Essex Gang and principal associate of Turpin in the years 1732–3. Her name was spelt both as

A modern photofit picture showing what Dick Turpin may have looked like. (Courtesy of the York Castle Museum)

Brazier and Brassier and she was a criminal in her own right, possibly born in Southchurch near Leigh-on-Sea, where she was known to the authorities. She was also indicted at the same Essex Assizes as Jeremiah Gregory and Joseph Rose and spent time in Chelmsford Prison at the same time as both. On that particular occasion she was up for stealing a bolt of damask worth 10d and along with several others was sentenced to be 'publicly whipped till their bodies are bloody'.

The gang was rarely out of trouble and often in the public eye. In 1733, before Samuel Gregory was dispatched to prison for a year, the local sheriff, wanting to make an example of him, asked for an allowance of £10 'for the expense of erecting a pillory at Epping' – being 16 miles distant from the county gaol – and putting the notorious deer stealer in it. He also requested a posse be raised to carry him there with a very strong guard. The request was granted and Gregory was displayed to the public but it was not long before his gang rode into town and he was rescued from under the sheriff's nose.

In 1734 there were eleven deer stealers in Chelmsford Gaol and as most of them were from the Gregory Gang, Waltham Forest saw a lot less poaching than usual. Jeremy Gregory and Joseph Roses finished their prison sentences by the middle of the summer but were immediately indicted for another offence so were not able to orchestrate the gang's poaching activities for quite a while.

Though the three Gregory brothers headed up the notorious brotherhood they were not known collectively as the Gregory Gang until all were captured and executed. At first they were simply a band of robbers who were reported by the newspapers as 'the gang with Gregory'. Newspapers also boasted that Samuel Gregory had admitted to being the leader as he often referred to 'his gang' but he also maintained his role within it to be a humble one, possibly because he was trying to play down his crimes. This was certainly believable as he was actually quite small, the opinion of many being that he was quite incapable of commanding twenty-one men. On the plus side he did sport a scar on his cheek, a 1½-inch memento of a kick from a horse in his younger days. Perhaps it was that distinctive mark that gave him a commanding air? Perhaps the title 'the Gregory Gang' simply referred to the number of Gregorys within it, as there were three brothers altogether: Samuel, Jeremy and Jasper (who the newspaper referred to as Joseph).

By autumn of 1734 the Gregory Gang were looking for a better financial return than they could get from deer stealing alone and so turned to other forms of crime. A publication called 'The Political State of Great Britain' noted that 'a large gang of rogues have lately been associated themselves together and have committed some very audacious robberies in Essex and other places'. The first of these occurred in October 1734 when the shop of Peter Split, a chandler and grocer of Woodford, was raided by five of the gang,

1724. Richard Reynolds, & Mary Osterland both of St Swithins April
Henry Silk of St Mary White-Chappel, & Mary Fewtin
of St James Clerkenwell - - - - - - - - May,
Jasper Gregory of Horn-Church in Essex, &
Charity Eve of Dagenham in the same - - - 29.
Richard Prichard of All-hallows Barkin, &
Sarah Harlwood of this Parish - - - - July, 1
Thomas Mullet, & Mary Heckington, both of this Parish 30.

The entry of marriage in the register of St Katharine Cree church, London, of Jasper Gregory and Charity Eve.

one of them armed with a knife. Days later, eleven of the gang carried out another robbery in Woodford, this time 'masked and armed', relieving a man called Wooldridge of all his brass and pewter, his clock, window curtains, beds and bed linen plus two fine fowling pieces (guns) and other items to the value of £200. Once the gang had drunk all the rum, brandy and ale they could they stole several horses, loaded up the booty and rode away.

The robberies continued, featuring all or some of the gang at any one time. On 14 December 1734, Samuel and Jasper Gregory, John Jones and John Wheeler broke into a house in Chingford and ransacked it in front of its owner, John Gladwin. It was a poor choice of victim as he, being a fellow of limited means, could only offer them a disappointing haul. Five days later on 19 December the gang forced their way into the home of Ambrose Skinner, a seventy-three-year-old farmer in Barking. When later Skinner gave evidence against the gang he told the courts that six armed men 'with their faces muffled and disguised burst into the house pointing their carbines to my breast and swore that if I made any noise or resistance they would immediately put me to death'. Bravely, for a man of his advanced years, Skinner put up a fight, but they tied his hands with his own garters, and he was made to show the gang where his money and effects were kept. As they had already taken his purse and keys they were also able to unlock all doors in search for money.

Skinner's maidservant Elizabeth King was locked in an upstairs room and when Skinner's wife and child returned during the raid, they too were threatened and bound. Once the ordeal, which had lasted three and a half hours, was finally over, Skinner had lost goods to the value of £300.

The robberies slowly grew in malice, and as in the case of William Morris at his home of Hainault Lodge in Essex, seemed to contain elements of revenge. Mason, as one of the keepers of Epping Forest, had been targeted for his part in the incarceration of at least five members of the gang earlier that year for deer stealing, and was badly beaten. It was a particularly unpleasant robbery, with Mason's house and the items the gang could not carry away gratuitously destroyed.

The Gregory Gang continued this reign of terror during the early months of 1735, even going south of the Thames to carry out a robbery on a farmer called Saunders in Kent. In Croydon, Surrey, five weeks later, the house of a gentleman, Mr Sheldon, was robbed 'by men masked and armed' who absconded with five sacks of booty. Back in Essex a two-man robbery was carried out in early January at Great Parndon, where clergyman Mr Dyde was absent, but his manservant was, as reported, 'cut about the face in a barbarous manner'. In February 1735 the gang robbed an elderly widow named Shelly in Loughton. Five of the gang menaced her at gunpoint, and threatened to 'lay her across the fire' if they were not told where her money was. The widow was made of stern stuff but her son, unwilling to see his mother hurt, gave the gang the information they needed. They found £100 on the premises and, seemingly sure of themselves and seeing no reason to hurry away, stayed and drank the wine and ale from the widow's cellars, even taking the time to cook some meat to accompany the wine!

It was now obvious the Gregory Gang were no local heroes. They had developed a ruthlessness that made them arrogant and extremely dangerous. They had no respect for property nor recognised that people should expect to be safe in their own homes. They had become violent men with no qualms about hurting the elderly.

With their notoriety growing, the gang raided less and less in Essex and decided to prolong their anonymity by making the alleys and backstreets of London their ultimate hideout. They lived in various places, but came together in the inns and alehouses to plot their next robberies. Turpin himself took lodgings at Whitechapel and Thomas Rowden in the notoriously dangerous district of Ratcliff Highway, with brothers Samuel and Jasper Gregory living nearby. Jeremy Gregory and William Saunders favoured Clerkenwell, Herbert Haines rented rooms in Shoreditch while Joseph Rose, Mary Brazier and John Wheeler lived at Dawes Street, Westminster, as did Humphrey Walker and John Fielder.

London was the perfect hideout. Information on suitable victims was easily available in the inns and taverns and it was in one such watering hole – The Black Horse in West Ham Broadway – that, on the afternoon of 4 February 1735, the gang gathered to plan two robberies that would prove to be their last. The first target was Joseph Lawrence of Earlsbury Farm in Edgware. Three days later Samuel Gregory, Turpin, Wheeler, Rose, Fielder, William Saunders and Humphrey Walker raided another farm, this one owned by William Francis at Marylebone.

The farm at Marylebone had two servants working outside when the gang arrived. These they attacked and tied up, and they tied up the owner, Mr Francis, when he wandered into the stable where the servants were being attacked. With the men firmly secured they turned to the farmhouse, bursting in with pistols drawn and attacking Mrs Francis, beating her about the head with the butt of a whip until her face was bloody. The daughter of the house and a maidservant were next to be beaten, and after having tied them up the house was ransacked, amid threats of even more violence if all monies and goods were not forthcoming.

In this instance the level of violence outweighed the gang's eventual haul, as the seven intruders made off with only £90 worth of goods and money. It was the sentimental value of goods stolen that made the victims' losses so personal; among them were mourning jewelry and a wedding ring inscribed 'God did decree our unity'.

Though London had easily shielded the gang it now gave them up just as easily when the youngest member of the gang, Wheeler, was caught and over time informed on his fellows to save his own skin. Wheeler was incarcerated in the New Prison (the Gatehouse, Westminster), initially for his own protection, but let out regularly to help the authorities apprehend the other gang members. Fielder and Saunders were soon sent to Newgate and on Monday 17 February three more members of the gang were apprehended – Joseph Rose, Mary Brazier and Humphrey Walker, all found drinking in the appropriately named 'Thieving Lane'. Rose and Walker were armed and put up a fight but were overcome and when their lodgings were searched two trunks of stolen goods were found. At their committal these goods were identified by the daughter of Mr Francis, whom the gang had so savagely beaten when they had attacked the farmhouse in Marylebone.

Wheeler continued to incriminate his former comrades and further arrests continued to be made. Of average height, fresh complexion and wearing a brown wig for his trial, John Jones, who had joined the gang as a carpenter, was duly implicated in a robbery at Chingford, and in four other robberies in Essex, Middlesex, Surrey and Kent. Rose, Fielder, Walker and Saunders were all tried at the Middlesex Sessions at the end of February 1735, found guilty of capital crimes and sentenced to be hanged on 10 March 1735. Walker however died in prison in the early hours of the very day he was to be executed. Fielder, Rose and Saunders, along with ten other felons, were taken from prison and driven off and executed at Tyburn, with three members of the Essex Gang sharing the same cart. After their deaths, all were cut down, taken to Edgware and their bodies hung in chains as a grim reminder of the consequences of such heinous crimes.

At the Essex Assizes in Chelmsford, also on that day, Jasper Gregory was sentenced to death. Evidence against him came not only from young Wheeler, but also from John Gladwin, a man in receipt of a 'Tyburn Ticket'. Such a ticket afforded Gladwin exemption from all manner of parish offices within the parish wherein the felony was committed', and was an incentive to those who freely testified against convicted criminals. Gregory was executed three weeks later.

Meanwhile the rest of gang was still at large and continued their crime spree in various parts of the country. Samuel and Jeremy Gregory were eventually apprehended by four men who arrested them after a brief armed struggle. The twenty-three-year-old Samuel lost the tip of his nose in the fight after a sword caught him in the face, while Jeremy was shot in the thigh. The pair were committed to Winchester Gaol, where Jeremy died of his wound. Samuel was transferred to London on 13 May 1735, handcuffed and feet chained under the belly of the horse he was riding all the while guarded by up to eight men. On the testimony of the informant Wheeler, Gregory was sent to Newgate under a strong guard.

Samuel Gregory was tried at the Old Bailey on 22 May 1735, standing in the dock at 5 feet 7 inches, fresh-faced in the brown wig he always wore. Before joining the gang he had been a furrier, but now was indicted on six counts, including the rape of Dorothy Street, and was sentenced to death. Executed on 4 June 1735, his body, like those of his former companions, was then sent to hang in chains alongside their rotting corpses. Next to be captured was twenty-four-year-old Herbert Haines, who after being confined for a time in Newgate was transferred to Chelmsford where, on 8 May 1735, in a brick-coloured cloth coat, he stood trial at the Essex Summer Assizes, was sentenced to death and executed in Chelmsford Gaol on 8 August 1735. It was said he met his end with dignity. A paper from as far away as Derby ran the following two stories:

Sunday, 14 August 1735
Tomorrow Herbert Haines, the Barber, one of Gregory's gang is to be executed at Chelmsford together with the others ordered by the judges for execution at the last assizes. This Haines had escaped to Holland but his mistress wrote him word if he would come to Gravesend she would come thither to meet him and go and live together and abroad; so he came and sent her word of him being there; but the letter being intercepted he was seized on board the Vessel at Gravesend and brought to Newgate some months ago, from whence he was removed to Chelmsford and there convicted. He will be hung in chains in Essex.

Thursday, 21 August 1735
Yesterday Haines, the Barber, one of Gregory's gang and John Waller the horse-stealer, in company with Edwards, Ellis and Peter Isham convicted of

Felony and Burglary, walk'd in their Shrouds from the Gaol at the bridge to the gallows; at the Black Boy, a man in a laced hat gave Haines a glass of wine as he walked by, and Haines desired him to take care what he told him, and whispered him, then the gentleman in the laced hat drank to him, he hop'd he would be happy before night which occasioned in the town an ill suspicion of that man. Haines has behav'd very well ever since he has been in our Gaol, in a sedate a grave manner never once being heard to swear and went calmly to the gallows and behav'd there like a man, decent but not impudent. Whilst he was in Gaol his mistress came to see him, a homely creature, and much older than he; she said, or pretended she was with child, and told him, she should not long survive...

Chelmsford also featured in the apprehension of one of the last of the gang to be taken, while he was trying to cross its well-known three-arched bridge. Built in the 1600s to replace the original constructed in 1372, it was mistakenly built too narrow, so that when in 1735 a fugitive, thought to be one of the Gregory Gang, was escaping from a crowd in pursuit of him and tried to go over it at the same time as a wagon, 'his horse became jammed against a post so that he could not get away and 'was taken with great ease'.

Back in April 1735 Mary Brazier had been held at the Gatehouse, Westminster, but now she was tried at the Old Bailey and for her connections with the Essex Gang received fourteen years' transportation to America. It took time to collect together enough transportees to make an Atlantic voyage viable and so Mary remained in England until December. John Jones, committed to Newgate but later transferred to Chelmsford, was also tried for his part in the robberies of the Essex Gang and found guilty. His initial death sentence was commuted to transportation and he, too, eventually sailed for America in December 1736, a year after Mary Brazier.

In the early months of 1735 the Essex Gang was a feared, successful, anonymous group of organised criminals; by the end of the year they were almost totally wiped out. The bodies of those hanged earlier were still rotting in London at the height of summer as a warning to those who would take to a life of crime. Only two of the gang were still at large: Thomas Rowden and of course Richard Turpin. It was at this point that Turpin finally turned to the highway robbery that he became so famous for.

As if in desperation, Turpin and Rowden carried out numerous highway robberies during the summer of 1735, many in Epping Forest, and rewards for their capture were regularly increased. As the year wore on they became reckless and were often cited in the press. The *Ipswich Journal* of 11 October 1735 reported, 'Last Sunday in the afternoon several gentlemen on horseback were robbed between Putney and Kingston Hill by two Highwaymen well mounted and known to be Turpin the butcher and Rowden the Pewterer, the remaining two of the late Gregory's Gang'. Later the newspaper also wrote, 'On Tuesday last Turpin and Rowden, two of Gregory's Gang had the insolence to ride through the city at Noon-Day and in Watling Street they were known by two or three Porters who Ply'd there but had not the courage to attack them.'

Eventually sense prevailed and Turpin and Rowden realised they had best lay low. Both left London and their highwayman lifestyle and Rowden returned to his old ways, namely counterfeiting. A small man with a pockmarked face, he did not last long alone and after spending time in Gloucester jail, where he was recognised, he was sent back to Essex to stand trial for his part in the Essex Gang crimes. Guilty, he was sentenced to hang on 20 July 1735. This, like the sentences of Mary Brazier and John Jones, was commuted to transportation and he sailed to Virginia on 9 June 1738. That same year the informant John Wheeler was released but died, it was said, of natural causes.

Turpin was now the only gang member left at large and the authorities, embarrassed they had not as yet been able to catch him, circulated rumours that he was in Holland as a cover for their incompetence. Nothing could have been further from the truth. Turpin was as large as life in England, having resumed his old ways and thrown in with another famous highwayman, Matthew King.

Turpin's first meeting with King had been less than auspicious, with Turpin prepared to rob him on the road at gunpoint, mistaking him for a wealthy gentleman. King recognised Turpin and suggested they join forces, declaring he would be glad of the company. With that, the two of them took up with a man named Potter and continued to terrorise the king's highway but now murder was added to their crimes, which took place mainly on the Loughton Road, in Epping Forest. The partnership did not last long as Turpin accidently shot King in a robbery that went wrong. It was not the first time Turpin had killed a man. With the south of England having issued a bounty of £200 on his head, Turpin decided he would ride north.

We shall never know if Turpin was comfortable with being a killer. We know he was bad tempered, indulged in provocative behavior and pushed boundaries, often threatening those that frustrated him as he journeyed towards York. He was also arrested for horse stealing, the crime for which he ended up in York jail. It was his stay here that was his final undoing. After languishing for four months under the assumed name John Palmer, the identity he'd used since he'd left the South, he sent a letter on 6 February 1739 to his brother in Essex informing him of his plight:

Dear Brother,

I am sorry to acquaint you, that I am now under confinement in York Castle, for horse-stealing. If I could procure an evidence from London to give me a character, that would go a great way towards my being acquitted. I had not been long in this county before my being apprehended, so that it would pass off the readier. For Heaven's sake dear brother, do not neglect me; you will know what I mean, when I say, I am yours, JOHN PALMER.

THE

TRIAL

Of the Notorious Highwayman

Richard Turpin,

At *York* Affizes, on the 22d Day of *March*, 1739, before the Hon. Sir WILLIAM CHAPPLE, Knt. Judge of Affize, and one of His Majefty's Juftices of the Court of *King's Bench*.

Taken down in Court by Mr. THOMAS KYLL, Profeffor of Short-Hand.

To which is prefix'd,

An exaƈt Account of the faid *Turpin*, from his firft coming into *Yorkfhire*, to the Time of his being committed Prifoner to *York* Caftle; communicated by Mr. APPLETON of *Beverley*, Clerk of the Peace for the *Eaft-Riding* of the faid County.

With a Copy of a Letter which *Turpin* received form his Father, while under Sentence of Death.

To which is added,

His Behaviour at the Place of Execution, on *Saturday* the 7th of *April*, 1739. Together with the whole Confeffion he made to the Hangman at the Gallows; wherein he acknowledg'd himfelf guilty of the Faƈts for which he fuffer'd, own'd the Murder of Mr. *Thompfon's* Servant on *Epping-Foreft*, and gave a particular Account of feveral Robberies which he had committed.

The SECOND EDITION..

Y O R K:

Printed by WARD and CHANDLER Bookfellers, at their Printing-Office in *Coney-Street*; and Sold at their Shop without *Temple-Bar, London*; 1739. (Price Sixpence.)

A contemporary account of the trial of Richard Turpin.

Unfortunately for Turpin the letter was returned unopened to the post office as Turpin's brother would not pay for its postage and it was consequently seen by Turpin's old schoolmaster Mr Smith, who recognised his handwriting. The letter was taken straight to the local magistrate, where it was opened and Turpin's false identity discovered.

Turpin was indicted for his crimes, condemned and sentenced to be hanged on Saturday 7 April 1739. He was also one of the biggest draws that York had ever had, documents reporting that he 'lived in as much pleasure as the liberties of the prison could afford, eating, drinking and carousing with anybody that would spend their time with him'. It also proved lucrative for the jailer, who made £100 for himself by selling the refreshments.

Turpin, in the light of our modern day, was not the dashing highwayman of legend. That ideal was the work of William Harrison Ainsworth, the author of a book called *Rookwood*, who took Turpin as his main character, gave him a horse called Black Bess and romanticised his exploits into fiction. The Turpin we now know was a man given to cruelty and violence, but he did live up to his own legend in his final hours on the morning of 7 April 1739, a day that had dawned cold. This we know from a contemporary account of the day before, which had been 'blustering cold' with wind, rain, hail and snow. Turpin was dressed in fustian frock and a pair of pumps he had bought for the occasion, and having climbed into the cart that he had paid five poor men 5 shillings each to follow as his mourners, he was taken to his place of execution; the gallows that was locally known as the three-legged mare.

Ironically for Turpin, he was actually executed by one of his own. York was without a permanent hangman and so according to custom the York Assizes allowed one condemned criminal to be pardoned if he agreed to act as executioner for the others convicted of a capital crime that day. It was Thomas Hatfield, himself sentenced to death for highway robbery, who volunteered that day. Turpin, however, took his demise into his own hands and after mounting the ladder, leaning for a moment against the leg of the gallows, looked about him and, saying a few words, threw himself off the ladder 'and expired directly'. The highwayman that had outrun the authorities for most of his life was dead. And to make sure he was dead, his corpse was left hanging on the gallows until three o'clock in the afternoon.

THE NOTORIOUS COGGESHALL GANG

For the part you have taken in this guilty transaction in robbing and injuring
Mr Dell, your life is forfeited to the laws of your country, and if I did choose to
interfere by recommending you to the merciful consideration of her Majesty, the
consequences would be that you would suffer an ignominious death. You have
been evidently not concerned in this alone; but the circumstances of the injury
to the prosecutor were not so great as to justify me in letting the sentence take its
course, therefore your life will be spared, but the rest of it will be spent abroad.

Judge's sentencing of William Ellis

In 1844, the Coggeshall home of Mr Charles Skinsley was broken into, his wine cellar ransacked and the whole property set alight. Fortunately on that November night he was not at home. But in future, other victims of the notorious 'Coggeshall Gang' would not be so lucky. During a four-year period from 1844 to 1848 this group of local Coggeshall men would terrorise their village and the surrounding countryside with their increasingly violent attacks on both people and property. Nothing extraordinary you might say, considering this sort of thing was going on all over Victorian England. But this particular spate of Essex crime was carried out by local people on their friends and neighbours, the 'spoils' divided up in alleyways, or in barns, the gang apparently having no regard as to who may be watching the division of their 'ill-gotten gains'. Such a nonchalant attitude was unusual among criminals, yet despite their lack of care and attention these men surprisingly managed to both outmanoeuvre the village constables and, for a time, outwit the whole of England's police force.

Interestingly the gang operated out of the village pub, the main hub of all village life and the perfect foil for their clandestine activities. Called the Black Horse, this pub was in Stoneham Street and, as listed in both the Post Office Directory of 1845 and White's Directory of 1848, the landlord at those times was William French. Born in 1807, he was married and approaching his middle years when the housebreakings took place. He was quite tall for a nineteenth-century man, being 5 feet 11 with a smooth complexion unmarked by smallpox, brown hair, and of proportionate build. His position in the village made him the gang's perfect 'receiver of stolen goods', able as he was to hide contraband in the cellars or roof space. He was also perfectly placed to sell things on quickly through the clientele that frequented his establishment.

French was not the leader of the Coggeshall gang; that distinction belonged to his half-brother, Samuel Crow, another well-known local character, whose job as a post-chaise driver meant he mingled with both rich and poor and could glean useful gossip from both. Armed with relevant information, Crow would then gather his gang at the Black Horse and rehearse them in his plans. The gang's first crime had been, as previously mentioned, against the property of Mr Skingley.

Mr Bell, the local grocer, was their next victim. From his premises the gang stole eight hams, worth £10, a quantity of bacon, 27 lbs of candles and approximately seventeen cakes from his warehouse. A second crime, later in 1845, was also close to home as their target was the Bird in Hand public house in East Street, the establishment of fellow villager Henry Polley Cook. With blackened faces and wearing caps to disguise themselves, they broke into the inn, Crow first removing a pane of glass with a knife before reaching in and fully opening the window so as to allow them entry. They forced the till and took approximately £1, cigars to the value of £10 and a 4-gallon cask of brandy. The stolen goods were then taken back to French's Black Horse Inn and hidden above a false ceiling in the inn's granary. French later bought a gallon and a half of the hidden brandy, for which he paid his brother's gang 28 shillings, together with two boxes of the cigars.

The gang at one time had up to fourteen members, the principal offenders being William Wade, William Tansley, William Springett and William Christoper 'Crusty' Ellis. For Wade and Tansley the gang's activities were also a family affair as they were brothers-in-law, Tansley having married Lucy, Wade's sister, ten years previously.

Possibly the gang's most atrocious crimes took place in Bradwell juxta Coggeshall in 1847. A crime involving four gang members, the house of an elderly gentleman, James Finch, and his housekeeper Elizabeth Wright, was broken into and despite the advanced ages of the couple – Mr Finch was sixty-two – both were tortured for almost three hours in the hope they would reveal where they kept their money.

A newspaper article of September 1848 carried much of the sorry tale: 'Before the gang members got to Finch's house Crow put a shirt over his clothes and a white nightcap over his head, holes being cut in it for his eyes and mouth; the others blackened their faces with something that Crow had brought with him for the purpose and then they all went into the house.' William Tansley acted as lookout; stout and of average height, he stayed at the front door while Ellis, Crow and Wade went to the back of the house, attempting to break in without making too much noise. In the event, nothing went to plan and when they all finally entered the house they met Finch coming down from upstairs to investigate the disturbance.

Not expecting a confrontation, Crow asked Finch at pistol-point if he had any money, only to be told there was not any. Crow with Wade and Ellis in tow went upstairs to look for themselves. After a short while Crow retrieved a few halfpennies but best of all found a small book belonging to the Witham Savings Bank.

Perhaps foolishly, Mr Finch still maintained he had no money, which set Samuel Crow to riffling through the pockets of the old man's discarded breeches where he found 5/- in the pocket. Crow pressed Finch for more, but was told that any money Finch had was all in the bank. Not a man to be crossed, Crow then took Finch into another room and, having placed a rope about his neck, proceeded to suspend him from a roof beam for almost a minute. At this point gang member William Wade intercepted. Later, Finch was to say that he had been half dead by the time he was actually cut down from the beam.

Unsuccessful with Finch, the gang then went into the housekeeper's room and the demand for money was repeated. Like Finch, the woman refuted that she had any, sending Crow into a fury during which he threatened that he would 'set her upon the fire' if she did not reveal where her money was. The lady could only point to some half-pennies in a drawer. Ellis and Crow took her next door to the 'keeping room' and put her on the grate in which Crow had lighted a quantity of straw. At this point she screamed out as her gown had caught fire. Later, as a witness at the gang's trial she confirmed that the prisoners did not actually lay her on the fire but held her over it and that Crow had held a large stick against her head and threatened to dash her brains out if she made any noise. Again Wade had intercepted and extinguished the fire, which had rapidly begun to engulf her nightgown.

Audacious to the last, and giving up on finding any large amounts of money, the gang then retired downstairs to the pantry. Here Samuel Crow helped himself to his victim's beer, bread and cheese, which he ate on the premises. Eventually sated, the gang finally left, taking with them four hams, 'two pigs faces' and half the contents of a tub of pickled pork. Ellis and Tansley left first and Wade followed, leaving Crow alone at the house. Crow, however, was waiting for them back at the stable of the Black Horse Inn where, despite it being between four and five o'clock in the morning, they divided up their meager haul.

Words on paper are nothing compared to the terror Finch and his housekeeper must have felt. Crow, as leader, obviously had a taste for violence, taking no account of the ages and dispositions of his victims. William Wade on the other hand was a man who was discovering he had scruples, his conscience increasingly troubled with the methods they were using to extract information. To his credit, his taste for gratuitous violence was nowhere near as strong as Crow's.

A pattern of violence was now running through the Coggeshall gang's crimes. In another raid that year, the gang entered a house and threatened the frightened householder with a pistol. They then put a mattress on top of him and piled it up with furniture and boxes, almost suffocating him. The gang remained in the house for several hours, during which time they consumed several bottles of wine before leaving with £5 in gold and silver. The same night the gang visited another farmhouse two fields away, where the occupier, spotting them approach, asked them what they wanted from an upstairs window. In answer the gang made their way into the house declaring 'we are come for money which we will have'. Though the man's daughter had bravely become involved by throwing chairs at the intruders, the gang soon got the upper hand, making off just before dawn with £3 in money.

It now appeared that all the gang's robberies featured some measure of actual bodily harm, as this story in the *Chelmsford Chronicle* highlighted: 'Mrs Smith on the night of the robbery recollected being awoke and finding a masked man standing by the side of the bed called out "murder!" Another man put his hand over her face and eyes and smothered her with bed things declaring if they made the least alarm they would blow their brains out. If they kept quiet they would come to no harm.' The report continued to describe how the man who had covered her face had held her hard enough to have left his fingermarks on her face.

In October 1847 the gang lay in wait on the Colne Road in order to carry out highway robbery on Mr Richard Latimer Dell as he returned from Coggeshall market. Totally confident in their infamy, the gang this time were bare faced, though at some time during the attack Crow put a handkerchief over his head and turned his coat. When Mr Dell reached them, Wade took hold of the bridle, while Crow pulled him off his horse and both gang members proceeded to search his pockets, finding a purse. When the gang later assembled to divide the spoils they had between £3 and £4 in gold and silver each.

Dell's account of his robbery was slightly different, maintaining he was nearly blinded and, being quite bloodied in the struggle, said 'I stroked my hand which was bloody over one of them so as to mark him.' He also admitted to having been almost suffocated from hands being over his mouth.

The gang up until this point had outwitted all attempts to bring them to heel, but the capture of William Wade finally provided the authorities with the breakthrough they so badly needed. The papers fell upon this development with a voracious appetite for justice. The *Essex Standard* included journalistic gems such as 'when rogues fall out then honest folk will come by their own' and pressing home the old adage of there being no 'honour among thieves'. This, as it turned out, proved to be more than true.

Wade, described in the press as a 'field gardener', was convicted at the Essex Assizes of the outrage at Bradwell, and at first had no intention on 'peaching' (informing) on his fellow gang members. He had stressed this to Crow during his committal trial, but only on the understanding that Crow would look out for his wife, Mary Howell, to whom he'd not long been married. Wade was obviously concerned for Mary, especially as census records for 1851 show that at the time of her husband's capture she was either pregnant or had just given birth to their firstborn, William. While in Chelmsford Gaol, news reached Wade that the gang was not honouring their agreement and, furious, he informed the governor of the prison of the identity of the other gang members. Warrants for the arrests of William Ellis, William Springett, William Tansley and Samuel Crow were immediately issued.

Abbey Mill today. After a police pursuit over the rooftops of Coggeshall, it was from here that that Samuel Crow made his escape, 'absconding over the meadows into Abbey Wood by Abbey Mill'.

Ellis, suspecting he was about to be arrested, escaped for a while after leaving his lodgings at Rivenhall, but Springett, a thatcher by trade, was seized on a farm in Feering. Tansley, a labourer, was taken in Meeting Street, Coggeshall. Crow however proved harder to apprehend, despite a large force of police officers surrounding the Black Horse Inn where he was thought to be hiding.

Crow's half-brother William French denied that Crow was on the premises, declaring he was likely to be either in Colchester that day, or Stanway. Unconvinced, the police searched the building, eventually finding a hole in the ceiling of an outhouse large enough to hide someone in the roof space. Sure enough, Crow was spotted crouching on a beam by a police officer named Nicholls. Fleet of foot, Crow escaped past the officer and made off over the roofs of Coggeshall before dropping down into the garden of Mr Hunwick, making his way by East Street and absconding over the meadows into Abbey Wood by Abbey Mill.

Unable to capture Crow, the police instead apprehended his younger brother, a young lad of between fifteen and sixteen, and charged him with helping Crow abscond. A search of the boy's cart showed that Crow had indeed hidden there under a canvas, borne out by the discovery of a hat and clothes plus a bloody handkerchief used to wrap the hand that Crow had badly cut making his escape. A reward of £20 was issued by some inhabitants of Coggeshall for the apprehension of Crow, but it seemed he was long gone. With his brother's help, the wounded Crow had made his escape across Tiptree Heath, through Maldon, Danbury and Brentwood to Stratford.

The search for Ellis took police offers as far south as Rayleigh, where it was discovered he had then made his way to Tilbury and over the river to Gravesend, where he had effectively disappeared. Police officers on that occasion had to return empty-handed. It wasn't until October 1848 that he was finally captured in Bury St Edmunds.

Such was the interest in the gang, that when finally caught and brought to trial at the Chelmsford Assizes on the first Monday in March 1849, the galleries of the courtroom were filled with 'fashionably dressed women'. William Wade was the prosecution's main witness, but it was strongly suggested to the jury that they treat his evidence with some caution. However, it was Wade's evidence and the identification of Samuel Crow by the elderly Mr Finch, who had suffered at the hands of the gang at his home in Bradwell, that convicted William Tansley, William Ellis and Crow of the crime in question after only twelve minutes' deliberation by the jury.

By the end of the trial, the majority of the gang found themselves facing transportation. Samuel Crow, William Tansley and Ellis were awarded life, while Everett and French received seven years. William Wade, as a result of turning queen's evidence, had his sentence reduced from fifteen years' transportation to just seven. As one of over 300 convicts transported on the *Rodney* to Van Diemen's Land (Tasmania), he spent ninety-seven days at sea in dubious conditions, arriving in Hobart on 28 November 1850. He laboured under the confines of his sentence on the farm of James Baynton at Browns River, four years later being granted a ticket of leave. In June 1853 his conditional pardon was finally approved. There is no evidence to date of him ever returning to England. Wade's young wife Mary and son William were staying with Mary's in-laws in Stoneham Street in 1851, but she had listed herself as 'unmarried' on the census form, though her wedding to Wade had definitely taken place in October 1846 at Coggeshall's independent meeting house. Had she already resigned herself to never seeing William again?

William Tansley was also destined to spend the rest of his natural life abroad. He was thirty-five at his trial; the nature of his felony was 'burglary accompanied with violence'. He too left behind his wife, Lucy, Wade's sister, and five children. It was a double blow for Lucy, losing both husband and brother, plus her youngest son's birth certificate would always carry the stigma of the words: 'Father – transported for life.' With no means of support during Tansley's imprisonment, she and the children were living in the Coggeshall Union Workhouse. But circumstances did improve. By 1851 she was a 'silk-harvester', possibly at the Orchard Silk Mill, the main employer in the area, working an eleven-hour day, six days a week and all for around three shillings. Lucy still recorded herself as married in 1861, but by now the mill had closed and she took in children to nurse. Her son William, now sixteen, was labourer to a blacksmith, and supplementing the family income. By 1871 Lucy styled herself 'widow', having heard of her husband's death of dropsy (oedema) on 15 August 1869.

Possibly the oldest member of the gang to leave England, aged forty-two, was 'receiver of stolen goods' William French. Making the journey to Western Australia in the ship *Pyrenees*, he arrived on 14 March 1851 in the company of fellow convict, William Springett, who managed to return home to England in 1863 aboard the ship *Light Brigade*. William Everitt was on the same ship and, a gardener like Wade, also left behind a wife and children. Australian records described him as '5 foot 4¾ tall; light brown hair; blue eyes; round face; fair complexion' and of 'stout build'. Records also indicate he was granted a conditional pardon in 1853 and contain the comment, 'to London 19 July 1866'. He died at sea, possibly returning to his family.

Due to Australian convict records it is possible that the member of the Coggeshall gang about whom we know the most is William Ellis. Born in Coggeshall in 1820 he was thirty-two when he left England, 5 feet 9 inches tall, brown-haired and grey-eyed; he had a round face, fresh complexion and stout build. On his arrival in Australia aboard the *William Jardine*, it was noted in medical records that he had wounds on his legs and given that prisoners were often restrained while on board these could well have come from leg irons. Once ashore, William served his time at the Swan River Colony, first set up in 1829 for free settlers, but later using convict labour to help stimulate its economy. Ellis, as a bricklayer, was certainly utilised.

Once in Fremantle, Western Australia, Ellis obtained a ticket of leave in 1854, just five years into his sentence, and used this supervised freedom to employ himself for his own benefit, live independently and acquire limited property. He obtained a free pardon four years later and spent many years in and around the Perth area. After so many years away from England he probably never intended to return, as he married Caroline Victoria Robinson on 24 April 1865 despite being married at home. Legally he was free to do so as seven years had passed since he and his first wife had been forcibly separated, but the new marriage did not last long. Ellis died only five days after the wedding.

As for the Crow brothers, William and Samuel – John Crow was given three month's hard labour for assisting in his brother's escape, yet Samuel Crow, violent, cunning and sadistic, never served his sentence. Ironically he died in Chelmsford Prison a year after the trial in 1850, while waiting for a ship to take him as far from Essex as it was possible to go.

7

WARLOCKS & WIZARDS

For going to Cunning Folk...

John Cave, indicted for Witchcraft, Romford, 1592

E ssex history is littered with the names of those accused of witchcraft. Our usual idea of a witch is a toothless hag, but it appears that the dark art has no preference as to the sex of its initiate and so as many men as women were accused, indicted, found guilty and hanged as witches. With religious tensions at breaking point in the sixteenth century, people, it seemed, were only too ready to accuse their neighbour before they themselves came under scrutiny. It was nothing short of dogged determination that saw the villagers of Danbury accuse John Smyth of witchcraft, as they did so first in 1560, then 1561, and then in 1572. A beer brewer, he was thought 'a common wizard' who had bewitched a man and a woman, who 'languished thereafter, the former for three weeks, the latter for three months, when they died'. He was hanged.

It was Henry VIII's Act of 1542 that was the first to define witchcraft as a felony, a crime punishable by death and the forfeiture of the convicted felon's goods and chattels. Later, King James I passed his Witchcraft Act in response to his deep-seated fear of that which he could not control.

In 1579 at the Essex Summer Assizes, Richard Presmary of Great Dunmow was indicted. It was said that he and his wife Joan bewitched Gabriel Smythe, a 'brickelayer', whereby he languished until he died on 17 July. The year before, Joan had been before the magistrates on her own account accused of bewitching three calves and two cows belonging to Nicholas Whale. Then, she was found not guilty. This time though both pleaded not guilty; it was ignored and both were hanged.

A fire on 10 March 1584 was, at the time, thought to have been started by sorcery. A barn, stable, cart, wagon and other goods belonging to Edward Burgess, the rector of Wivenhoe, caught fire through the 'magic and incantation' of one Edward Mansell, described as a clerk from Feering, He was also accused of using the same arts on 10 September 1581, causing Burgess to 'languish' for six months. Also in 1584, Stephen Hugrave was indicted for being 'a witch and common Brawler and sower of discorde between neighbours'. When accused, Mr Hawes of Steeple defended himself by saying he was simply a 'fore-diviner and southsaier'. John Smyth alias Salmon of Danbury also appeared before Essex Quarter Sessions, where he was found guilty of bewitching eight cows, six calves, three pigs and seven ewes belonging to Francis Simon of Stow Maries. He had been acquitted earlier, however, on a charge of bewitching to death Rose Larkin, also of Stow Maries. The sentence is not recorded.

According to several studies into Essex witchcraft there is a general consensus that male witchcraft differed from female witchcraft in that it was far less sinister. Where female witches were accused of *maleficium* – black witchcraft responsible for harm and injury and punishable by execution or imprisonment – men's offences leaned more towards enchantment, conjuring, charms, and sorcery. Men, it appeared, favoured 'bookish' witchcraft, used mainly to deceive, especially in love magic. The element of literacy in this theory suggests male and female witches were of a different social status. Whereas female witches tended to be the wives of labourers or widow women living alone, men accused tended to be higher up the social scale – artisans or yeomen with the benefit of education.

An example of this exists in a rare text from 1590 whereby Edmund Hunt, a yeoman, was indicted for witchcraft for being in possession of a parchment 'full of crosses, characters and strange names'. It was not Hunt's. He had in fact stolen it from a cunning man whose help he had sought in order to locate treasure that he had been convinced lay buried in the grounds of 'Byleigh' (Beeleigh) Abbey. Later Hunt was drinking in the White Horse Inn, Maldon with his friend John Mace to whom he showed the parchment explaining he had sought the help of a wise man. Suspicious of what his friend had shown him and the fact that Hunt had come to him 'enter[ing] into some speech concerning conjuration', Mace accused Hunt of witchcraft and he was charged. The association between male witchcraft and the magical use of written documents was as strong in the minds of simple Essex folk as the association of female witches being 'persons full of malice and sinful desires, who contracted with the Devil'.

Less detailed examples illustrate how men were indicted as witches all over Essex. In the ten years from 1566 there were, among others, John Hawes of Steeple, Mr Richmond of Creeksea, Nicholas Johnson and John Webb of Woodham Mortimer, Ralph Spacey of Southminster, Thomas Ward of Purleigh and William Walford of Cold Norton. Great Wakering could lay claim to William Skelton in 1572 and in 1578 Thomas Varker of Hockley, a surgeon, was cautioned 'not to conjure or invoke spirits'. In 1588 as the Armada threatened England's shores William Bennet of Finchingfield and

Edward Mason of Bardfield, both yeomen, were indicted for invoking 'an evil spirit with the intention of making great sums of money'. That same year Miles Bloomfield of Chelmsford was exposed as a 'cunning man'. But perhaps the most well known of those who dealt in the magic of the male witch was Hadleigh sorcerer James Murrell.

JAMES MURRELL (1785–1860)

I had wondered at a mere village cobbler possessing the knowledge of mathematics, astronomy, and botany which many of Murrell's notes and manuscripts displayed, but my wonder had been somewhat lessened by Buck's [Edward Murrell's] information that his father had been a stillman at a London chemist's

Arthur Morrison in 'A Wizard of Yesterday', 1900

James Murrell was an Essex character of wide renown: a man of many aspects and of course, Hadleigh's famous eighteenth-century white witch. For many he was a wise and harmless mystic, but to some he was an embarrassment and his legacy was burnt or buried. Though his chest of collections is now retained in a museum, it is empty of contents, and having been a poor man, only some forty years after his death there was no marker to his grave.

Author Arthur Morrison's novel about Murrell, plus a story in the *Strand Magazine* of 1900 kept the memory of the man very much alive, a passage from his work *Cunning Murrell* giving us possibly the best description of the Hadleigh warlock:

A trifle less than five feet high, thin and slight ... Quick and alert of movement, keen of eye and sharp of face, Cunning Murrell made a distinctive figure in that neighbourhood, even physically, and apart from the atmosphere of power and mystery that compassed him about. Now he wore a blue frock coat, a trifle threadbare, though ornamented with brass buttons, and on his head a hard, glazed hat ... Over his shoulder he carried a large gingham umbrella with thick whalebone ribs, each tipped with a white china knob, and from its handle hung a frail basket.

Murrell attributed his powers to being 'the seventh son of a seventh son' and insisted he worked on the side of the angels, often boasting he was the devil's master. He was a witch, but a white one; his interests lay in astrology, quack doctoring, exorcism, veterinary surgery, and the casting out of devils. He cured with charms and potions, divined for lost property, laid spells to counteract the devil's machinations and to assist the lovelorn. For a man whose trade was essentially a shoemaker, his sphere of influence was remarkable. Letters with unusual requests would often arrive for Murrell, some from sophisticated London addresses.

For a man who was adept at casting spells, Murrell was just as adept at breaking those of other witches. For this he employed the skills of the village blacksmith, Mr Choppin, who made him his famous iron 'witch bottles'. These bottles would be filled with items personal to the client such as hair and fingernail clippings; pins, blood and urine among other paraphernalia, which were then sealed by the blacksmith. Such bottles would be placed on the fire, where they were known to burst, so destroying the diabolical hex.

This practice was endorsed by a London newspaper in 1849 when it reported what a sister paper, the *Ipswich Express*, wrote about an event in 'a village a few miles from Rayleigh'. It could only have been referring to Hadleigh and Murrell. The article mentioned the manufacture of a witch bottle by the village blacksmith in aid of a girl who was subject to fits, for which a witch was believed responsible. The usual personal items were deposited inside the bottle, which was then placed in a roaring fire, even chained to the grate. The story did then go on to relay the fact that the occult aside, a bottle filled with any liquid and heated furiously would be subject to steam and thus explode, 'blowing away the grate-bars and the fire.' But even if the article did end humorously with the tagline, 'this was expected to do the girl good', it gave Murrell's skills credence by the mere mention of them.

In spite of his fame and connections, James never was a rich man, in fact it would appear from a document found in his chest that in 1823 he was 'not above the petty afflictions of common humanity', and falling behind with a year's rent on his cottage in Endway, to the tune of £4 he 'had to have the brokers in' to recover the amount.

Records show a James Murrell marrying a Hadleigh girl, Elizabeth Frances Button, on 12 August 1812. There followed, over the next twenty years, baptisms of sixteen Murrell children in St James the Less church, Hadleigh; eight sons and eight daughters. With infant mortality at a high, James and Elizabeth's first son William died aged only one month. Six more sons died as babies, including twins, and three daughters. Edward, Murrell's only surviving son, could not claim his father's magical reputation, as he was only the third son of a seventh son.

Philip Benton, in his 1867 publication *The History of Rochford Hundred* speaks of James Murrell as being

the cunning man, who lived at Hadleigh, and died in 1860. He was by trade a shoemaker, but partly procured the means of subsistence by telling fortunes, and pretended to have the power of counteracting the designs of witches and discovering thieves and where stolen property was secreted. He was a herbalist, and administered potions and drugs. He would purchase forty different nostrums at a time, his price being one penny for each, which he refused to have labeled. A sackful of letters were destroyed at his death, but enough remain to prove that an incredible amount of ignorance, credulity, and superstition exists.

Examples of some of the letters may give an insight into the problems of the day: 'Mr Murls I have rote these few lines to ask you if you can tell weather their is aney mony or Not hid in my fathers garden he is bin ded 4 years name william duce of mayland pleas say how much and what to pay you.' Another proves the immense faith people put into his powers: 'I have took the powder it made me verrey quear in the stummuk pleas send sum more.' Benton concludes that 'some letters addressed to him allude to the appearance of apparitions, and

"STUDYING THE HEAVENS."   James 'Cunning' Murrell studying the heavens.

from the tenor of others from women, mysteriously alluding to being in trouble, and hearing he can relieve them, we may suspect him of darker doings...'

All the same, some of Murrell's possessions became collectors' items. In Benton's possession were two of his human skulls, 'phrenologically marked', as well as certain of Murrell's books.

James 'Cunning' Murrell died on 16 December 1860, at seventy-nine years of age, of 'natural causes'. He had foretold his death to his daughter to the day and the hour. His son Edward – also known as Buck – later recalled his father held 'learned disputations' with Hadleigh's curate, the Reverend John Godson, on his deathbed, still maintaining his mystic powers, as he was the devil's master.

The funeral took place at the south-east corner of St James the Less churchyard in Hadleigh on the 23 December following. On the death certificate his occupation was recorded as 'Quack Doctor'.

For years after Murrell's death his spirit was said to have haunted the lanes and hedgerows of Hadleigh, collecting herbs in his little basket.

GEORGE PICKINGILL (1816–1909)

A tall, unkempt man, solitary and uncommunicative. He had very long finger-nails, and kept his money in a purse of sacking.

Eric Maple, folklorist

It is approximately 10 miles as the crow – or should one say witch – flies from Hadleigh to Canewdon, once the home of George Pickingill. Like Murrell he was a nineteenth-century cunning man but unlike Murrell had a reputation of being both a white and a black witch. Described by author Charles Lefebure as 'the Devil incarnate', his story first came to public attention as the focus of a study into witchcraft by Eric Maple in the 1960s. In the 1990s a descendant of the Pickingill family, Bill Liddell, claimed his distant relation was in fact a Pagan and Luciferian. The claims that he had sold his soul to the devil, knew the secret of the elixir of life and eternal youth and was master of nine covens operating all over England is thought highly unlikely, yet cannot actually be disproven. As just one of the supposed witches operating in Essex at the time, the enigma that was 'Old George', as he was locally known, is still the subject of debate today.

The date of George's birth is recorded as 26 May 1816, and he was the son of Charles Pickingill and his wife Susannah Cudner, who had married in Hockley, Essex the year before in 1815. George was to be the eldest of nine children. Rumour had it that the Pickingills were descended from Romany stock and that was where George's magical skills originated from. In later life he did gain the reputation for being an itinerant horse whisperer, a trait associated largely with the gypsy culture. What is certain is that George lived with his parents in Hockley from the time of his birth until the 1830s, and that in the 1851 census he was to be firmly located working on the farm of David Clemens in Little Wakering. He was twenty-six, unmarried and just one of seven farm labourers lodging there.

By 1856, George was a married man. Both he and his bride, Sarah Bateman, a native of Tilingham in Essex, signed their names with an 'x' in the register of St George, Gravesend in Kent on 19 May of that year. Two years later the couple were back in Essex living in Hawkwell, then Eastwood by 1861. Between 1863 and 1867 the Pickingills had located to Canewdon, the village in which they would raise their children and where they would remain for the rest of their lives.

Settled in Canewdon, George continued as an agricultural labourer, working almost every farm in the area but earning little. To underline their poverty, a report in *Chelmsford Chronicle*, Friday 7 November 1862 states that 'Sarah, also known during her married life as Mary Ann, wife of George Pittingale, of Eastwood, was charged with stealing two pecks of potatoes growing in a field, the property James Tabor, Esq.', the result being a 10s fine (the value of the potatoes) and 8s costs. It was money the Pickingills could ill afford but it was paid to prevent Mary from spending two weeks in Chelmsford Gaol.

Perhaps the money was paid from the small income George made from his reputation as a cunning man and gypsy sorcerer; after all he was the man the locals consulted when a dispute needed settling, a wart needed removing or for a charm if lovesick. But it could equally have come from the money farmers gave George not to work his land – as George, or 'Old Picky' as he was sometimes known, could dabble in the black arts and was not adverse to exploiting the villagers, allowing them to believe he could also summon local witches using his wooden whistle, plus employ imps to carry out his work in the fields while he looked on. One rumour suggested George, as master of a local coven of thirteen witches, even held midnight orgies in St Nicholas's churchyard. These had been largely ignored by the former vicar, who was terrified of Pickingill's powers, but later investigated one night by his young successor. On hearing one evening the sounds of revelry coming from outside the church he rushed out to meet the witches. Strangely, in the sudden silence, all he saw were thirteen white rabbits peeping from behind the gravestones. It had become the norm in Canewdon not to cross George Pickingill.

George Pickingill's name was known far outside the confines of Canewdon and it was said that people came from all over to seek his knowledge of the black arts. But even before Pickingill settled in the village it had a dark reputation. From 1826 to 1861 Eliza Frost Lodwick, at first a young widow, singlehandedly managed Lambourne Hall, originally built in the late thirteenth century, which together with her other properties amounted to a sizable 500 acres. A mysterious accident plus thefts of sheep, which resulted in punishments far outweighing the crimes, made the locals suspicious and along with her sister,

George Pickingill. (By kind permission of *The Cauldron Magazine*)

the vicar's wife, they condemned the women for witches. Then it was James Murrell, cunning man of Hadleigh, that was called by the villagers to intervene on the village's behalf. He duly visited but the vicar refused permission for Murrell to rid Canewdon of its witches, for as a descendent of one of the original residents recounted many years later the vicar 'didn't want to be ashamed afore all knowing that his wife would be among them'.

George Pickingill died on 10 April 1909 in Canewdon, Essex, his supposed age entered in the register as being 103. An entry added by the vicar on the left margin of the page next to the entry mentions that he was in fact only 'in his ninety-third year, having been born in 1816'. It is thought that Pickingill added years to his age to enable him to better qualify in his latter years for parish relief. But he was not about to divulge his deception willingly, in fact his age increased constantly in the telling. When news of his longevity reached the newspapers he was visited by a reporter from the *Essex Newsman* in 1908 and asked just how he had managed to live so long. He said simply, 'Yes, I'm a hundred and five, and feel good for another twenty years. You just go on living – that's all.'

8

EXPLORERS

CAPTAIN LAWRENCE EDWARD GRACE OATES
(1880–1912)

*Oates is splendid with them – I do not know what we should do
without him.*

Captain Scott speaking of Oates and his ability with the expedition horses

When Lawrence Oates was accepted as a member of Robert Falcon Scott's Antarctic expedition he was already thirty years old. Not only was it his knowledge of horses that saw him charged with the care of the nineteen ponies vital for sled haulage on the trip, it was his distinctive service in the Army. Promotions in 1901 and 1902, reaching captain in 1906 and active service in Ireland, Egypt and India had all made Lawrence Edward Grace 'Titus' Oates courageous and self-reliant. In other words exactly what Scott was looking for in those that were to accompany him to one of the most hostile environments on earth.

Scott's South Pole expedition has of course been well documented over the years and is as much a tale of the human spirit as it is of human endeavour. With the expedition organised in 1910, Scott's ship, *Terra Nova*, left London on 1 June bound for New Zealand. After the preliminary tasks of setting up a base camp and creating strategic food and equipment dumps along the route, the explorers who were to make the last dash for the Pole started off from McMurdo Sound on 1 November 1911. It was estimated that the 800 miles to the Pole would be covered by Scott, Dr Wilson, Captain Oates and Petty Officer Evans by Christmas. Unfortunately severe weather meant the party was still 145 miles short of their goal on 4 January 1912. When they finally arrived on 18 January they were devastated to find their rival, the Norwegian Amundsen, had already claimed the Pole on 14 December 1911, over a month before.

Lawrence Edward Grace Oates. (By kind permission of Discovery Point, the Dundee Trust)

The real hardship hit the men on the return leg. Heavy-hearted and empty-bellied, they headed back toward One Ton Camp, hoping for adequate supplies at the food and fuel stages along the route. But the extra time it had taken them to reach their goal had seriously depleted food rations and with plummeting temperatures frostbite ate slowly into their resolve as well as their flesh. Oates was the worst affected; feet blackened and swollen, he could barely walk, plus the side effects of scurvy had made into a fresh festering mess an old war wound he had sustained earlier in his Army career.

As they battled atrocious weather, seaman Edgar Evans fell victim to concussion, the result of travelling so long over rough ice, and died at the foot of the Beardmore Glacier.

Scott's meticulously kept journal is our icy window onto those last days of the expedition and the deteriorating condition of Oates, affectionately known on the trip as 'the soldier'. On 5 March Scott wrote, 'We are two pony marches and 4 miles about from our depot. Our fuel dreadfully low and the poor Soldier nearly done. It is pathetic enough because we can do nothing for him; more hot food might do a little, but only a little, I fear. We none of us expected these terribly low temperatures.'

A day later, he logged, 'Poor Oates is unable to pull, sits on the sledge when we are track-searching – he is wonderfully plucky, as his feet must be giving him great pain. He makes no complaint, but his spirits only come up in spurts now, and he grows more silent in the tent.'

As temperatures plummeted and travelling conditions worsened, Oates realised he was holding up his companions, something Scott reluctantly noted along with resigned thoughts of his own demise, 'Things steadily downhill. Oates' foot worse. He has rare pluck and must know that he can never get through. He asked Wilson if he had a chance this morning, and of course Bill had to say he didn't know. In point of fact he has none. Apart from him, if he went under now, I doubt whether we could get through. With great care we might have a dog's chance, but no more...'

That chance never came, despite an act of supreme self-sacrifice on the part of Oates. On 16 or 17 March, in a comfortless blizzard camp and crippled with the cold, Scott finally wrote,

Should this be found I want these facts recorded. Oates' last thoughts were of his Mother, but immediately before he took pride in thinking that his regiment would be pleased with the bold way in which he met his death. We can testify to his bravery. He has borne intense suffering for weeks without complaint, and to the very last was able and willing to discuss outside subjects. He did not – would not – give up hope to the very end. He was a brave soul. This was the end. He slept through the night before last, hoping not to wake; but he woke in the morning – yesterday. It was blowing a blizzard. He said, 'I am just going outside and may be some time.' He went out into the blizzard and we have not seen him since.

The three remaining men perished on 29 March 1912. A search party found the bodies of Scott, Wilson and Bowers on 12 November 1912, but never found that of Oates.

A well-respected and popular man, his death was met with genuine regret and sorrow, especially by his mother who was thought to have slept in his room from that point on. Neither was Oates's dearest wish – that his regiment be proud of him – a forlorn hope. On 8 November 1913, on behalf of his brother officers, Major-General Allenby unveiled a memorial to him in Gestingthorpe church which reads,

In memory of a very gallant Gentleman Lawrence Edward Grace Oates, Captain in the Inniskilling Dragoons. Born March 17 1880. Died March 17 1912. On the return journey from the South Pole of the Scott Antarctic Expedition – when all were beset by hardship, he, being gravely injured, went out into the blizzard to die, in the hope that by so doing he might enable his comrades to reach safety.

Subsequently, his mother visited the church every week to polish the brass plaque. She died in 1937.

But Oates had been an all-round hero and in the relatively short time he had lived had seen action and adventure of every kind. Born in 1880 in Putney, he had spent his formative years in the family home of Gestingthorpe Hall near the Headinghams, where his father was the hereditary lord of the manor, the title he himself adopted on his father's death. After Eton he joined up with the 6th Enniskilling Dragoons and was drafted into the South African war that Lord Kitchener was trying to bring to an end. Here he almost immediately contracted enteric fever, but managed a full recovery.

While lieutenant, he was in command of a small patrol party, which were heavily outnumbered by Boers. Refusing the opportunity to surrender he fought on as long as his ammunition allowed. Every one of his men survived the attack, not one being captured. He himself was severely wounded in the thigh, spending many hours in a ditch before eventually being rescued by ambulance. Later, invalided home to Gestingthorpe, he was mentioned in dispatches and awarded the Queen's Medal with five clasps.

As a memento, Oates kept the personal note from the enemy who requested his surrender under the cover of a flag of truce. The message on the slip of white paper read, 'Captain Fouche asks for immediate surrender. Life and private property guaranteed.'

On his return to Gestingthorpe in the summer of 1901 Oates was enthusiastically received. The whole village was entertained at the lord of the manor's expense and in return they gave their returning hero the following framed address:

> We the inhabitants of Gestingthorpe heartily desire to greet you on your return home after your terrible experiences in South Africa. Englishman's heart must have thrilled with emotion when he read the account of your conspicuous act of valour, when you and your little band of men were surprised by an overwhelming number of Boers, and in reply to their demand to surrender you answered you were not here to surrender but to fight. You did fight as long as your ammunition lasted and after all not a single man was taken. We say every Englishman rejoiced, but what shall we say for ourselves to whom you belong? We are indeed proud of you and trust that you may soon be restored to health and strength and able to rejoin your regiment, always realising no honour can be greater than the consciousness that you have nobly done your duty.

Due to his injury Oates limped for a while, but it was not long before he rejoined his regiment. To further commemorate the return of their hero the village opted to have the bells at Gestingthorpe church restored and dedicated on 4 January 1902. The fifth bell bears the following inscription in Latin: 'In gratitude to God for the safe return with honour of her beloved son Lawrence E. G. Oates from the dangers of South Africa, C. A. Oates has caused this, and the sixth bell, for a long time cracked and useless, to be re-cast, 1901.'

Once back in action Oates was promoted to captain and soon after applied and was accepted for the British Antarctic Expedition. Having inherited his spirit of adventure from a family that had always loved exploration, he would be following in the footsteps of both his father and uncle, who as members of the Royal Geographical Society had journeyed into the African interior. He was not to know such footsteps would be his last.

On Saturday 15 February 1913, in memory of a truly inspirational young man, a memorial service was held simultaneously at both Gestingthorpe church and St Paul's Cathedral.

AUGUSTINE COURTAULD (1904–1959)

He was very handsome with a lively dark-skinned face, black hair and eyebrows, and expressive green eyes. He was a romantic who would have been at home in the time of Elizabeth I, charting unknown seas, for he was a brilliant navigator and it was from his point of view, a sort of tragedy that so little of the earth's surface was left unexplored.

August & Rab, a memoir by Mollie Butler

Essex is quite adept at producing explorers. Perhaps it is our salt marsh coast that brings the fingers of the sea almost to knock at a young man's door that first stirs his wanderlust, later to draw his heart towards adventures beyond our shores. Perhaps it is our closeness to the Continent, our island history, our proximity to London that has made Essex the capital's backyard, a thoroughfare for both pilgrims and the persecuted that has given us our fortitude. From an old and distinguished Essex family, Augustine Courtauld was already a seasoned explorer by the time he joined the British Arctic-Air Route Expedition in 1930. As his fiancée, Mollie Montgomerie, said of the expedition she had no qualms about his safety as 'he had returned twice before from expeditions to Greenland'. Little did she realise he would become an international hero before she saw him again.

The expedition was the brainchild of Gino Watkins, whose intention was to take advantage of the expansion of air travel and, recruiting a group of young men to accompany him, discover the possibility of an air route to North America, via Iceland and Greenland. It was virgin territory both in terms of what the weather was like over the Greenland ice cap in winter and the fact that it would mean exploring great areas as yet uncharted on any map.

Once there, the expedition set up an ice cap station about 130 miles inland from their seashore base camp and began what would become a daily routine of record keeping including vital information such as temperatures, wind force, speed of clouds, and air pressure. It was decided that only two men at a time would man the isolated station, being relieved a month later by another two and so on. At least this was the plan.

The severe weather conditions that followed were no surprise except in their ferocity. Constant blizzards meant travel was impossible, forcing men to huddle together for warmth, the dogs outside, used to bad weather, buried up to their noses in snow. Thus the plan of regular relief of one team by another after a month at the ice cap station became more and more difficult, and when it was the turn of Augustine (affectionately known as August) and his team it took them an incredible thirty-nine days to travel the 130 miles they needed to cover to offer relief and much-needed provisions.

August's diary gives us a feel for the conditions:

Still blowing, tent shaking and beating all day. Towards evening the wind increased in violence and as darkness fell the tent was thundering and shaking as if it would be torn to pieces at any moment. Had to shout to make myself

Augustine Courtauld. (By kind permission of Julien Courtauld)

heard by Hampton who was only a foot away. Everything covered with rime and snow. Sleeping bags wet. We slept in our clothes and prayed the tent would stay up.

When they finally arrived to take their turn it was in desperately low temperatures and those they had come to relieve had been in the station for two months.

It had become apparent to August that this situation was untenable and so he came up with what he thought would be a solution. It was his idea that he alone would man the ice station for the rest of the year if the returning party would supply him with all the food and provisions they could spare. He told companion Freddie Chapman that with his books and a sufficient supply of tobacco he would be 'perfectly happy'.

It was an anxious decision, but the only one that would break the cycle of late handovers. In perfect weather the original plan would have worked, but with hold-ups forcing the relief team to break into the food stocks they were bringing out to the station to replace their own dwindling stocks, when they did finally arrive they were not only overdue but had little to deliver. There was no alternative but to accept Courtauld's selfless offer, and on 5 December, August watched his companions fade beyond the snowy horizon, knowing he would be seeing out the Arctic winter alone.

When they had gone August entered their departure in his diary: 'The silence outside was almost terrible. Nothing to hear but one's heart beating and the blood ticking in one's veins.'

August's home, if only he had realised, would be until 5 May 1931 a canvas dome only 10 by 6 feet, hung by tape from curved bamboo ribs at an altitude of 9,000 feet. A second skin encased the first, allowing for a ventilation pipe to protrude up from the first and then through the second. From this shelter August would venture out in the cold every three hours to take readings from the instruments, more often than not having to unblock the entrance with fingers that were increasingly succumbing to frostbite. But with an extraordinary ability to adapt to his circumstances, once back inside the tent August let his books transport him out of what could have been an overwhelming sense of abandonment.

He played himself at chess and indulged his passion for sailing by planning the perfect boat, how he would sail her and where he would go. Never did he feel truly alone. According to author Nicholas Woolaston, writer and traveller, himself the son of a doctor and botanist on the first Everest expedition in 1921, 'August buoyed his capacity for endurance with the feeling that he belonged to the expedition; of community with friends, as if a thin connection ran back like a vein down the line of half-mile flags from the ice-cap station to the coast. Knowing that the others were at the base, and trusting then to come back for him as soon as they could, helped to sustain him.'

August made it through three months to 22 March but then after a ferocious gale closed the snow over the tent's exit and entry point all looked lost. August's paraffin lamp, which was both his light and heat, was almost exhausted and from then on he tried to conserve as much of his energy as he could by lying down most of the time. His tent was almost an ice tomb. Woolaston's account goes on to describe how 'the walls bulging inward from the weight of snow, were lined with hoar frost that hung in icicles, reducing the space even further; they drifted and pieces dropped on him in the dark. Condensation turned to ice in his sleeping bag, so that his feet froze and he had to warm them with his hands.'

Despite frozen fingers, August was still able to write, and was in no doubt he would be rescued, even when he was down to only a couple of ounces of food a day. He was convinced, he wrote in his diary, that he was not 'fated to leave his bones on the Greenland ice-cap'. And he wasn't. When an initial search party returned to base after failing to find the ice station on 1 March they set out again on 21 April, this time with Gino Watkins in charge and determined to find him.

It was almost impossible. The landscape had changed over the months and it was as if the ice station had vanished, even the Union Jack had shredded

Augustine Courtauld after being rescued from the Ice Station. (By kind permission of Julien Courtauld)

away in the Arctic winds. It was only when a small black dot – the tip of the stovepipe – was spotted that the rescuers felt both exhilarated and wary. There was no sign of life at all and later Freddie Chapman recalled how all the men, from initial elation, had suddenly begun to have 'certain misgivings'. Watkins called down the stovepipe, not realistically expecting an answer. But then one came, unsteady but audible. They had got there just in time, as only ten minutes before, Courtauld's last drop of paraffin had burned away.

When August was finally dug out, he was unkempt and smoke-stained, with soot on his clothing, his skin desperately pale. Photographs with his rescuers show him to be remarkably composed after his ordeal, but he was exhausted.

As if that had not been enough for one lifetime, Courtauld almost immediately set off on another adventure, seemingly reluctant to go home to the media circus his exploits had created. Coming as he did from Huguenot stock, he preferred to shun the limelight. This new expedition was to take August, Watkins and one other on an open-boat journey 600 miles round the unexplored coast of southern Greenland, a trip that proved just as hazardous as Courtauld's recent icy incarceration. But with combined seamanship the party completed their mission and when August did return home he was proud to be the recipient of the Polar Medal, awarded to him by King George V.

A spirit as free as August's was always going to be hard to contain, yet this polar hero married his patient fiancée Molly and between them they raised six children to be as independent and self-sufficient as he was. The summer of 1939 saw Courtauld join the organisation founded by Churchill known as the SOE (Special Operations Executive), in which he once more took his life in his hands, gathering as much intelligence as he could by sailing his beloved boat *Duet* along the Norwegian coast.

But probably his best accolade is the high regard in which he was held by his children. Julien Courtauld remembers his father:

> When quite young we would be allowed to row the dinghy ashore in Burnham River often with a strong tide running against the wind. Wearing a lifejacket was never thought of by us or him. He was the epitome of Good Seamanship – everything just as it should be. He rejoiced in knowing what risk he could take and cutting safety margins as fine as possible, and throughout his life he was proved right time and again – although he terrified a good few people in the process.

9

GENTLEMEN OF LETTERS

DANIEL DEFOE (*c.*1659/61–1731)

*He is a middle-sized spare man, about forty years old, of a brown
complexion, and dark brown coloured hair, but wears a wig, a hooked nose,
a sharp chin, grey eyes, and a large mole near his mouth…*

Description of him when charged with writing a scandalous pamphlet, *c.* 1704

When Daniel Defoe's first novel, *The Life and Times of Robinson Crusoe*, arrived on the early Georgian literary scene in 1719 he was almost sixty years old. *Moll Flanders* followed in 1721, cementing his reputation as a novelist, but Defoe was no stranger to publishing. A prolific and versatile writer, he wrote more than 500 books, pamphlets and journals on various topics, was a pioneer of social and economic journalism and spoke out strongly in favour of education for women. But it is the fact that he resided both in Chadwell St Mary and Colchester during his lifetime, plus the travel guide *A Tour Through the Whole Island Of Great Britain* written between 1724 and 1727 that qualifies him, to the reader of this book, as an Essex boy.

Defoe said of his *Tour*, comprising seventeen very large circuits, or journeys, which took him over almost all of England, that 'the work itself is a description of the most flourishing and opulent country in the world'. It is from these travels that we now know so much about the Essex of yesteryear. It is also from Defoe's constant need to express himself in both word and deed that we now know so much about him.

Daniel Foe (the 'De' was added later to add gravitas to his name) was actually born in London, most probably Fore Street, in the parish of St Giles Cripplegate, a corruption of the Anglo-Saxon 'cruplegate' meaning a covered way or tunnel. The exact date of his birth is not known, but historians estimate the year to be either 1659 or 1660. His parents, James and Alice Foe, were dissenters –

Nonconformists – and so Daniel was raised outside of regular Protestantism, eventually attending a dissenting academy aged sixteen as, for Defoe and others like him, the doors of Oxford and Cambridge were definitely closed.

As was at first expected, Defoe did not become a minister. Instead in 1681 he followed his father and became a businessman, trading in general merchandise, which included hosiery, general woolen goods, and wine. He was marginally successful, cleverly navigating his way through the wheeling and dealing of business, always hoping that the rewards of his speculative ventures would outweigh the risks. But unfortunately Defoe was a man with ideas bigger than his budget and, as history shows, a man who was continually in debt.

Money did come to him in the shape of a young woman named Mary Tuffley whom he married on New Year's Day 1684 with the consent of her father as she was only twenty, and with whom he was to raise a large family. It was a love match, but sorely tested. With Defoe often abroad, in hiding and with constant financial instability, it was a wonder the union lasted the forty-seven years that it did. Despite the fact she had brought with her an enormous dowry of almost £4,000, Defoe still could not escape the shadow of bankruptcy, the years 1688 to 1694 seeing no less than eight lawsuits against him, some citing him for fraud.

A year after his marriage Defoe became briefly involved with the Monmouth Rebellion, an attempt to replace the recently crowned Catholic brother of Charles II, King James II, with his Protestant bastard son the Duke of Monmouth. The failed attempt culminated in Judge Jeffries' notorious Bloody Assizes, and to avoid being hauled up before the magistrates, Defoe laid low on the Continent, dealing, in his usual guise of merchant, in wine, tobacco and general goods.

Defoe faced financial ruin again in 1692, this time for a vast sum, and imprisonment was the penalty for being in such heavy debt. But as Defoe was to find, as the law stood, he, as with all other bankrupts, did not then have the power to recover himself. He found this deplorable, publicly speaking out against such an untenable situation: 'He, who is unable to pay his debts at once, may yet be able to pay them at leisure,' he wrote, 'and you should not meanwhile murder him by law, for such is perpetual imprisonment.'

To avoid stubborn creditors, Defoe went to Bristol, lodged at the Red Lion in Castle Street, and from there was able to negotiate terms that spared him the humiliation of debtor's prison. He began writing essays and pamphlets in earnest, his observations of the laws of bankruptcy leading to a change in legislation that had stood since the time of Henry VIII. He also found himself in the government's employ as 'commissioner of the glass duty', and subsequently the secretary of a brick and pantile works in Tilbury.

From this position he eventually became owner of the works, producing Dutch tiles, which up until this point London's builders had needed to source from Holland. Defoe's new venture ensured there was a supply of the blue-and

-white delftware on London's doorstep, plus he was manufacturing much-needed brick, which was going some way to paying off his creditors in full.

The brickworks as a going concern operated between 1694 and 1703, and employed about 100 labourers. A later biographer of Defoe, William Lee, in 1860 placed the works 'immediately on the west side of the Tilbury Station', observing that 'a large plot was being dug over to form potato-ground for the railway servants; and a deep trench had been previously cut through the same river to drain the Company's estate. In this way the whole of Defoe's brick and pantile works had been laid open, including the clay-pits, drying floors, foundations of kilns and other buildings.' In the nineteenth century there was still a 'Brick Kiln Marsh' and a 'Brick House' in the vicinity. In 1697 Defoe supplied red bricks for the Greenwich Hospital for Seamen, and there are reports that London's Greenwich Observatory was partly built with spare bricks from Defoe's works that were lying unclaimed at Tilbury Fort just east of Defoe's works. William Lee also applauded Defoe's enterprise: 'Judging from fragments recently dug up, he made good sound sonorous bricks.'

But contemporaries of Defoe were ready to pour scorn on his venture, especially those who did not agree with is politics. His 'pot-works at Tilbury' were compared with the pot-works in Egypt; it was said that Defoe was not so much deficient in straw as wages. Perhaps this was not so far from the truth. Some sources claimed that Defoe's labour force at Tilbury was at times 'questionable' and his relationship with them at times strained. Perhaps it was down to a lack of local expertise or the fact that Defoe, at a prosperous time in his life, could not or would not pay them adequately. Records state that at times Defoe was obliged to employ beggars and casual labourers, Defoe himself stating that 'I affirm of my own knowledge, when I have wanted a man for labouring work, and offered 9 shillings a week to strolling fellows at my door, they have frequently told me to my face that they could get more a-begging; and I once set a lusty fellow in the stocks for making such an experiment.'

Even the composition of his bricks was in dispute. Whereas the Dutch were able to stiffen or weaken their clay by the introduction of sand or marl, Defoe's opponents circulated rumours that his company simply took the Thames silt and thought about nothing but 'saving coals in the burning, by mixing the clay with coal-ashes or small cinders which would make the tiles very porous and not so fitting for turning the wet'. When Defoe's venture eventually closed it was not from overwhelming competition by the Dutch, but once again was a downfall of his own making.

Defoe's fervent sense of justice often led him into deep water and his essay 'The Shortest Way with the Dissenters' had infuriated the authorities, prompting him to flee his two-storey home (complete with a dairy, brewhouse, and large barn), called 'Brick House' on Chadwell Marsh, and go once more into hiding. He published a follow-up pamphlet to say that he had been misunderstood but the government had his original work burned by the common hangman and a substantial reward was offered for Defoe's arrest.

Betrayed by an informant, Defoe was caught in May in Spitalfields and confined in Newgate jail where he had comparatively comfortable lodgings at his own expense. His trial for seditious libel began early in July but was quickly over. Pleading guilty, as he technically was, and appealing for mercy on the ground that he had not meant to be taken seriously, he was sentenced by the notoriously sadistic judge Salathiel Lovell to stand three times in the pillory in London's busiest places, namely the Royal Exchange, the conduit in Cheapside and finally in Fleet Street by Temple Bar. Following his public humiliation, Defoe was taken back to Newgate to face further time in the prison, the prospect of release relying on the payment of a disproportionate fine and sureties for his good behaviour for seven years.

While Defoe languished in Newgate, the government deliberated on the possibility that a man of Defoe's popularity and skill could be better controlled if he worked for them rather than against them, and so he was set free, £1,000 was paid toward his outstanding debts, all with the proviso Defoe would become a government agent.

Though this particular sequence of events wasn't quite the 'miracle' Defoe later expressed it was, it did give him a chance to earn a living again and begin to keep the promise he had given his numerous creditors. He was also in new debt. As a casualty of his time in prison, his Tilbury tile works had closed, indebting him further to the tune of £3,000.

By 1705 Defoe was running a small newspaper, The Review, and had managed to reduce his debts from £17,000 to just £5,000 which included the £3000 debt he had incurred from his time in prison that led to the closing of his tile works. One creditor in particular was quite complimentary: 'I know this Defoe as well as any of you, for I was one of his creditors, compounded with him, and discharged him fully. Several years afterwards he sent for me, and though he was clearly discharged, he paid me all the remainder of his debt, voluntarily and of his own accord; and he told me that as far as God should enable him, he intended to do so with everybody.'

After yet another libel arrest in 1715, Defoe spent his time working on the novels that would see him in the public eye for the right reasons, such as Journal of the Plague Year and Moll Flanders written in 1722 and Robinson Crusoe in 1724. But for Essex, Defoe's most important work is of course his Tour Through Great Britain, also published in 1724, especially his focus on the eastern counties. It is from here we glean much of what we know about Essex in the early Georgian period.

It has to be said, however, that on occasion Defoe, in his eagerness to illustrate a fact, was prone to gilding the lily. An account that makes historians smile is Defoe's reportage of an encounter with a man who recounted why the death rate for females in the marshy areas of Essex was abnormally high.

I have one remark more before I leave this damp part of the world, and which I cannot omit on the women's account, namely, that I took notice of a strange decay of the sex here; insomuch that all along this country it was very frequent to meet with men that had had from five or six to fourteen or fifteen wives; nay, and some more.

And I was informed that in the marshes on the other side of the river over against Candy Island there was a farmer who was then living with the five-and-twentieth wife, and that his son, who was but about thirty-five years old, had already had about fourteen.

Indeed, this part of the story I only had by report, though from good hands too; but the other is well known and easy to be inquired into about Fobbing, Curringham, Thundersly, Benfleet, Prittlewell, Wakering, Great Stambridge, Cricksea, Burnham, Dengy, and other towns of the like situation. The reason, as a merry fellow told me, who said he had had about a dozen and a half of wives (though I found afterwards he fibbed a little) was this: That they being bred in the marshes themselves and seasoned to the place, did pretty well with it; but that they always went up into the hilly country, or, to speak their own language, into the uplands for a Wife. That when they took the young lasses out of the wholesome and fresh air they were healthy, fresh, and clear, and well; but when they came out of their native air into the marshes among the fogs and damps, there they presently changed their complexion, got an ague or two, and seldom held it above half a year, or a year at most; 'And then,' said he, 'we go to the uplands again and fetch another'; so that marrying of wives was reckoned a kind of good farm to them. It is true the fellow told this in a kind of drollery and mirth; but the fact, for all that, is certainly true; and that they have abundance of wives by that very means. Nor is it less true that the inhabitants in these places do not hold it out, as in other countries, and as first you seldom meet with very ancient people among the poor, as in other places we do, so, take it one with another, not one-half of the inhabitants are natives of the place; but such as from other countries or in other parts of this country settle here for the advantage of good farms; for which I appeal to any impartial inquiry, having myself examined into it critically in several places.

The vulnerability of the fair sex aside, Defoe did give his reader a fair insight into Essex, excusing its faults as much as he extolled its virtues. When in Barking, he remarked on the catastrophic breaching of the sea wall, and how the River Thames, with each tide, scoured out 'soil from Dagenham marshes'.

He described how 5,000 acres of land lay buried underwater and the great mud bank in the middle created by the river was causing a hazard to shipping and trade.

Defoe marveled at Essex's ability to not only support itself in 'corn, flesh, fish, butter, cheese, salt, fuel, timber, etc.', but the fact that it could supply England's capital with the same! He commended our abundance of fish and oysters, especially those oysters from Wivenhoe collected from a small bank called Woelfleet. 'They are the best and nicest though not the largest oysters in England,' and 'once barrelled up and carried to Colchester, which is but three miles off, they are sent to London by land, and are from thence called Colchester oysters.'

Defoe also observes how

the Rivers Chelmer, and Blackwater unite to make a large firth, or inlet of the sea, sometimes called Idumanum Fluvium, but by fishermen and seamen, who use it as a port, it is called Malden Water. Here in the inlet in Oocy, or Osyth Island, commonly called Oosy Island, so well known by our London men of pleasure for the infinite number of wild fowl, that is to say, duck, mallard, teal, and widgeon, of which there are such vast flights, that they tell us the island, namely the creek, seems covered with them at certain times of the year, and they go from London on purpose for the pleasure of shooting; and, indeed, often come home very well laden with game. But it must be remembered too that those gentlemen who are such lovers of the sport, and go so far for it, often return with an Essex ague on their backs, which they find a heavier load than the fowls they have shot.

Witham, Defoe records, is a 'pleasant, well-situated market town, in which there are many gentlemen of good fortunes', adding that it is becoming evident that as the wealth of the capital increases, 'London spreads itself into the country, and plants families and fortunes, who in another age will equal the families of the ancient gentry'. Kelvedon, he informs us, was once called Kill-Dane; apparently named because it was here 'where the massacre of the Danes was begun by the women', though he adds that the story needed confirmation. He also tells us that locally the village is known as Keldon and that 'their chief business is breeding of calves, which I need not say are the best and fattest, and the largest veal in England, if not in the world'.

Defoe devoted much of his description of Colchester to its history and it being 'large, very populous, the streets fair and beautiful, and though it may not said to be finely built, yet there are abundance of very good and well-built houses in it. It still mourns in the ruins of a civil war'. Harwich, on the other hand, drew a much shorter tribute, purely for the reason that it was 'a town so well known and so perfectly described by many writers, I need say little of it'. He did however say that he found it 'a town of hurry and business, not much of gaiety and pleasure; yet the inhabitants seem warm in their nests, and some of them are very wealthy'.

Defoe it seems had mixed feelings about his great tour of England, which was in effect a series of circuits undertaken over a lengthy period. 'A tedious and very expensive 5 year journey' was a comment he made in 1727 when looking back on his venture. Tedious it may have been for him, but this historian, and I suspect many others, are eternally grateful that he took it.

It seemed that Defoe could not help but try once more to set up a pantile works in Essex. This time the location was Colchester and he ran it briefly in 1724. It was not his only connection with the town. His eponymous heroine Moll Flanders was raised in the town in her formative years, a deliberate ploy to allow the journalist in Defoe to highlight the social problem of infanticide that was rife in the town. Defoe also had a personal interest in Colchester. It was here that Defoe had a good friend in the Revd William Smithies, rector of St Michael's, Mile End and who in 1722 negotiated a lease for Defoe of an estate called Kingswood Heath, or Severalls. Just outside of town, this was for the benefit of his daughter, Hannah, who 'lived upon her income in respectable gentility until her death in 1759'.

In 1725–6 there is a record in the borough chamberlain's account of Defoe possibly having leased Tubswick – a farmhouse in Mill Road, Mile End, Colchester – that details the payment of expenses for two journeys 'from London to Daniel Defoe's house at Newington in respect of estate at Mile End, Colchester, held by lease from Borough of Colchester'. He is said to have paid the then huge sum of £1,000 for the ninety-nine-year lease.

Daniel Defoe died of 'a lethargy' at his at his lodgings in Ropemaker's Alley, Moorfields on 24 April 1731. From a time of ease and relative fortune, he had once again slipped into troubles and poverty, writing a year before his death that 'I am so near my journey's end and am hastening to the place where the weary are at rest'. He was buried in a famous Nonconformist cemetery in Bunhill Fields, London. What follows is not his epitaph, but, succinct and to the point, it could well have been. Defoe wrote of himself:

No man has tasted differing fortunes more, And thirteen times I have been rich and poor.

PHILIP MORANT (1700–1770)

Venerable author who used to walk about Colchester with a powdered
wig and a gold-headed cane, and was a general favourite on account of his
learning and good nature.

Reverend Dr Henry Hutton

Phillip Morant of Colchester was many things in his lifetime; clergyman, archaeologist, author and historian, but it is unlikely he ever considered himself an accidental diarist. Nothing he wrote about his parishoners was on the scale of Pepys, but the detail of his parish registers he was obliged to keep give us an often poignant glimpse into another world, snippets recorded in his neat and distinctive hand showing us the minutae of eighteenth-century day-to-day existence.

Morant was born on Jersey, one of the Channel Islands, to Stephen Morant (also known as Etienne) and his wife Mary Filleul on 6 October 1700. His long association with Essex began in 1732 when he took on the curacy of Great Waltham, which stands on the River Chelmer, just over 4 miles north of Chelmsford. His path to that post was dedicated, his considerable education beginning at Abingdon Grammar School, then Pembroke College, Oxford, where in 1722 he was admitted to deacon's orders at St Martin-in-the-Fields, ending with his ordination as a priest in 1724. Not a man to embrace idleness, he continued to study as well as assist Nicholas Tindal, the vicar of Great Waltham, in his curacy. This duel role continued until 1732, with accounts in the parish showing that Morant was paid £11 in 1725 for 'preaching at Chapel, 77 Sundays' and in 1726, 'Paid to Mr Morant for preaching at Chappell, nineteen Sundaies £4. 15. 00.' By 10 October 1729 Morant was assisting Tindal armed with a Master of Arts degree he had earned from Sidney Sussex College, Cambridge.

Morant was a rising star. A nomination by Queen Caroline, wife of George II, saw him spend two years in Amsterdam, during which time he had also been given the curacy of Shellow Bowells, a post he resigned on his return. Over the years, he would take on the position of rector of Broomfield, Chignall Smealey, St Mary's Colchester, Wickham Bishops and finally Aldham. Occasionally he held more than one benefice at a time but never more than two.

So much more than a man of the cloth, Morant, while rector of St Mary-at-the-Walls, Colchester, wrote the first of the works he is renowned for. *The History and Antiquities of Colchester* was inspired by an interest he had developed for the town in which he now worked and lived, and was published in 1748. Over a decade later Morant followed this with *A History of the County of Essex*, this time written not so much from the heart as from a project his old mentor, William Tindal, had undertaken, assisted by Morant himself back in his university days.

Philip Morant.

Tindal, having acquired, in 1732, some 400 well-charged parish files of an earlier historian, William Holman, intended to finish what Holman himself did not complete. In turn the notes Holman had intended to use were from the collection of much earlier public records and observations collected by Thomas Jekyll (1570–1652). In the event Tindal only published two instalments of the proposed *Essex History*, allowing Morant to publish his own manuscript on the county of Essex much later in two volumes between 1763 and 1768. Today the tomes have become an invaluable research aid, but surprisingly at the time they failed to elicit much excitement from the city dignitaries, and enjoyed only a small print run of 200 copies.

These two inspired projects show Morant to be a man meticulous in detail and dedicated to his subject, but it is the parish records he kept as part of his everyday job as town and village curate that unintentionally open the twenty-first-century eye to the details of life for every man, woman and child in the eighteenth. Not the landowning gentry of his *Essex History*, these were ordinary people; people who came to register their life events, trials and tribulations, their joys, tears and heartbreak to a man invested with the authority, as the law required, to record them. This he did for over twenty-five years.

Some make poignant reading. The death of Abigale Todd, wife of Samuel, reveals that she was buried 'with an infant of hers, "anonymous"'. The child of an extramarital affair perhaps? And Mary, the mother of a child buried only three days earlier, was herself interred 'with her other twin infant and buried together'. Smallpox, the scourge of eighteenth-century Colchester, casts a long shadow in

Morant's records. Between 26 July 1741 and 14 October, twenty-two children who had died of the disease were buried, seven in a four- day period. One can only imagine the despair of the parents of William and Ann Taylor, 'two children of the smallpox', when they were given up for burial on 23 September 1741.

Child deformities that can be largely averted with medical advances and early care in these modern times were beyond intervention in Morant's day. On 5 November 1739 Morant noted that the son of Andrew and Mary Halls was baptised. He also noted that the poor infant was 'very much deformed, having a sharp forehead and a nose pressed flat to his face. It occupied the room of the upper lips of the middle part of the upper jaw, the nostrills were hid within the mouth, which was above 2 inches wide – it gaped horribly at the two sides.' A cleft-palate? Morant recored the child died after only twenty-four hours. Another deformed child was described as having 'little below the navel' and died after three weeks.

On an archaic note, Morant writes in an entry for March 1741 that 'Mary Macdonald', 'camp-trull' was buried, 'trull' being an old word for camp-follower or prostitute, of which there were many in Colchester serving the barracks in the town. Subsequently we also have a record of George Ruth buried, 'a soldiers child', and Mary Woodthorpe burying her 'base born' (illegitimate) son. At the other end of the social scale we have a Mrs Mary Mayhew 'interred in the family vault'.

Accidents, though few and far between, were recorded all the same. Christmas Day 1745 saw Mr Edward Bartholomew, 'master carpenter of this parish', die of the wounds he received 'due to the overturning of the Stage Coach in Ingatestone, on his returning from London to this town'. Earlier, a child, John Bental, 'had been drowned at Middle Mill'. Later in the records three men were 'killed by the 'carving of St Todd's well'. Misadventure too appears; 'the poor boy, name unknown who died in the street as passing through this parish', and a man named Alexander Riley, 'a soldier in General Hawsley's regiment', poisoning himself. The coroner, Morant records, found him to have been 'a lunatic'.

Morant describes with a certain charm and accuracy the aged ladies within his records, sometimes leaving us to surmise as to how old they really were or in fact if their ages were known at all. Mary Doe is described simply as an 'old widow' while Susan Folkes is 'an ancient widow'. Eliza Gibbs was labeled 'ancient widow aged 92'. On 2 March 1756 Morant entered Ann Spencer's name in his parish register, and the fact she had long outlived her husband. There is no age written alongside; perhaps it was unknown, but the note he added gives us far more information than a number ever could; it reads, 'She remembered the Plague here in 1665 and 1666.' Similarly, Mary, wife of William Branch, was recorded as having died at only seventy, which seems to us neither old nor ancient but Morant's note states that she 'had twenty children born. Perhaps such childbearing had worn her out? One can only imagine the joys and sorrows she must have witnessed.

Thirty years after the death of the infant who had died of the deformity to his face, Morant buried the boy's father, Andrew Halls, aged eighty.

Yet all was not doom and gloom. Morant records his own marriage to Anne Stebbing, daughter of Solomon Stebbing and Ann of Brook House, Great Tey, in the register dated 6 February 1739, adding the birth of their only daughter, Anna Maria, the same year. Morant, no doubt thankful for his wife's safe delivery and proud of his new status as a father, penned the entry 'Anna Maria daughter of Philip Morant Rector of this parish and Ann his wife, was born November 25 at half an hour after one in the morning and baptiz'd the 1st of January following.'

When not keeping his parish registers and writing, Morant was a keen antiquarian, with evidence of his having 'dug up many leaden coffins and urns and Roman coins, with enameled bracelet-like ornaments, female bodkins for headdresses and the like' in the fields west of Colchester. Such activities, plus the work he had invested in his *History and Antiquities of Colchester* led to his election in 1755 to the Fellowship of the Society of Antiquaries in London. Ten years later, after the death of his beloved wife, he moved from Essex to live in Surrey with his daughter and her husband, Thomas Astle, the Keeper of Records in the Tower of London. Although almost seventy years of age, in 1768 Morant gladly accepted an appointment by the sub-committee of the House of Peers to prepare a copy of the ancient official records of the English Parliament, otherwise known as the 'Rolls of Parliament', for publication. It was a substantial task that he continued til his death.

Morant, historian, scribe, antiquarian and clergyman, died on 25 November 1770, the day of his only daughter's thirty-first birthday, and was buried with his wife in the older church at Aldham, Essex. His son-in-law, Thomas Astle, wrote Morant's epitaph, fitting words for a man whose contribution to English historical scholarship, both intentional and unintentional, was so substantial:

To Philip Morant, A. M. Rector of this Church he was a man of great simplicity and purity of manners An assiduous friend to the good, benevolent to all: Abounding in every kind of erudition He investigated with success the origin of the families and the territorial divisions of this County; And contributed much to celebrating the lives of illustrious Britons. In those studies he spent all his time from earliest youth to his death Not for ostentation, but for the profit of the public. He died Nov. 25th, A. D. 1770, aged 70. And to Anne, his wife, who was an honour to her sex. She was descended from the ancient families of Stebbing and Creffield And died July 28th, A. D. 1767, aged 69.

To these, the best of parents, Thomas and Anna Maria Astle have dedicated this monument.

THE INGRAVE SCRIBES

St Nicholas church, Ingrave, has a secret. Hidden in plain sight it has a work of art that is both a mystery and a blessing, a puzzle that perhaps now, due to the passage of time, may never be solved. The canvas for this conundrum is the very fabric of the church, its outer wall to be precise, where over the years countless hands have left their mark literally, by inscribing their names and initials in the soft orange surface. Graffiti, you may remark, is a sign of our own discontented times – the means by which we may deface our surroundings with spray cans and garish paper, easily obtained. Not so. Man has always left his mark, and in the case of Ingrave, extremely elegantly.

We can only speculate as to the identities of those who etched into the wall of St Nicholas, a church built between 1734 and 1736, to unify the benefices of Ingrave and West Herndon, the former churches of both parishes then being near to ruin. Perhaps the walls of this new building were too new for waiting choir boys to ignore, too tempting for children attending a harvest festival to leave unadorned and so dates as early as 1737 now give us a link to the past. Who was 'John Tricker 1783', as yet not found in Ingrave documents, or 'S. H. 1890'?

In 1843 'W Purkis' was engraved on the wall; a Susannah 'Purkis' was born to a Frederick and Maryann, but unfortunately 'S' is not the initial; we are presented with 'W'. There were Ingrave families with the names Wiseman, Whitby, Wood, and Wade, which could account for the 'C.W. 1857' and 'G.W. 1789', but this author has not, after looking through census and parish records, been able to definitively establish a match.

A breakthrough was almost made when a Charles Wiseman was discovered to have been fourteen in 1857 and perfectly able to carve the initial 'C. W. 1857' on the wall. Yet after following him in documents to Erith in Kent where he married Emma Marchant it became apparent he and his new wife had signed the register with the usual 'x' for those that could not write. Perhaps he could still be our signatory if he had at least mastered his initials, but never went on to master his full name?

Sarah Richardson and Thomas Richardson lived and were born in Ingrave in 1766 and 1792 respectively but do not fit with the tantalising initial 'B. R.'

There is, however, a credible candidate for 'RY 1791', and that is Robert Young, born in the village in 1783. He went on to become Ingrave's 'beer-seller' at the Cricketer's public house for ten years from 1841, but could he have carved his name in stone at only eight? It is nothing if not an intriguing thought.

The Ingrave Scribes. An example of some of the initials and names engraved on the wall of Ingrave church. (Karen Bowman)

CHARLES DICKENS (1812–1870)

He is young and handsome, has a mellow, beautiful eye, fine brow, and abundant hair. His mouth is large, and his smile so bright it seemed to shed light and happiness all about him. His manner is easy negligent but not elegant. His dress was foppish; in fact, he was overdressed, yet his garments were worn so easily they appeared to be a necessary part of him. He had a dark coat, with lighter pantaloons; a black waistcoat, embroidered with coloured flowers; and about his neck, covering his white shirt-front, was a black neck-cloth, also embroidered in colours, in which were placed two large diamond pins connected by a chain; a gold watch-chain, and a large red rose in his button-hole, completed his toilet.

Eyewitness description of Charles Dickens as he appeared at a party given by Judge Walker in Cincinnati, Ohio, in April 1842

The date 7 February 1812 has gone down in the annals of history for three reasons. It was the day a series of earthquakes caused a small tsunami in America's Mississippi River, causing it to run backward for several hours, the poet Lord Byron made his first speech in House of Lords and Charles John Huffam Dickens was born in Portsmouth. Admittedly Portsmouth is a fair distance from Essex but this small boy, who read avidly and was destined to become the greatest Victorian writer this country has ever known, drew on many places and populated his books with the characteristics of those he encountered on his travels. For this reason, Essex, like many other places, was not unfamiliar to him.

Charles Dickens.

His earlier years as a reporter brought him to Essex to cover the Parliamentary election of 1835, the election in the south being held in the first few days of January and covering Chelmsford, Epping, Billericay, Maldon, Romford and Rochford.

The two Tory candidates were returned with little fuss and solid majorities: Mr Dare gained a 130 votes over Mr Bramston who himself gained a handsome 2,117. To celebrate, a dinner was held at the Black Boy, Chelmsford, with the honourable J. J. Strutt chairing the proceedings.

Whether Dickens attended the dinner we do not know. But Dickens had made the Black Boy Inn his headquarters not only for his coverage of the southern elections but also while he reported on the northern election held at Braintree on 10 January. Here too the Tories were victorious, namely Sir John Tyson Tyrell, who represented the farming community, and the right Honourable Alexander Baring who, disliked by some, was derided for his apparent interest in Essex when he did not appear to own a single inch of the county.

Dickens tells us that

> [I] drove myself to Braintree in a gig [one-horse carriage] tooling [contemporary word for driving] in and out of the banners, drums, conservative emblems, horsemen, go-carts with which every little green was filled.

It must have seemed exciting to a young man such as Dickens, as he continued,

> Every time the horse heard a drum he bounced into the hedge on the left side and every time I got him out of that he bounded into the hedge on the right. With the trifling exception of breaking my whip I flatter myself that I did the whole thing in something like style. The hustings was formed of wagons on the Fairfield and the election was decided quietly by a show of hands. Tyrell and Baring were elected. There followed a dinner at the 'White Hart' with upwards of four hundred conservatives. Again the Tories had won a decisive victory.

This fleeting sense of elation, however, did nothing to endear Essex as a county to Dickens. He was in fact quite scathing of his stay at the Black Boy, which, up until its demolition in 1857, was said to have belonged to the De Veres, who used it as a halting place on their journeys to and from London.

Dickens, used to the hustle and bustle of London, found it incredulous that a town the size of Chelmsford was literally 'closed' over the weekend he was there;

> I can't get an 'Athenaeum' or 'Literary gazette' no not even a penny magazine – and here I on a wet Sunday looking out of a large window at the rain as it falls in the puddles on the opposite; wondering when it will be dinnertime and cursing my folly in not having put no books in my portmanteau! The

only book I have seen is *Field Exercises and Evolution Of The Army* ... I've read it so many times I'm sure I could drill a hundred recruits from memory.

There was, he said, nothing to look at in Chelmsford save 'two immense prisons large enough to hold all the inhabitants of the county. Whom they can have built it for I can't imagine.'

Chelmsford, he reported, was to him the 'dullest and most stupid spot on the face of the earth!'

To be fair, he was not in the best of humours when he had arrived. That could well have been due to the fact that his life so far had been far from inspiring. In 1834, when he covered the election, Dickens was a young man of twenty-two and living in poor lodgings in Cecil Street, off the Strand in London. He could well have taken better rooms had he not chosen to be near his place of work, the *Morning Chronicle*, and recently had not had to pay out a sum of money to get his father out of trouble. John Dickens often 'borrowed' money that he inevitably could not repay and it often fell to Charles to support his mother and family. His salary, he commented in a letter to a friend, was 'mortgaged for weeks to come'.

It was in the grip of such dispirited feelings that he found himself assigned to cover the Chelmsford election. Perhaps not knowing how he would find the place he also remarked, 'It is a joy to get out of London.'

Chigwell, on the other hand, fared better. Dickens was very taken with the village, unable to contain his delight at how it pleased him in a letter to a friend: 'Chigwell, my dear fellow, is the greatest place in the world. Name your day for going. Such a delicious old inn opposite the churchyard – such a lovely ride – such beautiful forest scenery – such an out-of-the-way place – such a sexton. I say again name your day.'

Dickens's novel *Barnaby Rudge* benefited from such inspiration. Dickens both started and finished the novel in the town, John Willet and his 'Maypole' bearing more than a slight resemblance to Chigwell's own Kings Head and its proprietor. Words such as 'picturesque' and descriptions of 'the peaceful cottages clustered around' litter the pages, showing the author's obvious delight at the place.

But Dickens took the dark as well as the light from this, his 'undecided' county. Research for *Great Expectations* saw the author charter a steamer from Blackwall to Southend in May 1861, and subsequently our desolate coast, brooding low clouds, mists and salt marshes became the backdrop to the intense encounter between young Pip and the convict Magwitch. Some say they even recognise the Old Ship at Fobbing as an inn and the 'little, squat shoal lighthouse on open piles, crippled on the mud on stilts and crutches' as the lighthouse out on Mucking Flats.

10

SMUGGLERS

Of the prisoners confined in the Essex County Gaol, this day 16th April,
1832, nineteen are smugglers....

Essex Standard & Colchester County Advertiser

There is little romance in smuggling. Stylised notions of moonlit nights, secret tunnels and ponies with muffled hooves are the product of enchanting works of poetry and prose. Conducted on immense scale all over the country from the 1700s to the 1830s, the real thing was more akin to terrorism and treason. Intimidation on a vast scale was often coupled with vicious and bloody murder.

In 1661 a royal proclamation decried the work of 'smuckellors' branding them as 'leud people' who had seldom been heard of before the 'disordered times' of the English Civil War, and who 'make it their trade to steal and defraud his majesty's government'. To 'Smuckle', in early English, was to 'hide', or denoted a hiding place. Before that it was 'Smukkeln' in Low German.

A document of the late thirteenth century cites Henry Arderne as the first recorded smuggler, a London wool merchant of note who traded out of his ship *Fynch* of Colchester. Interestingly, one of the earliest customs officers was poet Geoffrey Chaucer. He once received £71 as his share of the proceeds of a wool sale forfeited by a wool merchant convicted of non-payment of duty. To prove just how lucrative the whole smuggling business could be this was to be weighed against his usual annual salary of only £16 13s 4d.

Smuggling began to impact England's revenue in the Tudor era, as expansion in trade saw opportunities open up for merchants and an increase in illegal activity. In 1536 Henry VIII's Exchequer sent investigators nationwide, but especially into Essex, increasing customs men at harbours and creeks regularly until 1586. Between 1688 and the end of the seventeenth century smuggling was getting easier on a practical level. With the introduction of fore and aft rigging on sailing vessels it was now possible to sail into any creek, negotiate tides, shallows and sandbanks and harness any wind that had been off limits to previous square-rigged vessels. In some cases vessels were specially constructed for smuggling, swift and maneuverable in shallow waters. But it was to be the eighteenth and nineteenth centuries when Essex smuggling would come into its own, with illegal contraband landed in secrecy, cloaked in an Essex mist as far upstream as tides would allow.

It was perilous. Sometimes smugglers found themselves grounded in low-lying channels, but at least it prevented detection by the authorities. The strikingly named Upsher Alefounder, a young Brightlingsea tide surveyor, was just one of a myriad of excise officers to be avoided in 1722, of whom riding officers, tide surveyors, land surveyors, tide waiters, and waiters and searchers were but a few. Smuggling thrived on the lawlessness that was the signature of eighteenth- and early nineteenth-century Essex – that, plus malaria, also known as marsh-ague. This in effect left the marshlands devoid of any figures of authority. Church livings were left vacant and the gentry, often magistrates, preferring not to live in their coastal estates, left the fine farmhouses to be occupied by bailiffs and even farm workers themselves.

Essex had everything for the smuggler. Holland was a short sea passage away and there was already established trade with the coastal towns of Harwich, Colchester and Maldon. The forests of Epping and Hainault were perfect to store smuggled goods while in transit, and in 1807 both forests were described as 'haunts of the most profligate and lawless men.' The heaths of Tolleshunt Knights, Tiptree and Daws Heath close to Leigh were rendezvous for illegal auctions with secret buyers for spirits, wine, tobacco and silk, and the indigenous populations of gypsies and squatters, along with gangs from London, would assist in distributing contraband in the markets of London or Colchester. Smugglers had become so audacious in 1748 that they thought nothing of breaking into Colchester Gaol to free their comrades from under the Excise's nose.

'HARDAPPLE', DOWSETT & WISEMAN

Smuggling may have been the wrong way of life, but for those in villages and hamlets up and down the coast of Essex it was the *only* way of life. Pagglesham was a case in point and it is recorded that despite its tiny size it had the most customs records of any other Essex Parish. According to documents dated 1780 there were no less than '50 Pagglesham men involved in running large quantities of smuggled 'Geneva". As there were only thirty-five families living in the village at the time it appears that almost everyone was involved! William Blyth, immortalised on the village sign, was no doubt one of them.

Blyth has a reputation for having been a ferocious man, his nickname 'Hardapple' suggesting he was a strong drinker who often ate the glasses he

Pagglesham Village Sign, which celebrates
the smuggler William Blyth. (Bob Bowman)

drank from. He is also reputed to have fought a bull and won; wrapped groceries
in the pages of the parish records he kept as churchwarden and enjoyed cricket.
He appeared in documents dated from 1784 to 1796 as both 'oyster dredger
man' and 'mariner'. Both were the perfect cover for his smuggling activities, and
he was known to have owned six vessels from the *Leigh Roads* to the *Hope*.

Once when he was captured, and his illegal goods were transferred to a revenue
cutter, he engaged his captors in conversation and brandy and patiently drank
them all senseless. He then transferred all his smuggled goods back to his own
boat and made his escape, none the worse for wear. Another tale has him aboard a
grounded cutter in chains with the captain compelled to ask for his help in getting
afloat. Blyth, replying that 'I may as well be drowned as hanged', obliged.

Like other Pagglesham smugglers Blyth made so many trips across the
channel and was so well known that he and his companions almost operated a
ferry service from Essex to France. Once landed, smuggled goods were hidden
in the most unlikely places; the vestry of St Peter's church, three hollowed out
elms at Pound Pond near East Hall where £200 of silk could be hidden at any
one time, and of course, down among the oyster beds.

As was usual for small isolated villages families were joined by marriage and
ultimately close smuggling partnerships were forged. In 1783, the Dowsett
family, namely William and John, plus James Wiseman, all related by marriage,
were known to the Customs Service as 'respectable oyster traders'. They were

also known to own between them two smuggling cutters and another small vessel. Emberson, a brother-in-law of the Dowsetts, was also known to be in possession of a small boat, crewed by four to five men, but it was the Dowsetts themselves who were the best-known smuggling family on the Crouch, the notorious William Dowsett having the reputation of being untouchable.

William's brother, John Dowsett, operated *Big Jane*, which carried six brass 6-pounders and had regular run-ins with Revenue cutters, one being in 1780, which took place after an eleven-hour chase. The Dowsetts were so well known that they were often used by locals to travel from France to England, but William's run of luck ended in 1778 when the Revenue cutter *Bee* chased the 40-ton cutter *Neptune* he was commanding off Foulness and ran him aground under fire. The Revenue's haul from the *Neptune* consisted of 391 half ankers (each four gallons) of spirits, two wholes of brandy, rum and geneva, 8 cwt tea and 3 cwt coffee. Two smugglers had died in the skirmish, with three wounded, and when the case came to court in Harwich, five more smugglers aboard were 'impressed' into the Navy.

Not to be discouraged, Dowsett was soon running another 40-ton cutter, *Waggon*, but was brought down again by the Revenue after only three weeks. The loss of two vessels in so short a time was a serious setback for Dowsett and his superiority over the River Crouch and beyond suffered. But he did not disappear completely, as in 1783 he still had two vessels, namely the *Hazard* and the *Lark*.

DANIEL LONDON

Daniel London was a Tollesbury smuggler, and an accidental one at that. In a time when Revenue men were overworked and smugglers were becoming cavalier about their activities, it was only a matter of time before dishonest goods fell into honest hands. This was the case in 1819 when London found himself neither on the side of right nor wrong but in equal trouble with both of them.

It was standard smuggling practice to simply throw contraband overboard if there was a likelihood of capture by the Excise, with the intention of reclaiming it later when the coast was, literally, clear. With the smugglers' superior knowledge of creeks and inlets, they were sure casks of brandy and tobacco would simply sink and remain unnoticed until they were picked up. This worked well, but occasionally hidden goods were found by honest folk and given to the authorities.

Daniel London found such a haul when he was honestly dredging for shellfish in Tollsbury's Old Hall Creek. A large number of waterproof barrels came up in his nets and after spending hours heaving them aboard his boat he took all 152 tubs next morning to the Maldon Custom House. Unfortunately there had been 163 barrels temporarily abandoned by the smugglers, which meant that London had forgotten to declare a further eleven barrels that he deliberately left behind in Mill Creek.

On his return from Maldon, a small party of smugglers was waiting for him and they demanded to know where their property was, even offering half of the goods worth once he had given them over. Daniel foolishly declined and had to outrun the men who were about to lynch him. Soon after, the Maldon excise officer found him and his son frightened for their lives in their house, and Daniel confessed to having held back eleven tubs of illegal spirits, hoping the man would reward him for his honesty and save him from the baying mob. As it was, London was accused of smuggling and found himself committed to Chelmsford Gaol. He was foolish to think he would be treated fairly once there and set free. Instead he was assaulted by his fellow prisoners and he also lost possession of his boat, the *George and Anne*.

It is a complicated tale played out in the letters and petitions London wrote to the authorities stressing his innocence of any real crime. But it was to no avail. The authorities picked up on the fact he had a previous conviction for a similar offence and had convinced themselves he was in league with the smugglers. Perhaps his time in prison served a purpose, as if he had been released he would have just as quickly fallen foul of the smugglers.

'COLCHESTER JACK' (1705–1746)

He was very unwilling to be hang'd, saying, that he was in hopes the wound he had gave himself would have prevented it, as the knife had lain half an hour in his breast before it was discover'd. He bled inwardly and his body was much swelled after he was dead.

Newspaper report, Friday 6 September 1746

The lives of most smugglers are shrouded in secrecy but 'Colchester Jack', real name John Skinner, is unique for the fact that his life was more than adequately documented, written down as it was in a twenty-four-page pamphlet, printed for J. Thompson, 'near the seffions- houfe in the Old-Baily' and could be easily obtained for 3*d* 'at the pamphlet fhops [*sic*] and of the news fellers, 1746'. It is a cautionary tale highlighting how ultimately smuggling and murder make comfortable bedfellows. This John Skinner discovered to his detriment, when in 1744, after shooting his manservant in a quarrel over goods, he was caught and hanged.

John was originally an educated Essex boy from a 'good and credible' family and, when of age, his parents apprenticed him to an 'oilman' and 'dry-salter' near St Andrew's church in Holborn, London. Indulged as a youth, he took the liberties all young men take while growing from boys to men, but successfully served his apprenticeship, his parents then setting him up with his own business in a 'neat and well furnished' shop near Aldgate.

John's business began to flourish and soon after, his thoughts turned to the need of a wife to share it with. He found one in his home county of Essex, a very pretty young lady by all accounts, with the small added bonus of a fortune of £5,000.

All was well for a time, but soon realising he was in possession of his wife's money he began to indulge himself in the seedier side of life, namely gambling and womanising. The pamphlet written of his last days describes him as 'launching out into all manner of Debauchery particularly gaming and whoring', reporting that 'he has been at a Bawdy House for ten days successively and spent sixty or seventy pounds, when he should have been at home minding his business'. Ignoring his wife, he took to riding hard and hunting for days in the company of dubious gentry until he acquired the name of 'Squire Skinner'. In the absence of their indolent master, his servants stole from him, and had little respect for his powerless wife. In 1736 he found himself bankrupt, the news of the disgrace of 'John Skinner, of Leadenhall-Street, London, oylman' reported in the London newspapers, and calling all creditors to meet at Old Tom's Coffee House to petition for recovery of what was owed them.

As sobering as this may have been for some, Skinner embraced the chance to leave behind an old life and embrace a new, namely that of smuggling out of the King's Head Inn at Rumford (Romford) before he finally settled in Colchester. But just as Skinner had found a way to keep his head above water his wife, now deserted, sank fast, 'reduc'd to such extremity that she was obliged to go into the Parish workhouse', and though Skinner could well have afforded to help her he 'never sent to her in her greatest necessity one shilling'.

It was not long before Skinner gained the reputation of being 'as great a smuggler as any in the county of Essex', and as his fame grew it became necessary to disguise his new-found way of life. Setting himself up as a respectable farmer, Skinner rented two farms, at Old Heath in the parish of St Giles, Colchester, locally known as the Tan Office and Cox's farm. Here contraband was stored and deals struck, until one day his servant and partner in crime removed some goods they had smuggled together without Skinner's knowledge, causing Skinner to fly into a rage, seek out the man and murder him.

Caught and imprisoned in Chelmsford Gaol, Skinner rested his defence on the fact that his servant Daniel Brett had been attempting to rob him, but it did not convince the prosecution who were taking Skinner's disreputable character as a whole into consideration. The witnesses who came to make statements were altogether quite damning of Skinner. John Rallett, a tailor, said that he had been at Skinner's house the day of the murder to discuss business and while there Elizabeth, Skinner's housekeeper, told Skinner that his servant Daniel Brett was coming to take away some goods. Rallett then said Skinner had flown into 'a violent passion at what she had informed him and bid him fetch his powder-horn for I will shoot him dead as a carrion crow'. Rallett then said Skinner loaded his carbine, and went out with the words, 'Now for conquest, Liberty or death.' Rallett testified that he had heard the next day that Daniel Brett had indeed been shot only hours after he himself had left Skinner's house.

Skinner was proved to have sought out his servant with 'premeditated malice' and, despite his paying several witnesses to vouch for him being a 'peaceable man', was condemned to death, his execution set for 29 April 1746. To his credit he behaved with modest and decency in court, hiding a genuine horror at his sentence, and once returned to prison told his jailers that they need not 'look so sharp after me for I do not want to run away'. While in Chelmsford Gaol he hoped for a reprieve and wrote to those that would listen of the distress of 'laying in irons' when it was common knowledge of how genteelly he had lived. He also wrote to his fellow smugglers advising them not to trust their servants with secrets, especially to keep them ignorant as to where their goods were kept, and, as if to condone his own smuggling against that of others, commented ironically that the king lost more duties annually by lace smugglers than all the smugglers in the kingdom and he was sure more French lace was annually worn in the three kingdoms than paid duty in ten years.

In a last attempt to avoid what he thought would be a shameful and humiliating death, Skinner made a vain attempt to cheat the gallows and stabbed himself on the morning of his execution, being found after half an hour by a terrified turnkey. A surgeon was summoned, who discovered that he had tried to take his own life with such force that the small knife he had used was lodged inside his belly, 'handle and all'. Consequently the surgeon had great difficulty removing it and sewing up his wound.

Unfortunately, his attempted suicide made no difference. Supported by two men, he was led to church to hear prayers, and then, too weak to speak, made no protest as the executioner carried out the sentence. After hanging for the usual time, Skinner's body was cut down and carried to Colchester, where it was decently buried.

PHILIP JOHN SAINTY (1754–1844)

It seems strange to call Philip Sainty a smuggler when he was lauded as one of the chief boat- and yacht-builders in the late eighteenth and the early nineteenth centuries. He had, though, been known to have said that there was 'not enough money in boatbuilding for bread and cheese', and so, possibly to supplement his income, he dabbled in illegal trade.

Philip John Sainty was born in January 1754 in Wivenhoe, and died on 21 January 1844 after reaching the venerable age of ninety. He married Abigale Wiley on 20 October 1776 in All Saints, Brightlingsea, by whom he had five sons. He also married Amelia Moseley on 5 May 1796 (when he was forty-two), by whom he had four sons and three daughters. He then went on to marry Elizabeth Pullen in May 1821 (when he was sixty-seven) in London at St Dunstan's church, Stepney. By Elizabeth he had three sons and three daughters. To marry frequently in a time when life was short and hard was not unusual, but it was rumoured that he was married to each of these women at the same time.

Proof against bigamy may well lay in a Brightlingsea burial record, which records that 'Abigale Wiley' was buried on Christmas Eve 1792, four years before Sainty married for a second time. Weight is added to this by the fact that a Nathaniel Wiley was buried the following year and, as either Abigale's brother or father had been a witness at the couple's wedding in 1776. Why though this woman would have been buried under her maiden name is certainly food for thought.

Sainty's boatbuilding success enabled him, on 21 January 1802, to take on an apprentice by the name of Thomas Wyatt, who was himself labeled 'shipwright' in the indenture document. Working out of a yard upstream of Wivenhoe Quay, between them they produced both fishing smacks and luggers, plus the faster cutters that were beginning to be favoured by the growing Customs Service. His knowledge of how to build fast yachts did not, however, go unnoticed and soon attracted the attention of men of wealth who wished to dabble in the new sport of racing under sail, one such man being Henry William Paget, the Marquis of Anglesey.

As well as building boats, Sainty also used them regularly to ply an illegal trade with Holland. Sainty sailed in boats with false sides and double hulls, only to destroy them on his return to Wivenhoe to conceal evidence, though to satisfy his superstitious nature he always used the copper nails from the burned boat in the construction of the next. At first, this appears wanton destruction on the part of a master boatbuilder, but it simultaneously put Sainty out of the reach of the Revenue men and enabled him to omit from the next vessel to be built any faults he may have encountered in the last.

It was during this time that Sainty made a trip to Holland in the *Ruswarp* with his son, also John Sainty, and brother-in-law, John Pullen, that proved 'inconvenient'. While there he encountered a smuggler, a whip maker from Colchester by the name of Brown, who had made the sea journey carrying a great number of 'counterfeit guineas' (coins) and who had been detected and detained there. It appears Sainty persuaded the authorities to release Brown and he brought the man back to Essex. It was at this point, perhaps in order to save his own skin, that Brown informed on Sainty and his small crew, telling the Revenue exactly where Sainty's smuggled goods were to be found. Brown

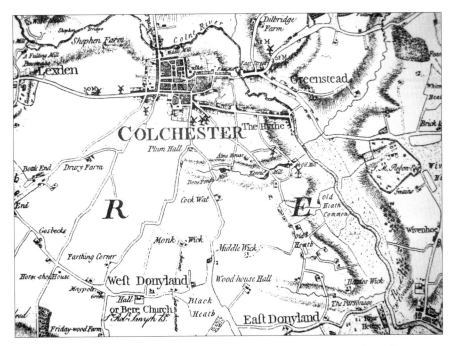

Old Heath, an area just outside Colchester where Philip Sainty rented two farms near to the Hythe to continue smuggling after leaving Romford.

received a lot of money for his information, and went on to settle in Colchester, buying a public house in Barrack Street. Sainty and his companions, meanwhile, were sent to Chelmsford Gaol, it was stated at the time, 'for life'.

It is not known how long Sainty was in gaol for before he was sought out by the Marquis of Anglesey himself, but it was long enough for him to have run up a significant debt with his jailer, something the marquis gladly paid in order to get Sainty released. Keen to indulge his passion for yachting, and recently returned from the war as Wellington's second in command at Waterloo, the marquis decided he wanted a fast ship to rival that of the Duke of Norfolk in a coming race, and, not satisfied with examples from the shipyards at Cowes or Poole, declared he would have none other than Sainty build him one. Finding Sainty detained at King George's pleasure in Chelmsford, the marquis embarked upon urgent negotiations for his release with the Prince of Wales himself after announcing that 'by God,' if Sainty 'were in hell, he would have him out!'

Sainty was indeed 'got out', but not after he had secured his own son's release by allowing him to answer to the name on the 'pardon' document as his name was the same as his own. He also requested his brother-in-law's freedom by saying that in a boat-building venture he could not do without him. When Phillip John Sainty did finally enter the employ of his benefactor, the marquis had paid the jailer and considerable fines to the Crown on Sainty's behalf and now found himself seriously out of pocket. In return, just a mile out from Colchester and drawing the curiosity of shipbuilders from all parts to see its progress, Sainty built him the *Pearl*.

David Starling, in his book *Nice-Looking Essex Girls Afloat* (2011) describes Sainty's *Pearl* as 'indeed a pearl among ships – Clinker built below the wales and carvel above, 92 feet from her stern to end of her bowsprit and measuring 127.5 tons, the pearl was a giant among the yachts of her time. In an era of straight stems and bluff bows she had a fine entry, a long run and a delicately proportioned counter. She was fast.' A retrospective article in the *Essex Standard* dated 1879 and called 'Yachting and the Colne' describes the *Pearl*'s ballast to have been supplied by a Mr Dorrell and being 'all cast iron balls and all behind the mast' for improved speed. It also records that the *Pearl* was launched in 1819 and registered with Lloyds in 1820.

Such was the *Pearl*'s success that the grateful marquis settled a handsome annuity of £100 on Sainty with the proviso that he refrain from building boats for anyone else. It was an unworkable agreement, as by 1831, Sainty had accepted offers from other patrons, building the cutters *Gypsy*, *Gazelle*, *Corsair* and *Ruby*, the *Swallow* and *Arundel* for the Duke of Norfolk plus the *Flower of Yarrow* for the Duke of Buccleuch. Sainty had also, since 1825, taken advantage of Wivenhoe becoming a salvage centre and so cashed in on building salvaging smacks. That plus the continued patronage of the marquis meant Philip John Sainty became an extremely successful man.

Unfortunately in 1833/4 his luck took a downward turn and the *Essex Standard* of Saturday 19 and 26 July 1834 carried notification of Philip Sainty's bankruptcy. It advertised a valuable dwelling house and shipyard to be sold at auction on 8 August at noon at the Rose & Crown, Wivenhoe. This was to be no small sale as Sainty had become a man of means, either by fair means or foul, and he was to lose spacious workshops, lofts, a boathouse, a paintshop, various sheds situated in Wivenhoe plus 'three good freehold substantial white-brick and sash fronted tenements in Bath Street'. The sale also advertised 'a good fast-sailing fishing boat called the *Gypsy*, copper fastened – burthen 18 tons of the port of Colchester, well found in stores and fishing gear' plus the hull of the schooner, *Unity*, 'lately rebuilt berthen 77 tons'.

Perhaps the indignity of bankruptcy was lost on Sainty, as it appears that he had been made bankrupt before, aged forty-six, in 1800, as reported in the *Ipswich Journal*. Sainty was eighty years old in 1834, and six years later in 1841 the first national census lists him as living in Wivenhoe Highstreet aged eighty-six. Sainty died aged ninety in 1844. He predeceased his young wife by almost forty years.

11

REVENUE MEN

Smugglers have grown to such a degree of insolence as to go in armed
gangs with swords and pistols even to the number of 40–50 ... the number
of Customs House officers who have been abused and wounded since
Xmas 1723 being no less than 250, besides 6 others actually murdered in
execution of their duty.

Parliamentary Enquiry Report of 1736

The job of the Revenue men was hard, thankless and moreover dangerous. For decades they were fighting a losing battle, a battle fought on both land and sea. Suspicious carriages and wagons were routinely checked by land carriage officers who also had the authority to search stagecoaches and cellars. Riding officers patrolled the shorelines and, inshore, boatmen were placed along the coast. Further inland, excise officers were stationed. These revenue officers could request help from mounted infantrymen or dragoons and should the need arise could call on local militia. At sea, revenue cutters were helped grudgingly by Naval warships, though evidence points to it often being the smaller, more nimble cutters that helped out the Royal Navy.

For the best part of 130 years there was no stretch of English coastline free of smugglers. Illegal goods flooded England; in the south from France, in the east from Holland (where Dutch ships also waited out in the deep water of the North Sea selling a variety of goods to passing vessels) and up towards the north from Denmark. The beleaguered revenue forces employed maximum effort for little return. Essex as a county was so bound up in smuggling that if smugglers were caught it was the devil's own job to get a prosecution. In 1736 a report informed the authorities that 'in some parts of the maritime counties the whole population is so generally engaged in smuggling that it is impossible to find jury that will upon trial do justice to an officer of the revenue in any case whatsoever'. More often than not it was the revenue officers who were indicted, not for corruption, but for causing injury and sometimes death during an act of self-defence against brutal and desperate smugglers.

Acts of violence against those trying to enforce the law, even in the early days of the smuggling epidemic, were common. In 1686 John Sewell, an inn holder, Stephan Watson, a labourer, and Richard Cooke, a weaver, all of Halstead, were indicted in the Sessions Rolls for 'the threatening to kill Mr Thomas Brooke, one of his majesties officers of the Excice [sic] or that he would do him harm by beating him or wounding him'. Later in 1692 William Cooch, Matthew Lambe and James Hunwick, all of Burnham, were called before magistrates to answer for assaulting Mr Wheatly Brabant and Edward Chillcott, gent., in the execution of their duties. As the Customs Office became a department of State, officers were appointed to sit on the board, with Sir Benjamin Mildmay of Moulsham, Chelmsford serving as Commissioner of Excise between 1720 and 1728. At Sunken Island, close to Salcott and Virley, a particularly grisly discovery was made when a Customs boat was discovered floating aimlessly with twenty-two corpses aboard, their throats having been cut. The men were buried together beneath their upturned boat in the local graveyard.

With supply and demand becoming the only masters men on both sides of the law were prepared to obey, co-operation between the services was not always convivial. An indictment heard before Essex Magistrates on 4 August 1713 described how two Excise officers, having information that a parcel of 'foreign brandy' was being hidden in the house of Peter Weston of Wivenhoe, sought the help of innkeeper and parish constable John Turner with the intention of apprehending Weston and recovering the brandy. Turner refused to help, instead assaulting the officers. Turner confessed to the assault, admitting openly that he had deliberately assaulted him, then added that if he had not been restrained by his position of parish constable, he would gladly have 'beaten his brains out'. Weston was arrested for taking the side of the smugglers and jailed a month later in September.

As with any service that has a duty to uphold the law, risk sits cheek by jowl with any perks, which, in the cases of Customs officers, were exemption from serving on juries, attending inquests or becoming parish constables. Later, protection from press gangs was added. But far from being champions of the law, Customs officers and their families often found themselves social outcasts.

The riding officer in particular was always recruited from the area to which he was assigned and so operated in a tangible 'silence' as he went about his business. Generally there was one riding officer for every 10 miles of the English coast, every 4 miles if traffic was really bad. If he did intercept a smuggling operation he was obliged to act, but in essence he was a man alone, with only a pistol and a cutlass against a criminal gang, heavily armed and supported by half the local community.

If caught by the smugglers, riding officers were often subject to violence and even death. In 1713 a riding officer was attacked by gang of villagers soon after he had seized smuggled tea at a farm in Colchester but luckily he was not badly hurt and the tea was successfully recovered by the villagers. Yet at the other end of the scale a riding officer in Ireland had his tongue cut out and his ears cut off. The gory trophies were nailed to the door of the Customs house as a grizzly warning to others not to meddle with smugglers. As changes were made to the Customs Service over the next twenty years, more men volunteered as riding officers, Edward Moseley and his son joining up at Clacton. Preventative officer Hugh D'oyley, who served from 1734 to 1743, is recorded as having a stroke of luck when he uncovered a stash of contraband by accident. It appears that while walking along the beach the ground gave way under his feet, exposing a store of nineteen half-ankers of brandy.

'Geneva', also known as 'Hollands', or gin, was another money-spinner for the smugglers. It was a drink of Dutch origin, originally a spirit flavoured with juniper berries, and in its day was more popular than beer. The seventeenth-century populace took to it so well that a saying has us believe you could get 'drunk for a penny but dead drunk for 2d'. Not only is this notion borne out by Hogarth's famous painting of 'Gin Alley', but records show that farm labourers in Essex were literally dying in the fields from drink. Gin was a very lucrative smugglers' market. In 1750 a smuggler could purchase gin in Holland for 9d a gallon and sell it in England for between 4 and 6 shillings a gallon. Helped by the fact that gin, by the late 1700s, was becoming a respectable middle-class drink, the Dutch even set up distilleries especially for the smuggling trade. In 1801 an affluent Fingringhoe farmer was more than happy to pay over the odds for 8 gallons of seized Geneva for re-sale from the Colchester Custom House.

Smugglers had no qualms about tampering with goods. Tea, a most popular and heavily taxed beverage, was sold off to inns and at fairs, but was not always what it seemed, as to turn a decent profit smugglers often mixed it with sawdust. This was also the case with tobacco and subsequently, since the seventeenth century, all tobacco manufacturers and tobacconists are required to be licensed by law.

Though legislation at first struggled to curb the smuggling epidemic, it did over time make some impression. An Act of 1698 extended a riding officer's powers, allowing the confiscation of smuggled wool up to 15 miles inland of the coast, and by 1717 smugglers who refused to plead guilty to their crimes were liable for transportation. This was strengthened by the wonderfully named 'Hovering Act', which allowed small vessels (under 500 tons) to be seized if found loitering within 6 miles offshore. By 1721 the number of oars allowed to propel a boat was limited to hinder boats conveying contraband ashore, and by 1746, for landing or even attempting to land contraband, a smuggler could be hanged on a gibbet at the scene of the crime. Newspapers such as the *London Gazette* were ordered to print the names of known smugglers, advising them they had only forty days to give themselves up – if they did not, they were convicted in their absence and punishment awaited them on capture.

In 1782 the Act of Oblivion was a pardon for smugglers on a sliding scale, promising that if a smuggler could persuade a number of his comrades to change sides and serve with the armed forces or produce two soldiers for the Army and two sailors for the Navy then he himself would escape prosecution.

One of the most instant and forward-thinking measures to take place was in 1783 when Prime Minister William Pitt the Younger cut duty on tea drastically by 114 per cent to reduce it to just 12 per cent. This took tea off the smugglers' shopping list. But to recoup the lost revenue money, Pitt then introduced the notorious 'window tax'!

WILLIAM LISLE

It was almost impossible to make a good living from being a riding officer. Wages were deliberately low; £60 a year, which was hardly more than those of an agricultural labourer, out of which he was expected to provide himself with a servant and cover the cost of a horse for transport. Such low rewards were designed to encourage extra effort in the tracking down and prosecution of smugglers and if successful there was a bonus of £20 per conviction. This rarely had the desired effect, as once a riding officer apprehended a smuggler it was down to him to pay for the costs of the prosecution.

William Lisle, however, managed to become very comfortable in a supervisory position within the riding officer network. He carried out his duties, namely regularly visiting his officers both during the day and at night, and kept a detailed log of his patrols. He also liaised with the local militia in his area to secure their support should he ever need them and he kept the Colchester Custom House abreast of all activity and action in his area. This generated his basic wage, which was in line with others of his rank at £50 per annum, but it seems as he was able to convince his superiors that as he needed an extra two horses to enable him to ride the 100 miles of coastline he patrolled every week, thus receiving a further £20 in allowances.

In 1734 he received the Customs Board's latest allowance of £5 for every smuggler apprehended, which afterwards rose to £12. Surprisingly, if not suspiciously, Lisle managed to arrest forty smugglers over the next year, inflating his income in excess of £300. 'Head money', it appeared, was a great incentive, but did not line his pockets for long as he still had to pay his expenses, among them a network of informants. One man in Lisle's employ was smuggler Edward Spells, who had spent a few weeks in Chelmsford Gaol and to whom Lisle paid a few shillings a week for any useful information supplied that led to Lisle apprehending yet more smugglers.

Lisle was a successful officer. A man who employed the necessary methods to keep him ahead of his game and ensure the smugglers he sent to Chelmsford Gaol stayed in gaol, his success rate had grown considerably by 1740, ensuring him an income of over £70 per year. But success is a double-edged sword and Lisle was making enemies, enough by 1744 to give rise to reports by the Customs House collector that Lisle had been kidnapped by smugglers. Lisle reappeared unharmed, apparently released on the condition that he did not tell anyone what he had seen or whom he had met. The circumstances of such an early and safe release raised the question as to whether he was in fact working hand in glove with the smugglers for a mutual benefit.

Lisle held his post in the employ of the Colchester Customs Service for twenty years from 1730 to 1750, and possibly died in possession of it at a ripe old age. An overworked institution, the Customs Service often ignored the age of their riding officers and overlooked replacing them, so that men were allowed to keep their posts well into their eighties. It does appear a strange policy, as at such an advanced age it is doubtful they would have been able to chase and apprehend a smuggler even if they had wanted to!

CAPTAIN ROBERT MARTIN (c. 1683–1763)

Like Lisle, Martin was employed by an infant Customs Service, but this time at sea. The son of George Martin and his wife Eleanor, Martin was born in Shelly, Suffolk, but lived most of his life in Essex, marrying Susanna Dennison in 1708 at Great Wigborough. His contribution to the war on smuggling was simple and effective, but as yet untried, and would address the imbalance between the maritime side of the Customs operation, and the land-based. Reticent to confront smugglers at sea because of the cost of maintaining Customs vessels, officers had to wait until contraband had been landed and was in the process of being dispersed before apprehending it. Pioneering an efficient and cost-effective way in which to offer the Customs Service the sail power they needed, Martin was the first to introduce the 'contract' system. As the Custom House maintained twenty sloops at the exorbitant cost of £500 per year (without the provision of firepower), Martin's idea of renting out the boats at two shillings and sixpence per ton (1730), all expenses and repairs the responsibility of the contractor, was certainly very appealing.

Martin himself was the most successful contractor. His family had made money from dealings in the East India Company and by 1729 Martin, his wife, three sons and six daughters lived on the quay at Rowhedge near to where Martin's own boats were berthed. Martin captained three cutters during 1729 to 1731, the first being a 63-tonner, *Walpole,* followed by the *Essex* at 67 tons, which was replaced by the small smack *Wivenhoe.* In the apprehension of seaborne smugglers, Martin and his crew were open to assaults, the results of one such affray costing the Customs Service a surgeon's bill for £5 3s in July 1729.

Despite personal dangers, Martin's rate of capture of illegal goods was consistently high, with the revenue benefiting twice in 1733 in the taking of two smuggling vessels, the *Dolphin* and the *Dennis,* the capture of nine smugglers and a vast quantity of tea. It was not without casualties, however, as Martin himself, and several of his crew, were wounded.

Graham Smith in his book *Smuggling in Essex* chronicles Martin's Customs career in great detail, following his successes with the *Cornelius* bought in 1738, which, though run that year at a cost of well over £200, had returns from the capture of illegal goods of over £600. Martin was deservedly appointed 'Surveyor of Sloops for the East Coast' in 1741, with the added control of all Customs vessels from Newcastle to Dover. While in this post Martin became commander of the *Princess Mary,* a large vessel of 79 tons whose exploits off Beachy Head that year were commented upon in the *Colchester Journal* dated 18 July.

On Sunday night Captain Robert Martin commander of the Princess Mary Sloop in the service of the Customs took a Spanish privateer with 29 men and four swivel guns which he took the day before off Beachy Head after a 2 hour engagement.

The ship was originally an English Cutter of 30 tons called The Jolly Boys and which the Spaniards themselves had taken from smugglers from the Isle of Wight and who instantly made a Privateer of her in order to cruise in the Chanel. On Monday the Spanish prisoners were brought to Colchester guarded by Martin and his men with drawn cutlasses carrying before them the captured Spanish colours. They were all confin'd in Gaol and used with great humanity, the captain is allowed to walk about the town in company with two soldiers. They say they belong to St Sebastian's, which place they left about a month since, were 40 in number and have taken three English vessels and sent them thither their men prisoners; they appear to be abandon'd wretches, ragged and dirty and shew no concern at their confinement. Two of them were wounded in the engagement but proper care having been taken to dress their wounds they are in a fair way of doing well.

Martin continued to be the scourge of smugglers at sea, with a later refurbished and heavier-gunned *Princess Mary*, plus the *Good Intent* and the *Mayflower*, seeing, in 1753/4, revenue secured by the seizure of illegal goods amounting to over £1,000 from the *Princess Mary* alone.

The vigilance with which Martin carried out his duties in the eighteenth century would be capitalised upon in the nineteenth by one Richard Gowland, commander of the cutter named, perhaps in tribute, *Vigilant*. Patrolling the shipping lanes closer to the Kent coast than those of Essex, he rarely failed to land a sizable haul and in 1847 he relieved the Maldon vessel *Hannah* of 6,043 lbs of illegal tobacco, and 530 lbs of snuff, repeated a year later when he captured from another Maldon vessel, *Charlotte*, 14,402 lbs of the same.

The 'contract' system Martin had established to such good effect was abolished in 1788, but not before Martin had made his fortune and around 1755 purchased the Manor of Great Holland, a substantial property near Frinton.

12

THE LORDS RICH

SIR RICHARD RICH, 1ST BARON RICH (1496/7–1567)

A man of whom nobody has ever spoken a good word.

Lord Dacre, historian

In Tudor England, a knowledge of the law was a sure way to get ahead in life and Richard Rich, the first Lord Rich (and Baron of Leeze), by making sure he knew every twist and turn of the judicial system, ensured he kept his head when most of those around him were losing theirs. An Essex man by virtue of acquiring much of the county by whatever means available, he became extremely 'well-heeled' if not well-loved. A man who could easily sacrifice his integrity, he went on to successfully serve all but one Tudor monarch. An expert opportunist, Rich went about achieving his goals by changing his politics and religion almost as often as Henry VIII changed his wives.

Rich was born around 1496/7 not in London but in Basingstoke, Hampshire, the son of John Rich and his wife, Agnes. He came to London as a child, perhaps living in the house in Islington that his father owned, and which he left his son when he died in 1509. With an eye to self-improvement Rich studied law, sought the patronage of influential men such as Thomas Audley, knight of the shire for Essex, and entered the Middle Temple. It was here that he first encountered Sir Thomas More, with whom he became acquainted. Unfortunately for More, Rich was to be the death of him, literally. In More's disputes of conscience with King Henry VIII during the early 1530s, Rich, now Solicitor General, saw further opportunities for advancement in the wake of Thomas More's impending demise. It was Rich who helped compile the evidence against one of the most honest men in Christendom.

After sixteen months and two difficult sessions of Parliament, More was brought to court and charged with four counts of treason; refusal to accept the king's supremacy over the Church in England; writing treasonous letters; seditiously stirring up the populace and 'maliciously, traitorously, and diabolically' denying Parliament's power to declare the king head of the Church in England. In the face of fifteen judges and twelve jurors More successfully defended himself against the first three, but it was the fourth that hinged on a single conversation between Rich and More, and which was one man's word against the other. In answer to Rich's libelous testimony More replied, 'In good faith, Master Rich, I am sorrier for your perjury than for my own peril.' As if to finally sum up Rich's duplicitous character, More then pressed home Rich's lack of credibility as a witness, and as a man, with this damning observation:

> And you shall understand that neither I nor any other man to my knowledge ever took you to be a man of credit in any matter of importance that I or any other would at any time deign to communicate with you. And I, as you know, for no small while have been acquainted with you and your conversation. I have known you from your youth since we have dwelled in one parish together. There, as you yourself can tell (I am sorry you compel me to say so), you were esteemed to be very light of tongue, a great dicer, and of no commendable fame.

Thomas More, Henry VIII's former friend and Lord Chancellor, was beheaded at the Tower of London, on 6 July 1535. Essentially now Henry VIII's right-hand man, Rich was strategically placed to oversee the Dissolution of the Monasteries, a move that would see His Majesty triumph over Catholicism, gather in the spoils, and allow Rich to substantially feather his own nest. He became Chancellor of the Court of Augmentations, a body designed to control the land and finances formerly held by the Catholic Church, and starting in 1536 all religious houses with an annual income of less than £200 per year were dissolved. By 1540, they had all gone, their incomes reverting to the Crown, with Waltham Abbey in Essex being the last to close. Though Henry allowed some monastic buildings to remain, on the proviso they were re-founded under the guardianship of a dean and chapter as opposed to monks and priors, most were disposed of by grant or purchase, and found their way into the hands of the wealthy.

Early on, in 1536, Leeze (Leighs) Priory, which Rich enlarged and made his home, came to Rich as a gift from the king, but this was not how almost 100 other Essex manors came his way. It was said of Rich that when the abbeys passed through his hands many of them 'stuck to his fingers', in fact several times Rich was called to clear himself of accusations of corruption, and defrauding the Crown. Interestingly, Rich also acquired, only to destroy, the lands and holdings of the Priory of St Bartholomew-the-Great in Smithfield.

He did, however, build the Tudor gatehouse that fronts what is left of the church and survives to this day.

Even before the suppression of the monasteries and his growing tally of Essex properties, Rich was active in the county. As early as 1528, he was part of the commission of the peace for Essex and Hertfordshire and, with the sponsorship of Thomas Audley, was returned for the Borough of Colchester in the Parliament of 1529, where Audley was Speaker. In 1530 he served on the Colchester Gaol delivery commission, and on 30 September 1532 he was chosen as Recorder of Colchester. In later years he was an active Justice of the Peace, his name along with those of other high-ranking Essex gentlemen; Maxey, Mildmay, Maynard and Sir Anthony Cook of Gidea Hall, appearing on county sessions documents as they settled disputes and dispensed justice, as seen in 1561 when one Robert Wryght of Debden, 'burglariously' broke into the house of John Brown, and stole the considerable sum of £56.

Rich's religious beliefs remained nominally Roman Catholic, but he subscribed to Henry VIII's Protestant reforms, and later those of his son Edward VI, under whose reign he was created a baron. It was Rich who, in 1551, on the orders of Henry VIII, rode to the Princess Mary at Copped Hall to forbid Mass in her household. He also supported the plot to settle the crown on the head of Lady Jane Grey, which was devised to prevent Catholicism returning should Henry's daughter Mary succeed the throne. The honour of Rayleigh came his way soon after as the price of his support. Perhaps not surprisingly, when the nine-day queen was beheaded and Mary rode triumphantly into London to begin a five-year reign and persecution of all Protestants, Rich re-embraced his old religion.

In 1553, as a privy councilor, he set about organising the queen's coronation, and as a Justice of the Peace in Essex he was at the forefront of Mary's Catholic backlash. He assisted Bishop Bonner in the burning of heretics and, as requested in a letter dated 18 March 1554, was present at the executions 'of such obstinate persons about to be sent down for burning in divers parts of the county of Essex'. He was also present on 3 June 1555, 'at Colchester, Manytree [Manningtree] and Hardwicke at such tyme as the offenders that are already condemned for heresie shalbe there executed'. Rich was also a participant in the only recorded torture of a gentlewoman, Anne Askew, at the Tower of London in June 1546. Before her execution she is known to have said of them, 'The Lord Chancellor and Master Rich took pains to rack me with their own hands, till I was nearly dead.'

Rich and his wife entertained Mary on her progress to the capital early in August 1553, but despite his cordial dealings with the queen, once she had realised how he had greatly profited from the dissolution of 'her' religious houses, forced him to restore some of the buildings and their lands. Once Elizabeth I became queen he was able to buy these properties back.

With the accession of the young Queen Elizabeth in 1558, Rich once more subscribed to Protestantism and although by now almost retired from court, was appointed to accompany Elizabeth upon her triumph into London. He never became one of the new queen's official privy councilors, but she retained his services, he being one of those who, early in her reign, spoke to her on the subject of her marriage and the succession. Rich himself had married Elizabeth Jenks before 1536 and when she died in 1558 at their London residence they had been together for at least thirty years and produced sixteen legitimate children, with a further illegitimate son and three daughters fathered by Rich. Elizabeth was buried in St Andrews, Rochford where it is thought he had the church spire erected in her memory.

Rich himself died on 12 June 1567 at Rochford Hall, the property gifted to him by Edward VI, his body then transported in a solemn procession

Richard Rich, 1st Baron Rich, died on 12 June 1567 at Rochford Hall. (Robert Hallmann)

across Essex to Felstead where he was buried on 8 July. At his death, Rich had an income of around £2,000, which was more than other peers, who on average were worth half of that amount. He left a total of sixty-four manors, two-thirds of which were former religious houses bought at favourable rates but which had also seen the Crown enriched to the tune of almost £10,000. In lieu of any outstanding debts, Rich's Will left a further twenty-seven manors plus St Bartholomew's Fair to his executors, for a period of seven years. Rich believed that his estate would be solvent within six years and that the seventh year would be pure profit for his benefactors. Most of his considerable estate was given to his son Robert though Richard, his illegitimate son, was provided for both financially and by a provision in the Will for the executors 'to purchase a female ward for marriage with his base son Richard'. His nine surviving daughters shared his movable goods.

It has been suggested that as Rich got older, his conscience troubled him, the ghosts of those he had wronged throughout his long political career coming back to haunt him. Perhaps that is why his Will also made a £50 provision for the founding of an Almshouse in Rochford for '5 poor men and 1 aged woman', and some years before, during Mary's reign, he founded a chaplaincy with provision for the singing of masses and the ringing of bells in Felsted church.

As a product of the Catholic Church, this was disallowed under Elizabeth, but the monies allocated were allowed to be transferred in 1564 to the foundation of a grammar school at Felsted, for instruction, primarily for children born on the founder's manors, in Latin, Greek and divinity. Was he trying to save his soul? Buy his way back onto the path to heaven?

What we know is that at his death he held twenty-eight 'advowsons' or the right to choose the vicar and therefore the religion of a parish. His choices, it is said, were to have provided the basis for the next two centuries of Puritanism in Essex.

THE RICH LORD RICHES

The dynasty Richard Rich established lasted until well into the eighteenth century, with the barony held by the Earls of Warwick from 1618 until 1759, when all titles became extinct on the death of Edward, the 8th Earl and 10th Baron. Robert Rich, 2nd Baron Rich, married Elizabeth Baldry and it was their son Richard who was to take up the mantle of advanced Protestantism, some say Puritanism, organising unauthorised gatherings and sermons in his father's great rooms at Rochford Hall. He in turn became father to Sir Nathaniel Rich of Stondon Massey who, following a moderate

Puritan path throughout his life, became a colonial adventurer and patron of the establishment of the American colonies.

With the second baron's death the barony passed to his son Robert, who also gained the title of 1st Earl Warwick in 1618 and who married and subsequently divorced the beautiful and independent Penelope Deveraux. Before this divorce, however, seven children had been born to this couple, daughters Lettice, Penelope, Essex and Isabel and two sons, the younger Henry, who became the first Earl of Holland, and then eldest and heir, Robert, 4th Baron Rich and 2nd Earl Warwick.

Distrusted by King and Parliament after twice changing sides during the English Civil War, Henry was executed in 1649. Meanwhile Robert, like his mother, being far too independent to be constrained by government and politics, looked far beyond Essex to satisfy his lust for adventure.

SIR ROBERT RICHE, PURITAN PIRATE (1587–1658)

Though he had all those excellent endowments of body and fortune that give splendour to a glorious court, yet he used it but as his recreation; for his spirit aimed at more public adventure…

Arthur Wilson, *History of the Reign of James I*

As great-grandson of Richard Rich, Sir Robert Riche, the 4th Baron and 2nd Earl of Warwick, was now a rich and titled man and about to become richer. Glad of his high connections but not wishing to sit on his laurels in England, Robert, after marrying in 1605 and producing two children, turned his head toward New England and his hand, in true Elizabethan style, to privateering.

In 1616 the Duke of Savoy granted him several commissions, which, being roving voyages to the East Indies, called for the fitting out of two ships, which would not only afford comfort to those on board but also facilitate the taking of 'valuable prizes'. Later that year Riche sent the ship *Treasurer* to Virginia where, commanded by Captain Elfrith, it plundered Spanish shipping and lined Riche's pockets. But such private enterprise saw him in trouble with the East India Company, plus it split the fledgling Virginia Company into opposing sides, its disagreements over the role of piracy in the colonies leading to a policy overhaul.

Riche's privateering career, however, did not stop. He maintained a small fleet of ships, which in turn continued to maintain his income at a cost to the Spanish. He also contributed into the establishment of the early colonies, especially Virginia on the American mainland, plus the Somers Islands, known

Robert Riche, 4th Baron Riche and 2nd Earl of Warwick, was the great-grandson of
Richard Rich, and was known by some as the Puritan Pirate.

today as Burmuda, named after a ship's captain, Juan de Bermudez, who
was attributed with discovering them. Riche was also a slave owner, with his
ships responsible for bringing 'good stores of neggars' to the islands to fell
the trees and clear great swathes of the interior in order to grow tobacco. His
'Southampton' settlement provided for at least 144 men, women and children
who, as slaves in the early days of Bermuda's development, were more akin
to indentured servants than the poor creatures that would survive the lack

of rights and deprivations of later centuries. The company for the plantation of the Somers Islands (Bermuda), and the Guinea Company, founded by Sir Francis Drake, and which Riche had substantial financial interest in, amalgamated in 1618.

In 1620 Riche gained a seat on the council of the New England Company and was a signatory on the charters awarded to the investors and settlers of the Plymouth colony, who each received 100 acres of land on which to start new lives. Over the next years he had influence in the Massachusetts Bay Company and was closely involved with the founding of Connecticut, the state that was to become the home of many of the Pilgrim Fathers and those who fled England in the Great Migration of the 1630s.

Not always in the Americas, when home in Essex, Riche served Charles I in whatever capacity his conscience would allow, and in 1627 the king, seeing his coffers dangerously empty, granted Riche a privateering commission to help lighten the loads of Spanish galleons. However, as the king's demands conflicted more and more with Riche's deep sense of justice, he became estranged from Court, disagreeing fiercely with the king's policy of arrest without due cause, and the levy of the infamous ship tax for which Riche lost his post as lord lieutenant in 1635.

A staunch Protestant, Riche used his power of advowson (the right to appoint ministers to churches within his jurisdiction), to protect Puritan preachers in all sixteen Essex parishes he had control over. One Essex gentleman declared that Riche was a great patron to 'the pious and religious ministry'. Also as a Protestant, Riche sided with the Parliament in the Civil War; a personal friend of Cromwell, he was later to become related to the regicide when his grandson married Cromwell's daughter Francis.

Riche predeceased his second wife, dying in April 1658 after achieving, in the last decade of his life, the position of Lord High Admiral and Governor-in-Chief of all islands and other plantations subject to the English Crown. Though interred at Holy Cross church, Felsted, close to the school his great-grandfather Richard Rich founded, his heart and no doubt independent soul still roamed the seas and resided at his 'Richeneck' plantation located in Virginia.

With an influence such as his it was not just his plantation that bore his name. Warwick River, Warwick Towne, and Warwick County in Virginia are all believed to be attributed to him, as are Warwick, Rhode Island and Warwick Parish in Bermuda.

13

MEN OF SCIENCE & VISION

WILLIAM GYLBERD (1544–1603)

... for believe me ... these books of yours on the Magnet will avail more for perpetuating the memory of your name than the monument of any great Magnate placed upon your tomb.

Edward Wright, a contemporary mathematician

In the chancel of the church of the Holy Trinity, Colchester, there is a handsome monument to William Gilbert Gylberd (Gilbert), once owner of the beautiful Elizabethan house Tymperleys. Son of Jerome Gilbert and his wife Elizabeth Coggeshall, he died in 1603 and has for over 400 years been hailed as the father of electricity. Born on 24 May 1544, he lived at a time when England had finally turned her back on the medieval, embracing instead a glorious renaissance in trade, prosperity and ideas. A greater understanding of the world was being brought about by innovations in mathematics and astronomy (Galileo), in medicines (William Harvey) and in philosophy (Sir Francis Bacon). The earth, its magnetism and the early recognition of electricity was to be William Gylberd's legacy.

When Elizabeth I was crowned in 1558, William was fourteen. His father was Recorder of Colchester (a minor judge), and with Colchester standing as the twelfth-richest town in England on the back of the wool trade, the Gylberds were a prosperous family in a prosperous town. Education was also expanding at this time and if not tutored at home, Gilbert most probably went to Colchester Grammar School, chartered in 1539 and one of many to be set up or expanded at the time. He went on to St John's College, Cambridge, a relatively new foundation (1511) that contributed to the Tudor expansion of university education. He followed a curriculum reformed by Henry VIII that was less ecclesiastical and scholastic and more humanistic.

Tymperleys, the magnificent Tudor house of William Gylberd (Gilberd), just off the road on a busy main street in Colchester. (Robert Hallmann)

It is documented that from Cambridge University 'he travelled beyond the seas', where 'he had the degree of doctor of physick conferred upon him'. This could well have been at the celebrated University of Padua in the Venetian Republic, where his contemporary William Harvey, who discovered the circulation of the blood, was also educated. What is certain is that 'Dr Gilbert' settled in London around 1573, an obvious destination for an ambitious physician, and rose rapidly in his chosen career with 'great success and applause'.

He was appointed a physician to the Royal Navy, visited Deptford dockyard, met Sir Francis Drake and the circumnavigator Thomas Cavendish, and made contact with expert mathematicians like Edward Wright. These reports of explorers fascinated Gilbert, and provided him with invaluable knowledge that triggered his investigations into the nature of the entire surface of the earth and ultimately electromagnetics. Latterly, as a Fellow of the College of

Physicians, he had gained such a reputation in his field that he was appointed physician to Queen Elizabeth.

A woman known for her strict bookkeeping, Queen Elizabeth was also a scholar, whose curiosity for all sciences saw her uncharacteristically award Gilbert a pension to aid him in his experiments. She also invited him to reside at Court. On the death of Queen Elizabeth, Dr Gilbert was appointed physician to her successor, James I, but he did not occupy that post for long. Plague hit London in 1603, starting in the bear pits and cock pits of Southwark, spreading to its theatres and brothels and eventually claiming the lives of 38,000 Londoners. It is widely thought that Dr William Gilbert was among them.

Gilbert died a bachelor, leaving no heirs, but by his Will he left 'all my bookes in my Librarye, my Globes, and Instrumentes, and my cabinet of myneralles' to the College of Physicians.

His real legacy was his treatise on electric and magnetic science entitled *De magnete, magneticisque corporibus, et de magno magnete tellure* (London, 1600), upon which later knowledge of electricity was based. Gilbert wrote of his studies with static-electricity using the semi precious stone amber as a lodestone. Amber in Greek was called *elektron*, leading Gilbert on to coin the phrase 'the electric force' to describe its effect. Long after Gilbert's death, Sir Thomas Browne, in 1646, was the first person to use the word 'electricity', deriving it from Gilbert's work, where the old medieval word 'electricus' had been used by Gilbert in relation to amber's (magnetic) 'attractive properties'.

Gilbert is also accredited with being the inventor of the first electrical measuring instrument, namely the electroscope, plus the reputed inventor of two instruments to enable sailors 'to find out the latitude without seeing of sun, moon or stars'. An account of the latter is given in Thomas Blondeville's *Theoriques of the Planets* (London, 1602).

JOHN PELL (1611–1685)

Of person he was very handsome, and of a very strong and excellent habit of body, melancholic, sanguine, dark brown hair with an excellent moist curl.

For the last twenty years of his life, one of the most eminent English mathematicians of the seventeenth century lived and worked in Essex. The man in question was John Pell, Fellow of the Royal Society of London, Doctor of Divinity, and latterly vicar of Fobbing church deep in the malaria-ridden marshes of south-east Essex as well as Laindon-cum-Basildon, an area which had earned the unsavoury reputation of being known locally as 'kill priest country'.

Pell was born on St David's Day (1 March) 1610 of a father also named John Pell and his wife Mary Holland. Mary was from Kentish stock, but John's father hailed from Southwick where John Jnr was born. He was the second of his parents' two sons, but time with his parents was short-lived, as by the time John was six his father had died, his mother following a year later and leaving him an orphan. The family was of moderate means but John's father did have a fine library, which John constantly referenced as he grew up, possibly contributing to John being accepted into Cambridge at only thirteen. Entering Trinity College, he was to gain a Bachelor of Arts degree in 1628 and a Master of Arts in 1630.

He was by this time an expert in Latin and Greek and, although it is not certain exactly when his training in mathematics began, it is documented that he was writing and receiving letters from Henry Briggs, a leading English mathematician and the man responsible for introducing logarithms still used in science and engineering today.

Leaving Cambridge a well-qualified man, he became a schoolmaster, first in Horsham, then at Chichester Academy in Sussex. Aged twenty-one he was in a position to marry, and so wooed and wed Ithumaria Reginolles, by whom he had four sons and four daughters. Five years of teaching mathematics in London kept the family in a comfortable position, but then Pell took up a post in Amsterdam, first as Professor of Mathematics at the Gymnasium Illustre in 1643, then three years later, in a similar post at the University of Breda with a salary of 1,000 guilders a year.

In 1652, at the outbreak of the First Dutch War, Pell returned to England, and as a man with Cromwellian sympathies, he was appointed by Oliver Cromwell himself to a teaching post in London. When hostilities had ceased Pell once more went abroad, this time sent by Cromwell on a diplomatic mission to Zurich. Detained there for longer than he had anticipated, Pell eventually returned to report back to Cromwell but was denied the chance as the Lord Protector had died shortly before.

Pell had Cromwellian sympathies for much of his life, but at the Restoration in 1660 Pell subscribed to the monarchy, though he was no Royalist. In 1661, when Pell took orders and enrolled in the priesthood, his wife of almost thirty years, Ithumaria, died. She did see him made a deacon at the end of March that year, but never saw him become a Doctor of Divinity, a position he attained in 1663. From the year of her death, Pell became vicar at Fobbing church in Essex, adding to that in 1663 the parsonage of Laindon with the attached chapel of Bartlesdon (Basildon). This was by decree of the Bishop of London, who also observed 'which benefices are in the infamous and unhealthy (feverish) hundreds of Essex'. Pell was none too enamoured of his posting at first, complaining one day to his bishop of the unhealthiness of his benefice, upon which his learned companion replied, 'I do not intend that you shall live there.' 'No,' said Doctor Pell, 'I shall die there.' At Laindon, within sixteen years Pell lost at least six of his curates to 'marsh fever'.

The change in location from the sunnier climes of Europe to the salty marshes and islands of Essex struck Pell as a sharp contrast. Entries in the Fobbing registers from the time he was vicar illustrate all too well the poverty of Pell's new marshland parishes: 'Saturday 12 September the son of Edward Charwell was buried. Thursday 15 the day the other son of Edward Charwell was buried ... Sunday 10 November 1657 the Concubine of Edward Charwell was buried.' 1 July 1661 – 'a poore boy, a beggar, his name unknown was buried at the parish charge'. Later that same year, 'August 11 1661 – Old Christopher Gowers, without a coffin.'

Sometime before 1669 Pell remarried and though his two parishes were large enough to bring him an income of £200 per year, Pell could not seem to amass more than £60 per annum from them. But Pell was not a man of worldly affairs, preferring to concentrate on producing his theories and doctrines on mathematics and astronomy and his tables of squares and of antilogarithms, which became famous aids to calculations.

Thus he was unaware that in his declining years his tenants and relations often cheated him of profits and kept him so impoverished that he could not even afford necessaries, such as paper and ink. Towards the end of his life he spent some time in the King's Bench Prison for debt, but then in March 1682, was invited to live in the College of Physicians. Here he stayed until his health dictated he live with his grandchild in Westminster. He died, however, at the house of Mr Cothorne, reader of the church of St. Giles-in-the-Fields, 12 December 1685, in the seventy-fourth year of his age, 'not having a sixpence in his purse when he died'.

MYLES GRAYE, BELL-FOUNDER (1575–1649)

Myles Graye, the prince of founders.

Canon J. J. Raven, 1889

There is little on earth that sings the praises of the heavenly host better than the peal of a bell. It lifts the soul and for a moment makes us believe we are in the company of angels. Similarly, nothing can ground the heart like a single bell's mournful toll. Without bells, our forebears would have been unable to mark out their days, to be called to prayer and to the fields. Theirs were the days of the Seeding Bell and the Harvest Bell; the Pancake Bell, which was rung to remind them of Lent, and the Oven Bell to warn that the lord of the manor's ovens were hot and they could bake their bread. Even today our modern timepieces derive from the Dutch word for bell – *klok*. But it wasn't until the advent of a mechanism that allowed the bell to be swung though great angles, instead of just from side to side, that 'peals' were introduced and bells truly celebrated. It was now that the 'bell-founder' came into his own, one of the most important foundries of this time being that of Myles, or Miles Graye at Colchester.

'Miles Graye made me' was a recurring inscription on the church bells of the eastern counties during the seventeenth century; it is thought there were over three hundred made. *The Church Bells of Essex,* published in 1909, gives us an idea of just how prolific the Graye family was. Of the two bells in Althorne church, an 'ancient one' was made by Thomas Harrys of London around 1480, the other by Miles Graye in 1638. Mayland's church had only a single bell, marked 'Miles Graye made me 1622', and of the five bells of Purleigh all but one are marked Miles Graye. At Steeple with Stansgate Miles Graye made one of the two bells in 1636, and the little church of Stow Maries had only one bell, marked 'Miles Graye made me 1686'.

Graye made two of the three bells of Woodham Mortimer church, but only one of the bells at Woodham Walter. It was the custom here for a bell to ring a death knell twenty-four hours after a death; the formalities being three for male, two for female. It was also a regular feature to ring a gleaning bell. Gleaning was the act of collecting leftover crops from farmers' fields after they had been commercially harvested, and in nineteenth-century England such practice was a legal right for cottagers. The sexton of a village would ring a church bell at eight o'clock in the morning and again at seven in the evening to tell the gleaners when to begin and end work. It was never rung on a Sunday – gleaners were expected to be in church!

It is not always easy to distinguish who was who in the Graye family; their genealogy has proven complicated, with the forename 'Myles' or 'Miles' appearing regularly down the male line. The lack of standardised spelling at this time further complicates matters by presenting the surname as either Gray, Grey or Graye, which this book has faithfully reproduced when the name appears in documents. Yet if dates are followed we can generally conclude that we are looking at grandfather, father and son. It can be gleaned from records that Miles Graye was born around 1575 and 'apprenticed to Richard Bowler', the earliest known Colchester bellfounder. Myles married his master's domestic servant, 'and subsequently another'. A paternity suit could have been the reason Miles married initially, aged twenty-two. An appearance before the Borough of Colchester Quarter Sessions examinations on 11 November 1598 reports the 'confession of Miles Graye, bellfounder, that he is father of the child with which Alice Mullings is pregnant'. A marriage to Alice possibly followed soon after.

Miles Graye was to become the most celebrated bell-founder of the seventeenth century, affectionately known in the industry as 'Colchester Graye'. His work far outstripped that of his contemporaries, and he acknowledged his work with a simple and succinct Latin inscription, '*MILES GRAYE ME FECIT*' (Miles Graye made me), but it was always beautifully crafted in the Gothic lettering learnt from his master, Richard Bowler. Even Miles's own sons could not match his expertise, though the younger, Miles (born September 1628) was marginally better than his elder brother Christopher (born January 1625), who was universally known to be 'in every way an inferior founder to his father'. About 270 bells by the older Miles still remained in the east of England, 'about one-half in Essex itself', so said John James Raven in his book *The Bells of Suffolk*, published in 1890. Of all these, Graye's masterpiece is accepted to be the tenor bell at Lavenham, Suffolk.

Graye's bells were cast from his foundry at Head Street, Colchester, and later taken to their destinations all over Essex, Suffolk and Cambridgeshire. If this was not possible or if a repair was small then the Grayes operated out of local foundries, or even set up temporary works close to the church in question if there was plenty of wood and water at hand. Often the materials to make repairs were in short supply and had to be gathered from different sources,

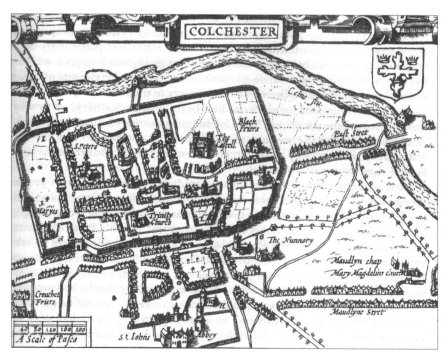

A copy of John Speed's map of Colchester dated 1610. In the lower left-hand corner is Head Gate, and it is documented that Myles Graye's bells were cast from his foundry at Head Street close by.

though it was reported the church adamantly drew the line at collecting pewter house to house from parishoners.

We can assume that the Graye bell-founding business was a family concern for part of its existence; between 1632 and 1642 Miles the elder was employing both his sons as his agents in the counties of Hertfordshire and Bedfordshire as well as Cambridge. It is also known that during this time 'the younger Graye' made Saffron Walden his headquarters; a convenient centre in every way for dealing with the district he was responsible for. Here he settled for thirteen years, the children born to himself and his wife Jane Banishe, whom he married in 1622, recorded in the local parish register from the year 1630 to 1643.

Accounts of work carried out by the Colchester bell foundry still exist. In 1637 the wardens of Ickleton church in Cambridgeshire accounted for work done to their bells by Graye and others. Thirteen shillings was paid to 'to Graye of Saffron Walden, bellfounder, for running and casting tower bells belonging to the Church of Ickleford aforesayd'. The itinerary continues, 'Item payd to James Jackson for carriage of some of the sayd bells by cart to Saffron Walden and for recarriage of them, 20s. Item for carriage of the other of the sayd bells thither and for recarriage of them by this accomptant's owne carte and horses, 20s. Item to — Graye for mending a bell clapper, 3s. Item to a messenger to go to Saffron Walden. 2s 6d.'

Miles Graye the elder died in 1649 aged seventy-three, his Will stating that he was 'erased with age and weak in body, but yet in p'fect mind and memory'. He could have been ailing for some time but what is certain is that he would have suffered, and was possibly worn out by the privations endured in the eleven-week Siege of Colchester the year before he died in 1648. It had been a siege of attrition, where after initial skirmishes and an early attempt by Lord Fairfax and his Parliamentary forces to storm the town walls, Fairfax was happy to watch as the town was left to 'stew in its own juice'. In this initial fighting, Graye's bell foundry was burned down, the Will of Miles Graye dated 17 May 1649 alluding to the loss of the foundry in connection with a building known as 'The Swan with two Necks', a corruption of 'nicks', the marks on a swan's bill that denoted it was a king's swan. It was a house in Head Street, Colchester, once occupied by Miles Graye, and bequeathed to his second wife Dorothy: 'Rents, issues, p'fits, cominge, growinge, and arisinge out of the east end of the capitall messuage or tenement, lately burned downe, scituate and beinge below Head Gate, in Colchester aforesayd, commonly called or knowne by the name of the Swan with two Necke.'

We also learn from the Will that Miles left almost everything to his wife and that his son Christopher is not mentioned at all – a family rift perhaps? Son Miles received only a shilling as did daughters Ann Darbye and Mary Starlinge. Another son, James, gets the remainder of some leasehold property 'to him and to his heyres for ever'.

What prompted old Miles Graye to leave his son Christopher out of his Will we will probably never know, but we do know that Christopher frequently worked in Cambridgeshire, mostly from 1666 to 1684, using Charles Newman's iron foundry at Had Denham. A clue may come from a reference to Christopher in 1669 when improvements were made to a St Edward's church, Cambridge, for the recasting of two bells, the founder being 'a degenerate son of Colchester Graye'. Nevertheless, Christopher must have been a competent bell-founder, as among others he cast four bells at Yelling (1666), all three at Piddle-cum-Fenton (1675) and five at Afford Darcy (1676), plus Charles Newman began casting bells himself under Christopher's guidance, his first in 1684.

After three generations, the Graye family lost the Colchester bell foundry on the occasion of Christopher's death in 1686. The foundry was purchased by Christopher's successor, Charles Newman, and fellow Sudbury bell-founder Henry Pleasants, who cast his first bell at Colchester in 1691.

THE NATHANIELS HEDGE (1710–1795 & 1734–1821), CLOCKMAKERS OF COLCHESTER

It is almost impossible to imagine a time without clocks. Today our lives are ordered and organised. Meticulously measuring to the digital second, we exist in a world full of time-filled precision. Modern time uniformity came about with the advent of the railways and Greenwich Mean Time. Before the 1840s people kept time by the sun, their clocks set to 'local mean time', which meant there could be up to an hour's time difference between villages at opposite sides of the country and coach travel, as well as being notoriously uncomfortable, was equally unreliable time-wise.

Blacksmith-clockmakers can be found in Colchester in medieval times. Evidence dated March 1483 records, 'I toke to the clokkemaker of Kolchester for emending the clokke … 2 shillings and fourpence.' It was predominantly the blacksmith craft that was needed, as the type of repairs needed were not so much precision-based as structural repairs to what was then 'turret-type timepieces' found in churches.

The first recognisable English domestic clock was the lantern or chamber clock, also known as the 'birdcage clock'. This evolved around the beginning of the seventeenth century and at first London was where most clocks were made. It didn't take long, however, for men from the surrounding counties, especially Colchester in Essex, to become skilled enough to challenge the best. One early clockmaker was Thomas Clough, born between 1565 and 1575, who was sent for by the villagers of Braintree to repair their turret clock in 1602. As travel then was not simple or safe, the villagers must have valued his reputation to have asked him to travel the 15 miles from Colchester to undertake their repair.

James Wheeler, another Colchester clockmaker, born in 1604, had begun his clock- and watchmaking career as a locksmith. He married in St Botolph's parish and fathered three children, his eldest son attending Colchester Grammar School in 1639 aged thirteen. His son's admission papers record James Wheeler as 'Horologici', the Latin for clockmaker. He traded successfully between 1625 and 1636 until tragedy befell the family. Other clockmakers, such as William Bacon, John Groome and Henry Woodward, followed with successful businesses. Thomas Harvey, 'of ye parish of St Nicholas in Colchester, in ye county of Essex Clockmaker', became successful enough to leave considerable amounts of money to his children, shares in seagoing vessels and investments in ventures overseas. By 1712, Colchester had eight experienced craftsmen.

Nathaniel Hedge (1710–95) was one such man and, from the eighteenth to well into the nineteenth century, the Hedge family – through several generations and many 'Nathaniels' – perfected and so dominated this local industry.

Nathaniel's grandfather, also Nathaniel, was the founder of this dynasty but not as a clockmaker. Nathaniel senior had inherited a successful business making what had been known from the 1540's as the 'new draperies'. The manufacture of broadcloth had long been in decline, and now, with the introduction of the spinning wheel, lighter cloths were in demand. It was in 'bay and say' manufacture that Nathaniel senior had made the family moderately prosperous, able in 1682 to sell two tenements near Magdalen Green, St Botolph parish, to James Harrison, Maltster, for the princely sum of £78.

His son, Nathaniel, when of age, was apprenticed to a weaver and after seven years, in 1700, became a free burgess of Colchester, able to set up his own business and take on an apprentice of his own. Unfortunately it was a precarious living, with Colchester still suffering the ravages of plague, war and siege plus a hefty Parliamentary fine. Perhaps that is why we see in records of 1705 a Nathaniel Hedge convicted of stealing wood and ordered to pay 2/6d to the poor. A repeat offender, in 1707 he was also committed to gaol for 'misbehaviour'.

Nathaniel's two sons, Thomas, born 1700, and Nathaniel, born 1710, were to work with him, but it soon became apparent that the cloth business could not support the three of them and so young Nathaniel found an apprenticeship with John Smorthwaite, clockmaker of All Saints parish, at a cost to his father of £10. This was obviously a concessionary rate as Smorthwaite's last two apprentices had had paid him £20 and £31 respectively. Nathaniel's apprenticeship began on 1 May 1728 when he was eighteen. This was a little old for an apprentice, but does illustrate that Nathaniel's father did try to give his sons work for a number of years. John Smorthwaite promised to teach, keep and clothe Nathaniel until his apprenticeship was served, and likewise Nathaniel acknowledged the terms of his indenture and promised he would not marry, gamble, or visit taverns.

For five years Nathaniel kept his part of the bargain, becoming in that time a competent journeyman, until common sense deserted him and at twenty-three he fell in love with his master's daughter, Sarah, who was six years his senior. Love overcame reason, and soon the young couple had cemented their relationship, the resulting pregnancy having to be kept secret, as Nathaniel knew John Smorthwaite, successful businessman and important member of Colchester society, would think him an unworthy match. Speed was of the essence and on 2 October 1733 Nathaniel applied for a marriage licence with the intention of using it in Alresford, a nearby parish, in the hope news of their marriage would not reach Colchester. The application shows that Nathaniel lied about his and Sarah's ages to make the difference less of an issue:

Appeared personally ... Nathaniel Hedge of the parish of All Saints' Colchester, aged 26 and alleged he intended to marry with Sarah Smorthwaite of the parish of All Saints', Colchester aged 27 years. License them to be married in the parish church of Alresford in the county of Essex. 2. October 1733.

Although Alresford was a quiet backwater, rumours of the wedding did reach Smorthwaite's ears and, unforgiving, he turned both Nathaniel and his pregnant daughter out of the house, never to see them again. In his Will dated 18 May 1736 there was no mention of his daughter, his son-in-law or of his grandchild.

But Nathaniel was also made of stern stuff. Despite his incomplete apprenticeship, he went into partnership with his friend and former pupil of John Smorthwaite, William Cooper. They traded as Cooper and Hedge until 1739 when Nathaniel's old master and Sarah's father died. Not one to let an opportunity pass, Nathaniel seized the chance to negotiate with his old master's widow and, buying up Smorthwaite's 'stock in trade', tools and the reputation of his clockmaking business, he set up to trade under his own name. His venture was not without obstacles as first he needed to be a free burgess of Colchester, but got over this by claiming 'patrimony' from his father instead of completing the last two years of his apprenticeship. Courage to take an opportunity is not the same as being able to afford one, and Nathaniel at the time of breaking out on his own was very aware he was giving up a secure income from his association with Cooper. At first his income and outgoings were hugely disproportionate and it is possible that his payments to suppliers and Smorthwaite's widow fell behind. But his gamble eventually turned to profit, and soon Hedge of Colchester was one of the town's most prosperous and highly respected clockmakers.

Until Nathaniel Hedge went into business, most Colchester clockmaking was run on a small scale. Hedge ran his workshop on the lines of a well-equipped factory before there ever was such a concept. His clocks catered for two markets and he produced both high-grade longcase clocks and cheaper thirty-hour longcase clocks designed for the tradesmen and farmers in the area, as well as to satisfy markets further afield. The term 'cheaper' did not, however, denote sub-standard. The main difference was in the wooden cases and general ornament of the clocks. Local tradesmen were employed to use simple woods; natural pine was lacquered and oak polished to give a good but affordable finish. In all instances, the movements inside each and every one of Nathaniel Hedge's clocks was of the highest quality. There are over one hundred still working today.

Nathaniel's more exclusive clocks were eight-day longcase clocks with 11- or 12-inch square or arched brass dials. He paid individual attention to the design and production of these clocks and consequently no two of them were ever the same. Alongside these, he also produced hooded wall-bracket clocks, and devoted considerable time to producing watches, housing them in either gold or silver. It is estimated that between the years 1739 to 1778 the Hedge clockmaking business produced no less than 4,500 watches.

On one occasion Nathaniel's shop was broken into by Joseph Broadbent and Richard York, both labourers, and Nathaniel had to appear at the Colchester Borough Sessions to give evidence at their indictments. Found guilty of felony, Richard York was 'whipped in the cart from the Gaol to the Three Crowns from hence to St Nicholas Church and back again to the Gaol on Saturday, between the hour of twelve of the clock and one'. From there, hopefully a lesson learned, he was discharged.

When Nathaniel retired aged sixty-two he still kept a watchful eye on the business as his two younger sons traded on his behalf under the names 'Thomas & John Hedge'. Nathaniel's eldest son, also Nathaniel, had set himself up separately some years before, trading successfully from his own premises. His branch of the business was to become the survivor of the two, as his brother's partnership gradually dissolved after Thomas died aged only forty-five and John fell back on his interests in local government and his sideline company, which supplied post coaches to London and Suffolk. When Nathaniel himself died in 1795, the original business he had built after he and his pregnant wife had been turned out on the street by John Smorthwaite was all but gone, but his eldest son's efforts were still proving to be as fruitful as his own.

This Nathaniel, like his father, had concentrated on watch- and clockmaking, preferring to tender out the casings and engraving of dials. He concentrated on making traditional clocks, the finest of which he cased in oak and ebony, but was also commissioned to make a turret clock for the parish church of Colchester, which was an opportunity his father had never had. His design was an eight-day clock with two dials facing both east and west which would, with sufficient support, project about 8 feet out over the pavement. Because of this projection it was fondly known by Colchester folk as the 'frying pan clock'.

To distinguish his clocks from those of this father, he signed his full name, Nathaniel Hedge, as opposed to simply 'Hedge', the moniker his father used. As business grew he moved to larger premises in St Runwells parish on the south side of the high street opposite the Three Cups, six years later moving three shops to the west, but effectively now trading in the parish of St Peter's.

Like his father before him, this Nathaniel also had sons, but only his second son, Charles, took an apprenticeship. Once returned from London he occupied the premises next door to his father and as silversmith and engraver carried out the delicate ornamentation of the clocks his father passed to him.

By 1800 Nathaniel was a respected craftsman with a fine reputation and in that year he was asked by a Colchester MP if he would design a public clock for the townspeople. It was a distinguished commission and was to be housed in the newly repaired old Bay Hall on the north side of the high street. An investment of £100 was made to construct a tower to hold the clock, which was to face south, east and west. The honour of installing the clock was given over to Nathaniel's journeyman Joseph Banister, who in 1807 became Nathaniel's business partner, the pair trading under the name Hedge & Banister. Business boomed, as a year later in 1808 the business advertised in the *Ipswich Journal* for watch finishers, promising that 'a good workman may have a constant employ, on application or by letter post to Hedge & Banister, Colchester'.

But, as so often happens, tragedy follows fortune and a year later in 1809 Nathaniel's son Charles suddenly died. Though no longer a young man, Nathaniel (senior) advertised in the local paper that he would be stepping in to run his son's silversmithing and jewellery-making business, 'with proper assistance', for the sake of his son's widow and children. To allow him more time to do this he asked his business partner, Banister, to buy him out, something Banister did most generously. From that point the manufacture of watches and clocks would be in future conducted by Banister alone. Three and a half years later, on 8 December 1818, Nathaniel died, and with him the Hedge name that had dominated clockmaking in Colchester for a century.

Banister continued the business, but favoured the manufacture of watches over clocks. His standards, like Nathaniel's, were never in question but once he almost lost the 'Hedge' reputation due to no fault of his own. Despite the decline of longcase clocks, the clocks themselves still needed maintenance and repair, and Banister was at one time summoned to a county house in Colchester to discover why its clock stopped at odd times and was unable to start up again. Banister made several visits to clean the movements and look carefully for faults but, at a loss to find the cause, set up the clock again and left.

It was during a later visit and while watching the clock with its case door open that he saw a cat's paw suddenly dart out from a knothole in the back of the case and stop the pendulum. The hole was filled and the reputations of three of Colchester's finest clockmakers saved.

HUMPHRY REPTON (1752–1818)

Upon first visiting every new subject I am obliged to conceive in my own mind such a plan as I afterwards render visible to others; and endeavour to fix on my memory the several leading features of each place by making sketches, without which from the multiplicity of various situations it would be impossible for me to pursue any regular system of improvement...

H. Repton, 1795

When, in 1797, the new owner of 'Highlands' House at Widford, outside Chelmsford, employed Humphry Repton to overhaul their parklands, they did so knowing him to be the most innovative successor to England's most famous landscape gardener, Lancelot 'Capability' Brown. Repton was to transform Hyland's grounds and add to his standing as an outstanding designer who dominated his field in the late eighteenth century. But this was not Repton's first commission and, by the time he was working his magic on this, the new acquisition of Cornelius Kortright, he had already been consulted on over one hundred commissions, his first paid project being Catton Park, Norfolk in 1788. His first Essex project, however, was Rivenhall Place near Silver End.

Humphry Repton's path to success was not a straightforward one. He was born on 21 April 1752, in Bury St Edmunds, Suffolk, son of John Repton, a prosperous collector of excise duties, and Martha (*née* Fitch), from Suffolk. Aged twelve he was sent to Holland to learn Dutch and prepare for a mercantile career. On his return he was apprenticed to a textile merchant, then, after marriage to Mary Clarke in 1773, set himself up in business. He was not successful and after then trying his hand at journalism, dramatics, painting and finally politics, he realised his prospects did not look good.

In 1786/7, after losing the small inheritance his parents had bequeathed him on their deaths, he moved himself and his family, in 'straightened circumstances', to Romford, where he took a small four-bedroomed cottage on the main road in Hare Street. Now, aged thirty-six and with no secure income, he decided to indulge his love of sketching with his love of nature and try his hand at landscape gardening, a term he himself invented. Initially calling himself 'an improver of the landscape', Repton advertised his services in pamphlets and by contacting those he knew from his many previous enterprises. His very first Essex patron was Baron Western of Rivenhall.

Western was a short, wiry little man who was Member of Parliament for Maldon and Essex and who would go on to sit in the Commons for a total of forty-two years. Though in some circles Western was referred to as 'the Squire' or, less politely, 'Old Stiff Rump', he was in fact a gentleman of surprising vision and culture. Well educated, he had undertaken the Grand Tour to Italy in his youth and from that point had become an enthusiastic collector of Roman antiquities. When he came of age in 1788 he set about improving and redesigning Rivenhall Place and its park. Fortunately for Repton, Western was willing to take a chance on him.

Repton had flair for design, possibly learnt when he was abroad in Holland as a youth, but he was also very practical. His approach to his work was very personal and he would stay with his clients at their homes to acquaint himself with all aspects of the landscape before even putting his pen to paper. Instead of plain sketches, he then produced small folios; miniature notebooks (13.5 by 8.5 inches) containing attractive watercolour paintings, beautifully bound in red Morocco leather. Repton would then produce an overlay or a second painting as his improved prospective. This, by means of lifting the latter off the former, would show a 'before' and 'after' effect, and the full impact of Repton's design could be fully appreciated. These would come to be known as Repton's famous 'Red Books' and one, although now lost, was produced for Western at Rivenhall.

Repton first visited the estate in August and again in September, finding Rivenhall Place 'gloomy', with the appearance of being 'low and damp'. He told Western that there was indeed work to be done, stating that the designs of former days 'has indeed, rendered the improvement and restoration of its natural beauties a work of some labour; yet, by availing ourselves of those natural beauties, and displacing some of the encumbrances of art the character of the place may be made picturesque and cheerful'. He recommended removing the stables and all the bushes in the low meadow and converting this into a 'pleasing piece of water in the front of the house'. In the next year he made two further visits in May and September.

Repton offered two designs for the house – one classical, the other favouring the medieval 'Gothic'. The classical design was chosen perhaps for personal taste, though Western had just bought Felix Hall close by and his budget was stretched. What is known is that, as the adjoining estate, it was Felix Hall that Western retired to for the duration of Repton's renovations.

With his general dislike of red brick, Repton tended, where possible, to finish his houses with a render of lime, mixed with both yellow and black minerals, to suggest the house was constructed, in Repton's words, 'of the most costly materials', and which was not so hard on the eye. The house today still has a dusty yellowish hue.

By the time Repton got to work on Hylands he had become an astute businessman and worthy successor to 'Capability' Brown. Unlike his predecessor, however, Repton was not above 'borrowing' an already established effect. Whereas Capability Brown may have started from scratch, Repton used a point of interest, working with it to draw the eye, incorporating a church spire as the focal point of a new vista as opposed to hiding it. Repton was also not averse to taking on smaller commissions, possibly influenced by the fact he was working through the less affluent years of the Napoleonic Wars, but though smaller in size they were no less impressive. Repton did, nevertheless, subscribe to Brown's observation that 'nature abhors a straight line', adding his own belief that natural beauty could always be enhanced by art. With the world fast entering an age of romance, and without the hindrance of planning permissions, Repton became known for giving his clients of all incomes the private and peaceful 'Arcadian' estates in which they wanted to live.

By the time Repton got to work on Hylands, he had become an astute businessman and worthy successor to 'Capability' Brown. (By kind permission of Hylands House, Chelmsford)

HUMPHRY REPTON.

The Grade II neoclassical villa we see today, set within its 232-hectare Hylands Park land south-west of Chelmsford, was not the 'Highlands' Repton first knew. The original house was large but unpretentious, and built around 1726 in the grounds of Shakestones manor, which had been bought by respectable lawyer Sir John Comyns. At that time Comyns lived close to the cathedral in the centre of Chelmsford in a house called 'Guy Harlings', but despite its linen-fold paneling and modest decoration Comyns wanted a house that reflected his station in life. 'Highlands' was completed four years later; an elegant two-storey red brick building with stone quoins (cornerstones) detailing around its doors and windows, 'pilasters carrying a pediment, and crowned by a dormer roof rising behind a high parapet'. Its grounds were set out in the geometric style of the time, all within a 100-acre park, plus 300 acres of farmland. Two gates allowed access to the house, one on the Widford side and one on the London side.

On the death of John Comyns in 1740, the estate was claimed by a nephew, as there were no male heirs, the house in turn being inherited by his son John Richard Comyns in 1760. It was to pass out from the Comyns family after three generations, being bought at auction in 1797 at the Black Boy Inn, Chelmsford, for £14,500. The new owner was Repton's latest client, Danish merchant Cornelius Hendrickson Kortright, a man who had acquired his fortunes through the sugar and slave trade in the West Indies.

Kortright was definitely a man of means, and gave Repton a free hand to suggest improvements to Highlands. With 213 extra acres Kortright had added to the estate to extend his boundary up to the banks of the River Wid, Repton soon set about modernising, landscaping and redesigning the whole area.

Repton first changed the way visitors first viewed the estate by replacing the old approach to the house. He re-aligned the direct route from the Widford gate towards a new Serpentine Lake to the north, before leading the visitor through a wooded area so that the house itself could only be seen once you had emerged from the trees. Highlands, with all its changes, was then in full view – or was it? Now approached by the new drive, which swept round from the east towards the house, what was seen was a fashionable bow-fronted east wing in all its glory. The other side of the house, with the less attractive servants' quarters, was perfectly hidden from view.

Under Repton's direction, the old house slowly disappeared behind new extensions, bow windows, a colonnaded conservatory, a fashionable Palladian façade and white stucco rendering. This was to hide the old Georgian building of red bricks that Repton so disliked and in this instance commented that it 'put the whole valley in a fever'. It was a wonderful ongoing transformation observed by Kortright's many guests at the house, the *Ipswich Journal* dated 3 July 1801 reporting, 'His Excellency Count Bernstorff and his brother Count

Cornelius Kortright, the man who engaged Repton to transform the house and grounds of Hylands House, Chelmsford. (By kind permission of Hylands House, Chelmsford)

Frederick of Copenhagen left London on Sunday bound for Hylands House Essex, the very elegant seat of Cornelius Kortright. They will be staying for a few days on their way up to Harwich.' Similarly, during the Napoleonic Wars, a large military contingent was based nearby in Galleywood, and the *Essex Herald* in January 1810 reported Kortright's hospitality: 'An elegant ball and supper at his beautiful seat Highlands ... at which all the fashionables in the neighbourhood were present, including many military gentlemen.'

However, as Kortright's family grew the house became unsuitable and so it was the next owner of the house, Pierre Labouchere, who saw Repton's vision for the house finally completed.

With his career spanning thirty years, Repton worked on over four hundred commissions, some in Essex such as Claybury Hall, Dagnam Park, Stubbers in North Ockendon, Wanstead Park, Hill Hall, Theydon Mount and Woodford Hall. He also had a hand in the laying out of London's Russell Square in Bloomsbury and the redesigning of Kensington Gardens, landscaping and terracing aristocratic homes such as Longleat, Harewood House, Tatton Park and Woburn Abbey, counting among his clients the Dukes of Portland and Bedford.

Repton suffered an unfortunate accident in 1811, when, after his carriage turned over and he was thrown, he sustained injuries to his back that seriously restricted his movements. From that point he relied more and more upon his two sons, George Stanley and John Adey Repton, to carry out his commitments. He died in 1816.

In his last published work, written just before his death, we are given a rare glimpse of the quiet, industrious man behind the genius that was Humphry Repton. And surprisingly it concerns the modest house he found in Romford when he was in such 'straightened circumstances'. For a man who loved beauty in all things, he had originally found it 'incommodious', with 'foot passengers, wagons and stage coaches passing close to the entrance and a butcher's stall festooned with legs of mutton and shins of beef clearly visible from the windows'. But it soon became an elegant bolt-hole – a refuge. 'For more than thirty years,' he wrote in his deliberate and practiced hand, 'I have anxiously retreated from the pomp of palaces, and the elegancies of fashion.' Describing the experience of transforming his home, he added it was 'the most interesting subject I have ever known'.

14

HUSBANDS, LOVERS & ROGUES

Today marriage is regarded as a partnership of equal individuals. But as we have seen, those principles did not apply in the past. A husband had complete control over his wife and her affairs, to the point where a woman did not even exist in legal terms. But it was a double-edged sword. Though a man, as late as the 1770s, had the right to chastise his wife with a stick or whip hung above the bed, which he was permitted to wield should his wife not be as docile as he desired her to be, even deny her the right to eat at his table or speak if she were not spoken to, he also had, sometimes to his detriment, the sole charge of her behaviour, good or bad.

Since a wife was regarded as a minor, if she committed any crime in her husband's presence he was held responsible for it. In cases where she damaged anyone's property the damage was viewed as if carried out by a domestic animal and the husband answerable for it. All debts run up by the wife were also the husband's problem. Should a man find himself wishing he had never committed to matrimony there was little or no recompense.

On 28 February 1783 Ambrose Ellis of Chelmsford put out a public notice that he would not pay any debts contracted by his said wife, she having left him 'upward of two years' and having to his knowledge contracted various debts in his name. A year later on Friday 2 July 1784, Edward Hunt, incensed by the fact that his wife Mary had eloped with another man a month before in June, put an advert in the *Chelmsford Chronicle* stating, 'I, the said Edward Hunt will not pay any debts she may contract from the above date!'

In the eyes of the church it was actually a sin for married couples not to cohabit. The church only allowed couples to 'live asunder' if the aggrieved spouse had sufficient grounds to obtain a judicial separation. For the poor this was rarely possible and in most cases the courts ordered the couple to 'live together again'. For some husbands (and wives) this was not a tenable solution and so they sought other forms of relief from their unhappy unions. Cases of desertion and unlawful cohabitation were the bread-and-butter cases of the county courts.

In May 1784 a notice was posted in the local newspaper concerning Richard Thorn, a Blacksmith of Rochford, Essex. Apparently he had run away from his wife and child about ten days previously, and was described as being 5 feet 5 inches tall with black curly hair and black eyes and a dark complexion. It was suggested that if he returned to his wife and child in a few days, 'the parish would forgive him', if not, the parish would punish him according to the law.

There was a £2 reward issued in the *Chelmsford Chronicle* on Friday 28 July 1854 for a wanted man named John Heard. This curious bounty placed on his head was not for the usual crimes of robbery or assault but for desertion. John Heard, a labourer of Witham, Essex, had deserted his wife and children, leaving them chargeable to the parish. He was described as aged thirty-one, 5 feet 4 inches tall with dark hair and whiskers, grey eyes, and had been travelling about Essex with a donkey and cart buying rags. The reward was to be paid to any person who could give any information that could lead to his apprehension and should apply to the 'relieving officer' at Witham.

Wives too deserted their husbands. In 1786 husband Thomas Monk advertised in the local newspaper inquiring as to the whereabouts of his wife Elizabeth. He described her as a thin woman of twenty with darkish hair who had left him and run away with a one-eyed man who also had dark hair and 'had on a brown cloth jacket'. As they both, or separately, had stolen 'four gowns and several other diverse things' from Thomas – no doubt to finance themselves – a reward of 1 guinea was being offered for the return of the said items or information as to the whereabouts of the runaway couple, 'exclusive of reasonable expenses'. In the same year John Wash from Southminster issued a notice that should anyone harbour his wife, who had left him 'last Saturday evening', or indeed 'trust her', they would be sorely disappointed in her and be prosecuted for doing so.

In some cases the wife in question had left the marital home many years before as with the wives of William Patmore and John Harwood from Rochford, who had been missing for more than ten years. In other cases the husband wanted his wife back and took the trouble to give accurate descriptions of the missing spouse.

On Friday 9 June 1786 a message appeared in the paper requesting the whereabouts of Maria Gosling and to inform her, should she read the message, that should she return to her husband, Robert Gosling, she would be 'most kindly received'. Maria, described by her husband as being a short, thick person with light brown hair, had eloped with a man of about thirty years of age named John Lee but who preferred to be known as Great Jack. There is a good description of John Lee and it is fair to say that it is probably derogatory as the description was undoubtedly supplied by the wronged husband. He was described as being 'about 5 feet 10 inches high, red hair, wears a smock coat with a flowered collar, a flannelette waistcoat, with 2 rows of buttons, buckskin breeches, often wears pumps but occasionally water boots ... and is employed in walling or marsh ditching'. The message contained both a warning and a reward of 3 guineas for any information as to their whereabouts but also prosecution for those who harboured either Maria Gosling or her paramour.

Occasionally, if she had sufficient funds, a woman retaliated, as with Ann, daughter of Farmer Bates, born in Suffolk but latterly the wife of Jon Redman of Greenstead near Ongar, Essex, and Great Ormond Street, London, gentleman. Having 'eloped' from her husband it was said she had 'formed improper connections and confidants, contracted persidious debts and insulted and harassed her husband by employing attornies [*sic*] against him. The affair was settled by the husband settling a separate maintenance on his wife, but her name was blackened by Mr Redman declaring to 'all persons, shopkeepers and others both in town and country not to trust the said Mrs Redman' and that he would not recognise any debts incurred from that point on.

A case of wishing to be rid of one's wife and family could not be more bizarre than this man in Chelmsford. He sold his wife and child, a sow and eleven pigs for 6 guineas, to a bricklayer of the same place. 'He this day made a demand of them, and received them with open arms, amidst a prodigious

A contemporary print dated 1820 of a wife being sold at market.

concourse of people. NB. The knowing ones think the bricklayer has a very hard bargain.'

Wife selling in England was a way of ending an unsatisfactory marriage at a time when divorce was almost impossible, and it was usually done with the consent of both parties. It is commonly thought to have originated at the end of the seventeenth century, lasting well into the nineteenth, but there is a record from the early 1300s that states that a man 'granted his wife by deed to another man'.

A formal ceremony of marriage before a clergyman was not a legal requirement in England; before the Marriage Act of 1753, marriages were unregistered, and all that was needed to marry was for both parties to agree to the union. Women were completely subordinated to their husbands after marriage, the husband and wife becoming one legal entity, a legal status known as 'coverture', or as it stood in law, 'The very being, or legal existence of the woman, is suspended during the marriage, or at least is consolidated and incorporated into that of her husband: under whose wing, protection and cover, she performs everything.'

As a custom, wife selling was not upheld by the law and often resulted in prosecution. In 1833, the sale of a woman was reported at Epping. She was sold for two shillings and sixpence, with a duty of sixpence. Once sober, and placed before the Justices of the Peace, the husband claimed that he had been

A page from the Purleigh Parish Register recording the birth of a daughter of Moses Stebbing and a wife delivered to him in a halter. (Essex Record Office)

forced into marriage by the parish authorities, and had 'never since lived with her and that she had lived in open adultery with the man Bradley, by whom she had been purchased'. He was imprisoned for having deserted his wife. By the same token, particularly from the mid-nineteenth century onwards, clergy and magistrates chose to turn a blind eye. At least one early nineteenth-century magistrate is on record as stating that he did not believe he had the right to prevent wife sales, and there were cases of local parish constables and Poor Law commissioners using the practice to their advantage by forcing husbands to sell their wives, rather than deserting them and then leaving them on the parish. There is one baptismal record in Purleigh dated 1782 that states, 'Amie Daughter of Moses Stebbing by a bought wife delivered to him in a Halter.'

*

Essex history is littered with tales of damsels in distress and images of women fighting off unsuitable suitors, but on further investigation it sometimes appears a very real price a female had to pay for being a woman in a man's world. With marriage as binding as death and taxes, there was no way out of an unhappy union. Desperate men resorted to desperate measures and for some, to put aside one wife and bigamously marry another was the only solution. Bigamy, it appears, was rife among those pillars of the community, namely the clergy. The curate of Hadstock, one Mr Brane, was brought to court to answer a charge of bigamy in 1589 – he was charged with having 'two wives living'. One wife was with him at Hadstock while the other was in Canterbury, the place where his letters of ordination were also suspect, and so neither wife nor position was genuine.

Another candidate was Robert Hunter, minister of East Horndon, who was charged with having 'two wives alive'. He managed to explain the charge away with the following lengthy explanation:

> In the time of Queen Mary's reign, before he was made minister he was indeed married to Margaret Watte, that she died as he hath heard about twelve years agone, and that within three or four years after her departure from him he was married to Elizabeth Turner of South Weald in the parish church there, with whom he lived for twenty-eight years. He married her while Margaret Wattes was still living, for that he saith Margaret was then the lawful married wife of Richard Mingsden of Maidstone in the county of Kent.

He was also accused that he 'givith ill example of life by unquiet living, beating and chaining of his wife to a post, and is a slanderer of his neighbours'. The second marriage was, however, allowed.

JAMES EMERY (1796–1821)

As I walked down by Chelmsford Jail
I heard a youth in sorrow sigh
In anguish he did sore bewail
Saying, I am condemned to die…

Nineteenth-century gallows ballad

In 1821 at the Chelmsford Assizes the death sentence was passed upon eighteen prisoners. Two of them were described as 'wilful murderers', one being James Emery, indicted for the murder of Sarah King on 29 May earlier that year. A newspaper reported that the case 'excited uncommon interest from the atrocity of its circumstances' as the unhappy victim 'had been seduced and become pregnant by the prisoner'. To get himself out of his predicament Emery had given her arsenic, a poison by which she died in agony.

The crime had taken place in White Notley. Emery, coming from an adjoining parish and being a labourer in a gentleman's employ, had shown continued interest in the young Sarah Knight, having the intention of seducing her. Sarah, at twenty, lived at home with her father and some younger brothers and sisters in a small three-roomed cottage. She fell in love with 'the well looking man', to her detriment.

About a week before the girl's death Emery had gone to see Sarah and, while deep in conversation at the back of the house, did not realise that Sarah's younger sister was listening. Sarah was overheard telling her visitor, 'Emery, I am with your child.' Emery was heard to reply that 'if you like any body better than me, you may swear the child to him'. Sarah informed him that 'I have not been with any other person than yourself; and therefore I shall swear it to you'. Sarah's sister, who was witness to the whole conversation, swore later in court that the pair parted, apparently very good friends.

Emery visited Sarah again, this time on the evening before she died, and again Sarah's sister eavesdropped on the conversation, this time held in the parlour. When Emery asked after Sarah's health she replied strangely that she felt unwell. Immediately Emery produced a box of pills, recommended she take them and that if she did so willingly he would give her a pound. Suspicious behaviour it may have been but Sarah, perhaps blinded by love, did as she was bid and at eight o'clock that night after a hearty supper she took seven of the pills and went to bed.

In the newspaper that reported the trial we are told that in the night Sarah awoke 'in great torture and was violently sick', the pain so bad that she sent her sister to a neighbouring public house to get a measure of gin to take with some warm water. But this only aggravated the pain. It must then have suddenly dawned upon poor Sarah that all was not well and so to protect her lover she then told sister to take the pills, their box and several other phials containing mixtures Emery had been giving her, and hide them in a field at the back of the house. Apparently more concerned for Emery than for her own life, she cried out that 'Emery will be hanged – they will hang Emery' and as her pain increased, dispatched her sister to get some beer. When the sister returned, again in the words of the *Chronicle*, 'Sarah was a corpse'.

Her post-mortem revealed that she'd been poisoned with arsenic, and that the pills Emery had given her were so strong that it would have only taken half of one of them to kill her. On hearing of Sarah's death, Emery absconded with only a few clothes, having sold the rest to one of his master's servants. He kept one step ahead of the law for a time, appearing once at a Roxwell inn, where he excused himself for travelling, saying, 'I dare say you have heard that I have come away on account of that cursed wench who was poisoned at Nottley.' To another drinking companion he apparently stated that he had indeed 'got the girl the stuff', but that he had never meant her any harm.

It came out at Emery's trial that this statement was blatantly untrue. A fortnight before Emery began to give Sarah arsenic he had consulted with the neighbourhood blacksmith as to what the best method of bringing about a miscarriage would be. He did not find his answer there as the blacksmith refused to be associated with his query. Instead he went to Copford and bought the poison on the pretext that he was ridding his lodgings of rats and mice that were chewing his furniture and clothing.

As confirmed by Sarah's hiding of the several bottles and phials of mixtures that Emery had sent her, it was clear Emery had been supplying his pregnant lover for many weeks. The jury found no problem finding him guilty and he was ordered for execution at Moulsham Gaol a week after the trial. Strangely, in the words of the reporting newspaper at the time, 'the prisoner was resigned to his fate and appeared very little affected'.

REUBEN COLLINS

At the same Assizes in 1821, Reuben Collins was indicted for 'willfully, maliciously and unlawfully administering to Hannah Stammers, a pregnant woman but not yet quick with child, certain noxious drugs for the purpose of procuring miscarriage'. The prisoner was a young man aged twenty-one who had been a writer in the employ of a Mr Pattison, a solicitor at Witham. This solicitor had also employed the young woman in question as a house servant.

It appears that Reuben had seduced Hannah with repeated promises of marriage, but after she became pregnant he urged her take pennyroyal, steel filings and a corrosive mixture over several weeks in order for her to lose the child. His attempts to get Hannah to carry out his wishes failed, as at the time of his trial Hannah was very much pregnant.

The jury did not hesitate to find him guilty, allowing the judge to pass sentence upon Reuben Collins with the following elequent address:

> You have been convicted by a Jury of your country after a long and patient investigation of a very great crime. This crime is most enormous indeed; and I am afraid it is too commonly comitted. Your case seems to be attended with some very outrageous circumstances because it is clear that you have seduced this unfortunate girl, under a promise of marriage. Having so seduced her, you left her to shift for herself as she pleased. Although in your letters you have professed the warmest attatchement and promised to marry her, yet from some perversity of disposition, you thought it fit to change your mind and afterwards abandon her. There cannot be a worse instance of crime under this act of Parliamant; for in order to prevent her bringing forth that child of which you are the father you had recourse to the expedient of administering noxious drugs. You administered no less that 4 different things for that pupose.
>
> By way of defence you have greatly agravated your crime bcause you attempted to lay the blame entirely upon her, and you have ventured to state that she, in fact, had seduced you. Therefore I say you have made your case a great deal worse and it is highly necessary for the sake of public example that you should be severly punished and I think myself bound to go to the utmost extent of the law. The sentence of this court on you therefore is that you be transported for the term of fourteen years to such place as his majesty by the advice of this council shall think proper to order and direct.

Until that moment the prisoner had shown great fortitude and self-composure, but once sentence was passed the unfortunate youth was removed from the court in a flood of tears.

It appears that Collins first awaited his transportation on the ship *Leviathon*, arriving on board on 22 September 1821. He was then transferred on 21 June 1823 to the *York*, which was moored at Portsmouth. By 15 April 1824 he was three years into his sentence, and now aboard the *Retribution*, moored at Woolwich, still awaiting his fate.

A LAST WORD... 'UPON DUELLING...'

You are a damned [sic] where [whore] you have bin ridd above twentye tymes
by severall persons before you againe came in this countrey, you are a bawdy
bitch and came out of a bawdy house, and you are a dounghilly where...

Thomas Glascoch of Danbury about Bridget, wife of Robert Audley, 1657

For officers and gentlemen wishing to defend the objects of their desire there was always 'saber rattling' or in other words, the duel by which slander and disrespect, like the slanderous words above contained in a document in the Essex Record Office and directed at the wife of Thomas Audley, could be challenged and the perpetrator brought to account. The reason this particular incident was brought to light was that it was contrary to the laws against 'challenges and duels and all provocations thereunto'. If legislation existed in 1657 to outlaw duelling, it was mostly ignored, as the practice was still being decried towards the end of the eighteenth century as an outmoded form of redress, its cause often 'high words' and 'provoking language', and what began in comedy often ended in tragedy.

In 1787 a letter from a reader of the *Chelmsford Chronicle* declared, 'I wish a law was immediately enacted that the survivor at a duel should suffer as a murderer; and the "seconds" inflicted with transportation or imprisonment for life!'

The House of Commons in 1746 sought to 'extinguish the bloody and dangerous practice of Dueling which prevails more than in any other country in Europe, to the great scandal of our laws religious and civil to both of which it is equally repugnant'. But as late as 1806 the *Chelmsford Chronicle* records a fatal duel on Galleywood Common between two soldiers stationed at the barracks there.

The last recorded duel in England took place in Hampshire, between a Naval captain and a civil engineer. The former died of his wounds and the latter was arrested by the Metropolitan Police, and charged with murder, but received only a short sentence for manslaughter. An Act of Parliament did become law after that incident, which from then on made it possible for the relatives of anyone murdered or maimed in Britain to claim damages from the party responsible. The once romantic and gallant practice of satisfying honour first by blade and then by bullet seemed, after that, to lose much of its appeal.

BIBLIOGRAPHY

Anon, *The Life and Behaviour of John Skinner, who Murdered Daniel Brett, his Servant* (J. Thompson, 1744)

Aveling, James Hobson, *The Chamberlens and the Midwifery Forceps* (J. & A. Churchill, 1882)

Bebel, August, *Woman and Socialism* (Project Gutenberg ebook, 1910)

Benham, Hervey, *Once Upon a Tide* (George G. Harrap & Co. Ltd, 1986)

Benham, Hervey, *The Smugglers' Century: Story of Smuggling on the Essex Coast, 1730–1830* (Essex Record Office Publications, 1986)

Benton, Philip, *The History of Rochford Hundred* (Unicorn Press, 1991)

Bernhard, Virginia, *Slaves and Slaveholders in Burmuda* (University of Missouri, 1999)

Bothwell, J. S., *The Age of Edward III* (York Medieval Press, 2001)

Brown, A. F. J., *Essex People, 1750–1900* (Essex Record Office Publication, 1972)

Burrows, John William, *Southend-on-Sea and District: Historical Notes* (Standard Printing Works, 1909)

Butler, Mollie, *August & Rab, A Memoir* (London: George Weidenfield & Nicholson Ltd, 1987)

Captain John Perry, R.N., London Borough of Barking and Dagenham Local Studies Library Information, Sheet No. 37

Carlton, Charles, *Royal Mistresses* (Routledge, 1991)

Chadwick, William, *Life and Times of Daniel Defoe* (Franklin, 1969)

Christie, Christopher, *The British Country House in the Eighteenth Century* (Manchester University Press, 2000)

Clarke, Archibald, 'The Forest of Waltham under the Tudors and Stuarts', *Essex Review* (1926)

Clarke, William, *The Clarke Papers. Selections from the Papers of William Clarke, Secretary to the Council of the Army, 1647–1649, and to General Monck and the Commanders of the Army in Scotland, 1651–1660* ed. C. H. Firth (Camden Society, 1894).

Conan, Michael, *Bourgeois and Aristocratic Cultural Encounters in Garden Art, 1550–1850* (Harvard University Press, 2002)

Defoe, Daniel, *A Tour Through the Whole Island of Great Britain* (Penguin Classics, 1978)

Dictionary National Biography

Donagan, Barbara, *War in England 1642–1649* (Oxford: Oxford University Press, 2008)

Dyer, Christopher, *Everyday Life in Medieval England* (Continuum International Publishing, 2001)

Ellis, Sir Henry, *Great Britain Record Commission* (G. Eyre & A. Spottiswoode, 1833)

Fisher, William, *The Forest of Essex* (Kessinger Publishing, 2010)

Frith, Roger, 'Smuggling on the Blackwater', *East Anglian Magazine*, Vol. 20 (1960–61)

Gleig, George Robert, *The Veterans of Chelsea Hospital*, Vol. 2 (R. Bentley, 1842)

Goose, Nigel and Janet Cooper, *Tudor and Stuart Colchester*, Extract VCH (OUP, 1994)

Greaves, Richard L., *Society and Religion in Elizabethan England* (University of Minnesota Press, 1981)

Green, Abishai James, *The Essex Martyrs – Carefully Compiled Without Judgement from Foxe's Book of Martyrs* (1853)

Hart, Cyril, 'The Mersea Charter of Edward the Confessor', *Essex Archaeology and History*, 12 (1981)

Hildyard, W., *Pancratia, or, A History of Pugilism* (London: W. Oxberry, 1812)

Hunt, John Dixon and Peter Willis, *The Genius of the Place: The English Landscape Garden, 1620–1820* (HarperCollins, 1975)

Jarvis, Stan, *Smuggling in East Anglia 1700–1840* (Countryside Books, 1987)

Kent, E. J., 'Masculinity and Male Witches in Old and New England, 1593–1680', *History Workshop Journal* (2005)

Lavery, Brian, *Empire of the Seas* (Conway, 2012)

Leyin, Alan, *Thurrock's Past: Echoes from a Place* (Lejins Publishing, 1997)

Lockwood, Martyn, *The Coggeshall Gang* (Essex Police Museum, Issue No. 29)

Markku, Peltonen, *The Duel in Early Modern England: Civility, Politeness, and Honour* (Cambridge University Press, 2006)

Martin, Frank, *Rogues River* (Ian Henry Publications Ltd, 1983)

Martin, G. H., 'Introduction', in P. Morant, *The History and Antiquities of the County of Essex* (1978)

Mason, Bernard, *Clock and Watchmaking in Colchester: A History of Provincial Clockmaking from the Fifteenth to the Nineteenth Centuries in the Oldest Recorded Town in Great Britain* (Hamlyn Publishing Group Ltd, 1969)

Minto, William, *Daniel Defoe* (Macmillan And Co., 1879)

Morant, Philip, *The History and Antiquities of the Most Ancient Town and*

Borough of Colchester (1st edn, 1970)

Neale, Kenneth, *Essex in History* (Phillimore & Co. Ltd, 1997)

Pevsner, Nikolaus, *The Buildings of England* (Essex, 1954)

Planché, J. R., *The Conqueror and His Companions* (London: Tinsley Brothers, 1874)

Postgate, Raymond, *Out of the Past, Some Revolutionary Sketches* (Labour Publishing, 1922)

Power, Eileen, *Medieval People* (Create Space Independent Publishing Platform, 2011)

Rackham, Oliver, *The History of the Countryside* (Phoenix, 2000)

Raven, J. J., *Church Bells of Cambridgeshire* (Cambridge Antiquarian Society, 1882)

Rawson Lumby, Joseph (Ed.), *Henry of Knighton's Chronicle*, 2 Vols (London: HMSO,1889–95)

Richetti, John, *The Life of Daniel Defoe: A Critical Biography*, (Wiley-Blackwell, 2005)

Ridley, Jane, *Bertie: A Life of Edward VII* (Chatto & Windus, 2012)

Roe, Frederick, *Essex Survivals* (Methuen, 1929)

Sawyer, P. H., *Anglo-Saxon Charters* (London: 1968)

Smith, C. Elizabeth, 'Tea and the Free-traders of East Anglia', *East Anglian Magazine* (July 1956)

Smith, J. R., *Pilgrims and Adventurers: Essex and the Making of the United States of America* (Essex Record Office Publications, 1992)

Solly, AR, 'From Smuggling to Respectability', *East Anglian Magazine* (July 1949)

Spraggs, Gillian, *Outlaws and Highwaymen: The Cult of the Robber in England from the Middle Ages to the Nineteenth Century* (Pimlico, 2001)

Starkey, David, *Henry: Virtuous Prince* (Harper Press, 2008)

Starr, Christopher, *Medieval Mercenary: Sir John Hawkwood of Essex* (Essex Record Office Publications, 2007)

Walters, H. B., M.A., KS.A., *Church Bells Of England* (OUP, 1912)

Weintraub, Stanley, *Edward the Caresser: The Playboy Prince who Became Edward VII* (Simon & Schuster, 2001)

West, Richard, *The Life and Strange Surprising Adventures of Daniel Defoe* (Da Capo Press Inc., 1998)

Wright, Thomas, *The History and Topography of the County of Essex*, Vol. 1 (Kessinger Publishing, 2010)

INDEX

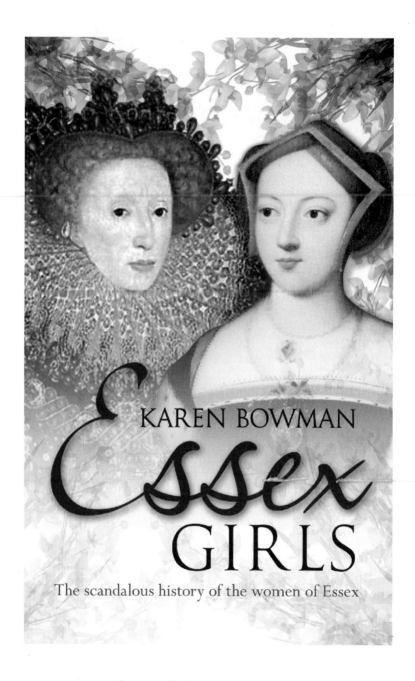